THE INTERPRETATION

OF

The Book of Revelation

By Prophetess Lisa Outlaw

This book is dedicated to my grandchildren. May they continue to promote the gospel of Jesus Christ to their generations. I also wish to give thanks to God first and then to my mother and spiritual parents. Without you, this book would not be possible. Finally, to my children and husband, thank you for inspiring me to write this book. You reminded me to continue to follow my dreams.

The Interpretation of the Book of Revelation is as follows:

Church Age, Tribulation Period or Eternal Damnation The Choice is Yours!

Blessed is he that readeth, and they that hear the words of this prophecy, and keep those things which are written therein: for the time is at hand.
— *Revelation 1:3 (KJV)*

Definitions:

Church Age - Accept Jesus during the church age to avoid suffering during the Tribulation Period. Because Jesus paid the price for the believer's sins on the cross, Jesus will spare the believer from the wrath of God. — *Revelation 7 (KJV)*

Tribulation Period - If Jesus is accepted during the Tribulation Period, the believer will experience the wrath of God by dying as a martyr. Because the believer did not accept Jesus during the church age, the believer must pay for his salvation with his own life. However, the believer will be spared from eternal damnation. — *Revelation 20:15 (KJV)*

Eternal Damnation - If Jesus is **<u>not</u>** accepted at all, the unbeliever will receive the final judgment of eternal damnation. Hence, all unbelievers shall be casts into the lake of fire, which is the second death. — *Revelation 20:15 (KJV)*

Prophecy - The action of foretelling the future.

Interpretation - The action of explaining the meaning of something.

THE INTERPRETATION OF CHAPTER 1

The Selection of the Prophet

I John, who also am your brother, and companion in tribulation, and in the kingdom and patience of Jesus Christ, was in the isle that is called Patmos, for the word of God, and for the testimony of Jesus Christ.
— Revelation 1:9 (KJV)

CHAPTER 1 introduces the Prophet John who was selected to communicate this end time prophecy. God chose the Prophet John, who was banished to the Isle of Patmos, to relay this end time message to the Christian Church. John was given the great commission to write this prophecy to the seven Christian churches that were established in Asia, to warn of the events that will occur before the heavens and earth pass away and before Jesus' Kingdom would come to replace the earthly kingdoms.

As it relates to earthly kingdoms, the Book of Revelation continues the prophetic message where the Book of Daniel ends. The Book of Daniel chronicles the status of Israel under the rule of various earthly kingdoms until the crucifixion and resurrection of Jesus the Messiah. This ushered in a heavenly kingdom on earth, which is the Christian Church. The Book of Revelation then picks up the message with the status of the Christian Church up until the Final Judgment of the earthly kingdoms and the second coming of Jesus.

The Book of Revelation uses symbols to prophetically represent many things. In Chapter 1, the Prophet John mentions that he saw seven golden candlesticks and seven stars. He explained that the seven stars were in the right hand of a spiritual being that looked like the Son of Man. The beauty of the Book of Revelation is that it interprets itself by either providing a direct interpretation or using the same symbols given to prophets in other books of the Bible. Revelation Chapter 1:18-20 interprets for us the Spiritual being that John saw and the meaning of the seven golden candlesticks and the seven stars. Revelation 1:18 explains that the spiritual being John saw was Jesus. This is known because the Spiritual being describes himself as having gone through death on the cross and resurrection. Revelation Chapter 1:20 explains that the seven golden candlesticks represent the seven churches: Ephesus, Smyrna, Pergamos, Thyatira, Sardis, Philadelphia, and Laodicea. The seven stars represent the angels of the seven churches, which are the designated leaders of those churches.

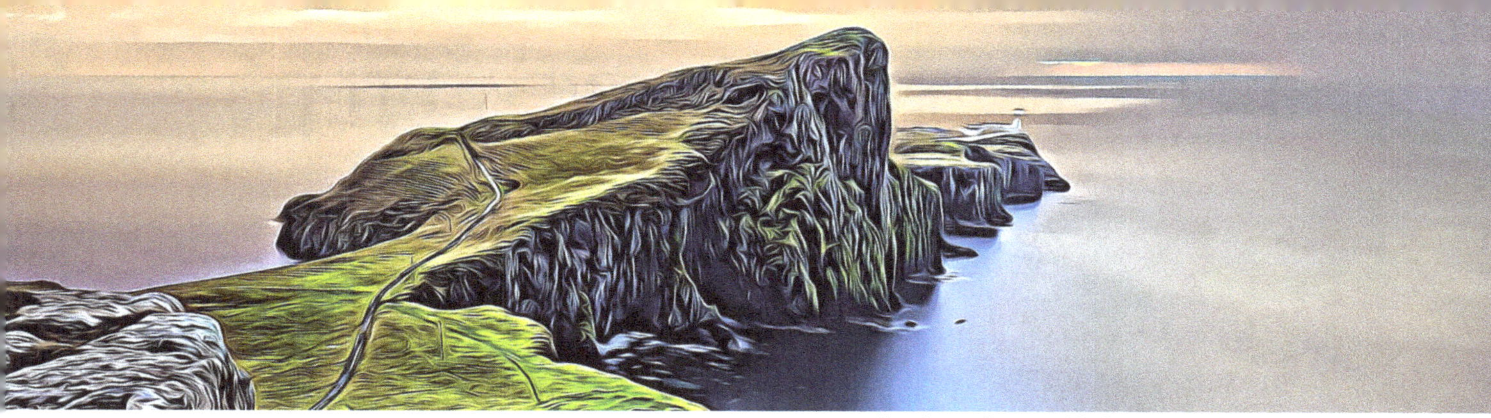

Revelation Chapter 1

1. The Revelation of Jesus Christ, which God gave unto him, to shew unto his servants things which must shortly come to pass; and he sent and signified it by his angel unto his servant John.

2. Who bare record of the word of God, and of the testimony of Jesus Christ, and of all things that he saw.

3. Blessed is he that readeth, and they that hear the words of this prophecy, and keep those things which are written therein: for the time is at hand.

4. John to the seven churches which are in Asia: Grace be unto you, and peace, from him which is, and which was, and which is to come; and from the seven Spirits which are before his throne;

5. And from Jesus Christ, who is the faithful witness, and the first begotten of the dead, and the prince of the kings of the earth. Unto him that loved us, and washed us from our sins in his own blood,

6. And hath made us kings and priests unto God and his Father; to him be glory and dominion for ever and ever. Amen.

7. Behold, he cometh with clouds; and every eye shall see him, and they also which pierced him: and all kindreds of the earth shall wail because of him. Even so, Amen.

8. I am Alpha and Omega, the beginning and the ending, saith the Lord, which is, and which was, and which is to come, the Almighty.

9. I John, who also am your brother, and companion in tribulation, and in the kingdom and patience of Jesus Christ, was in the isle that is called Patmos, for the word of God, and for the testimony of Jesus Christ.

10. I was in the Spirit on the Lord's day, and heard behind me a great voice, as of a trumpet,

11. Saying, I am Alpha and Omega, the first and the last: and, What thou seest, write in a book, and send it unto the seven churches which are in Asia; unto Ephesus, and unto Smyrna, and unto Pergamos, and unto Thyatira, and unto Sardis, and unto Philadelphia, and unto Laodicea.

12. And I turned to see the voice that spake with me. And being turned, I saw seven golden candlesticks;

13. And in the midst of the seven candlesticks one like unto the Son of man, clothed with a garment down to the foot, and girt about the paps with a golden girdle.

14. His head and his hairs were white like wool, as white as snow; and his eyes were as a flame of fire;

15. And his feet like unto fine brass, as if they burned in a furnace; and his voice as the sound of many waters.

16. And he had in his right hand seven stars: and out of his mouth went a sharp two-edged sword: and his countenance was as the sun shineth in his strength.

17. And when I saw him, I fell at his feet as dead. And he laid his right hand upon me, saying unto me, Fear not; I am the first and the last:

18. I am he that liveth, and was dead; and, behold, I am alive for evermore, Amen; and have the keys of hell and of death.

19. Write the things which thou hast seen, and the things which are, and the things which shall be hereafter;

20. The mystery of the seven stars which thou sawest in my right hand, and the seven golden candlesticks. The seven stars are the angels of the seven churches: and the seven candlesticks which thou sawest are the seven churches.

THE INTERPRETATION OF CHAPTER 2

The Prophetic Letters to the Churches

John writes Prophetic Letters to the four churches: Ephesus, Smyrna, Pergamos, Thyatira.

CHAPTER 2 contains the prophetic letters to four churches. In this Chapter, John writes the prophecy to the churches as given to him by Jesus. In summary, the following is the content of the prophetic letters written to the churches:

1. Ephesus – *"Left thy first Love"* In other words, this church left the teaching of the gospel of salvation and the teaching of receiving the gift of the Holy Ghost. Jesus acknowledged the works of the church and agreed with their policies, but found fault because the church had left its first love. Jesus commanded that they do their first works over again or he would remove this church. Acts Chapter 19 versus 1- 6 explained that the founding members of the Ephesus church were asked, "Have ye received the Holy Ghost since you been saved?". Following this, they were all filled with the Holy Ghost. This was the first work of this church, to pursue Salvation through Jesus Christ and receive the Holy Ghost.

2. Smyrna – *"Experienced Great Tribulation"* Jesus encourages this church to be faithful to Him even unto death and He will give those who endure to the end a crown of life. He also reminds the church that the individuals who overcome tribulation shall not be hurt of the second death. The second death is the lake of fire which is mentioned in Revelation 20:14.

3. Pergamos – *"Believers of False Doctrine and Corrupt Church Leadership"* Jesus acknowledged the works of this church, but found fault with their doctrine. This church believed in the doctrine of Balaam who taught Balak, an enemy of God, through prophecy how to cause the children of Israel to sin against God. Balaam was a prophet from Mesopotamia who was willing to pervert his prophetic gift for money. (Numbers 31:16) The Pergamos church also believed in the doctrine of the Nicolaitans. The Nicolaitans in their day are equivalent to corrupt religious church leaders in our day. These corrupt leaders gained power over the church through false teaching, for their own personal gain. They compelled the members of a church to submit to their own authority and power. (1 Peter 5:1- 3)

4. Thyatira – *"Allowed False Prophecy"* Jesus acknowledged the works of this church, but found fault because they allowed false prophecy to seduce their members into sin. This chapter introduces this point by stating the following: "thou sufferest that woman Jezebel, which calleth herself a prophetess, to teach and to seduce my servants to commit fornication, and to eat things sacrificed unto idols." Revelation 2:20.

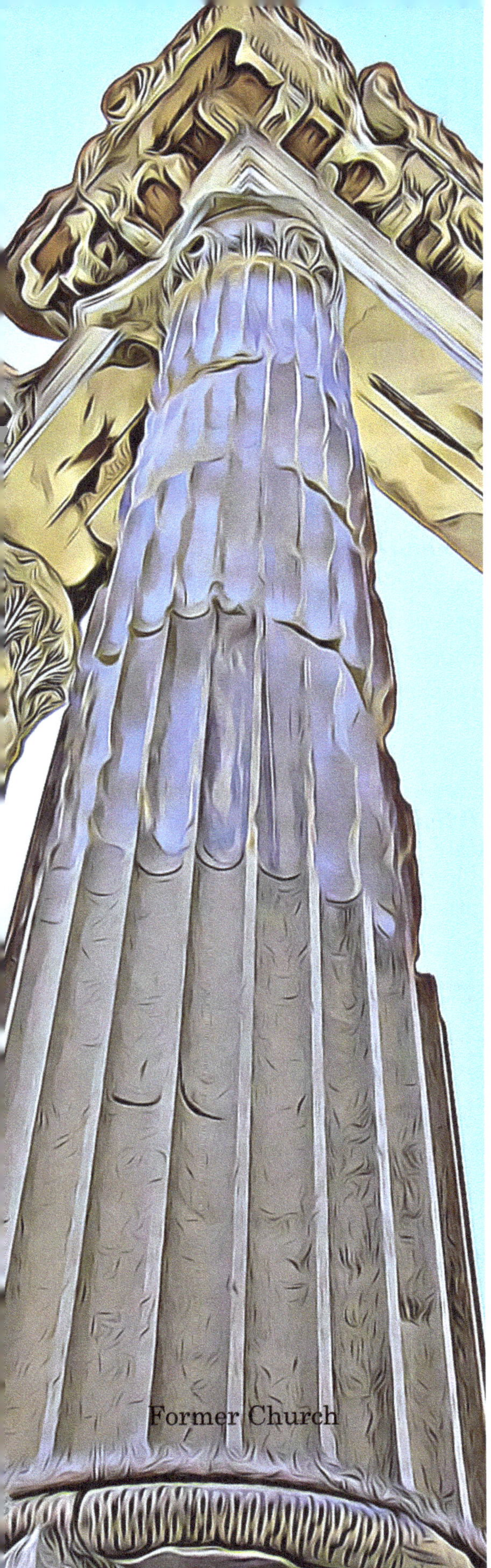

Revelation Chapter 2 King James Version (KJV) Public Domain

1. **Unto the angel of the church of Ephesus write**; These things saith he that holdeth the seven stars in his right hand, who walketh in the midst of the seven golden candlesticks;

2. I know thy works, and thy labour, and thy patience, and how thou canst not bear them which are evil: and thou hast tried them which say they are apostles, and are not, and hast found them liars:

3. And hast borne, and hast patience, and for my name's sake hast laboured, and hast not fainted.

4. Nevertheless I have somewhat against thee, because thou hast left thy first love.

5. Remember therefore from whence thou art fallen, and repent, and do the first works; or else I will come unto thee quickly, and will remove thy candlestick out of his place, except thou repent.

6. But this thou hast, that thou hatest the deeds of the Nicolaitans, which I also hate.

7. He that hath an ear, let him hear what the Spirit saith unto the churches; To him that overcometh will I give to eat of the tree of life, which is in the midst of the paradise of God.

8. **And unto the angel of the church in Smyrna write**; These things saith the first and the last, which was dead, and is alive;

9. I know thy works, and tribulation, and poverty, (but thou art rich) and I know the blasphemy of them which say they are Jews, and are not, but are the synagogue of Satan.

10. Fear none of those things which thou shalt suffer: behold, the devil shall cast some of you into prison, that ye may be tried; and ye shall have tribulation ten days: be thou faithful unto death, and I will give thee a crown of life.

11. He that hath an ear, let him hear what the Spirit saith unto the churches; He that overcometh shall not be hurt of the second death.

12. **And to the angel of the church in Pergamos write**; These things saith he which hath the sharp sword with two edges;

13. I know thy works, and where thou dwellest, even where Satan's seat is: and thou holdest fast my name, and hast not denied my faith, even in those days wherein Antipas was my faithful martyr, who was slain among you, where Satan dwelleth.

14. But I have a few things against thee, because thou hast there them that hold the doctrine of Balaam, who taught Balak to cast a stumbling block before the children of Israel, to eat things sacrificed unto idols, and to commit fornication.

15. So hast thou also them that hold the doctrine of the Nicolaitans, which thing I hate.

16. Repent; or else I will come unto thee quickly, and will fight against them with the sword of my mouth.

17. He that hath an ear, let him hear what the Spirit saith unto the churches; To him that overcometh will I give to eat of the hidden manna, and will give him a white stone, and in the stone a new name written, which no man knoweth saving he that receiveth it.

18. **And unto the angel of the church in Thyatira write**; These things saith the Son of God, who hath his eyes like unto a flame of fire, and his feet are like fine brass;

19. I know thy works, and charity, and service, and faith, and thy patience, and thy works; and the last to be more than the first.

20. Notwithstanding I have a few things against thee, because thou sufferest that woman Jezebel, which calleth herself a prophetess, to teach and to seduce my servants to commit fornication, and to eat things sacrificed unto idols.

21. And I gave her space to repent of her fornication; and she repented not.

22. Behold, I will cast her into a bed, and them that commit adultery with her into great tribulation, except they repent of their deeds.

23. And I will kill her children with death; and all the churches shall know that I am he which searcheth the reins and hearts: and I will give unto every one of you according to your works.

24. But unto you I say, and unto the rest in Thyatira, as many as have not this doctrine, and which have not known the depths of Satan, as they speak; I will put upon you none other burden.

25. But that which ye have already hold fast till I come.

26. And he that overcometh, and keepeth my works unto the end, to him will I give power over the nations:

27. And he shall rule them with a rod of iron; as the vessels of a potter shall they be broken to shivers: even as I received of my Father.

28. And I will give him the morning star.

29. He that hath an ear, let him hear what the Spirit saith unto the churches.₄

THE INTERPRETATION OF CHAPTER 3

The Prophetic Letters to the Churches

John writes Prophetic Letters to the three churches: Sardis, Philadelphia, and Laodicea.

CHAPTER 3 contains the prophetic letters to three churches. In this Chapter, John writes the prophecy to the churches as given to him by Jesus. In summary, the following is the content of the prophetic letters written to the three churches:

1. Sardis – *"Be watchful and strengthen the things which remain…. If not, I will come on thee as a thief"*- Jesus did not find the works of this church perfect before God. Jesus warned them to be watchful and strengthen what was left of the church or they would be caught off-guard when He returns to rapture the church from the earth. Jesus acknowledges that even in this church, there are a few that have not defiled themselves with the perverted works of this church. He wanted to let those saints know that they will be rewarded.

2. Philadelphia – *"Because of patience and good works, Jesus will make their enemies their footstool and rapture this church before the great Tribulation"* Jesus encourages this church because of its good works. Jesus gives them opportunities and shuts down hindering spirits that are against the members of this church. Because they kept the word of patience, Jesus promised that He would keep them from the hour of temptation, which refers to the great tribulation that will come from the Anti-Christ.

3. Laodicea – *"Thou art lukewarm, and neither cold nor hot, I will spue thee out of my mouth"* This church believes that they are blessed of the Lord because they are rich, but God sees them as the opposite and calls for them to repent. The usage of water temperature allows the church to clearly understand their issues. Laodicea had water issues in that day, where their water was known for being "lukewarm." In other words, the water was known for **not** having the power to heal or refresh anyone. It was neither cold to refresh or hot to heal. No matter how rich the Laodiceans were, they could not fix this water issue. Having the Prophet utilize this analogy to describe the state of the Laodicean church would have allowed the Laodiceans to understand their spiritual condition.

The letters to the seven churches not only applied to the physical seven churches in Asia, but it also prophetically spoke of the various spiritual conditions and stages that the Christian churches would find themselves in during the Church Age (the time from Jesus' Resurrection until the rapture of the church from the earth).

Revelation Chapter 3

1. And unto the angel of the church in Sardis write; These things saith he that hath the seven Spirits of God, and the seven stars; I know thy works, that thou hast a name that thou livest, and art dead.

2. Be watchful, and strengthen the things which remain, that are ready to die: for I have not found thy works perfect before God.

3. Remember therefore how thou hast received and heard, and hold fast, and repent. If therefore thou shalt not watch, I will come on thee as a thief, and thou shalt not know what hour I will come upon thee.

4. Thou hast a few names even in Sardis which have not defiled their garments; and they shall walk with me in white: for they are worthy.

5. He that overcometh, the same shall be clothed in white raiment; and I will not blot out his name out of the book of life, but I will confess his name before my Father, and before his angels.

6. He that hath an ear, let him hear what the Spirit saith unto the churches.

7. **And to the angel of the church in Philadelphia write;** These things saith he that is holy, he that is true, he that hath the key of David, he that openeth, and no man shutteth; and shutteth, and no man openeth;

8. I know thy works: behold, I have set before thee an open door, and no man can shut it: for thou hast a little strength, and hast kept my word, and hast not denied my name.

9. Behold, I will make them of the synagogue of Satan, which say they are Jews, and are not, but do lie; behold, I will make them to come and worship before thy feet, and to know that I have loved thee.

10. Because thou hast kept the word of my patience, I also will keep thee from the hour of temptation, which shall come upon all the world, to try them that dwell upon the earth.

11. Behold, I come quickly: hold that fast which thou hast, that no man take thy crown.

12. Him that overcometh will I make a pillar in the temple of my God, and he shall go no more out: and I will write upon him the name of my God, and the name of the city of my God, which is new Jerusalem, which cometh down out of heaven from my God: and I will write upon him my new name.

13. He that hath an ear, let him hear what the Spirit saith unto the churches.

14. **And unto the angel of the church of the Laodiceans write;** These things saith the Amen, the faithful and true witness, the beginning of the creation of God;

15. I know thy works, that thou art neither cold nor hot: I would thou wert cold or hot.

16. So then because thou art lukewarm, and neither cold nor hot, I will spue thee out of my mouth.

17. Because thou sayest, I am rich, and increased with goods, and have need of nothing; and knowest not that thou art wretched, and miserable, and poor, and blind, and naked:

18. I counsel thee to buy of me gold tried in the fire, that thou mayest be rich; and white raiment, that thou mayest be clothed, and that the shame of thy nakedness do not appear; and anoint thine eyes with eyesalve, that thou mayest see.

19. As many as I love, I rebuke and chasten: be zealous therefore, and repent.

20. Behold, I stand at the door, and knock: if any man hear my voice, and open the door, I will come in to him, and will sup with him, and he with me.

21. To him that overcometh will I grant to sit with me in my throne, even as I also overcame, and am set down with my Father in his throne.

22. He that hath an ear, let him hear what the Spirit saith unto the churches.

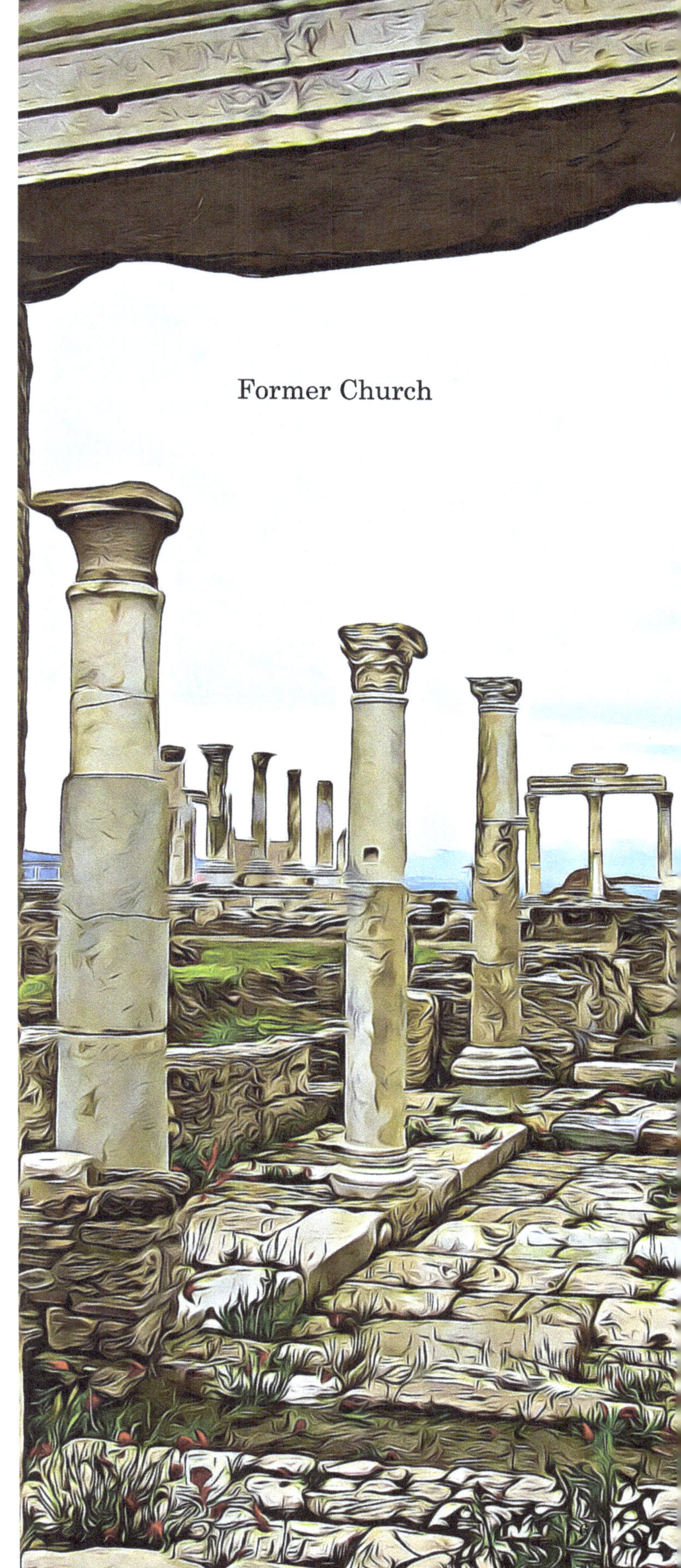

Former Church

THE INTERPRETATION OF CHAPTER 4

The Vision of God's Throne

And immediately I was in the spirit: and, behold, a throne was set in heaven, and one sat on the throne. — Revelation 4:2 (KJV)

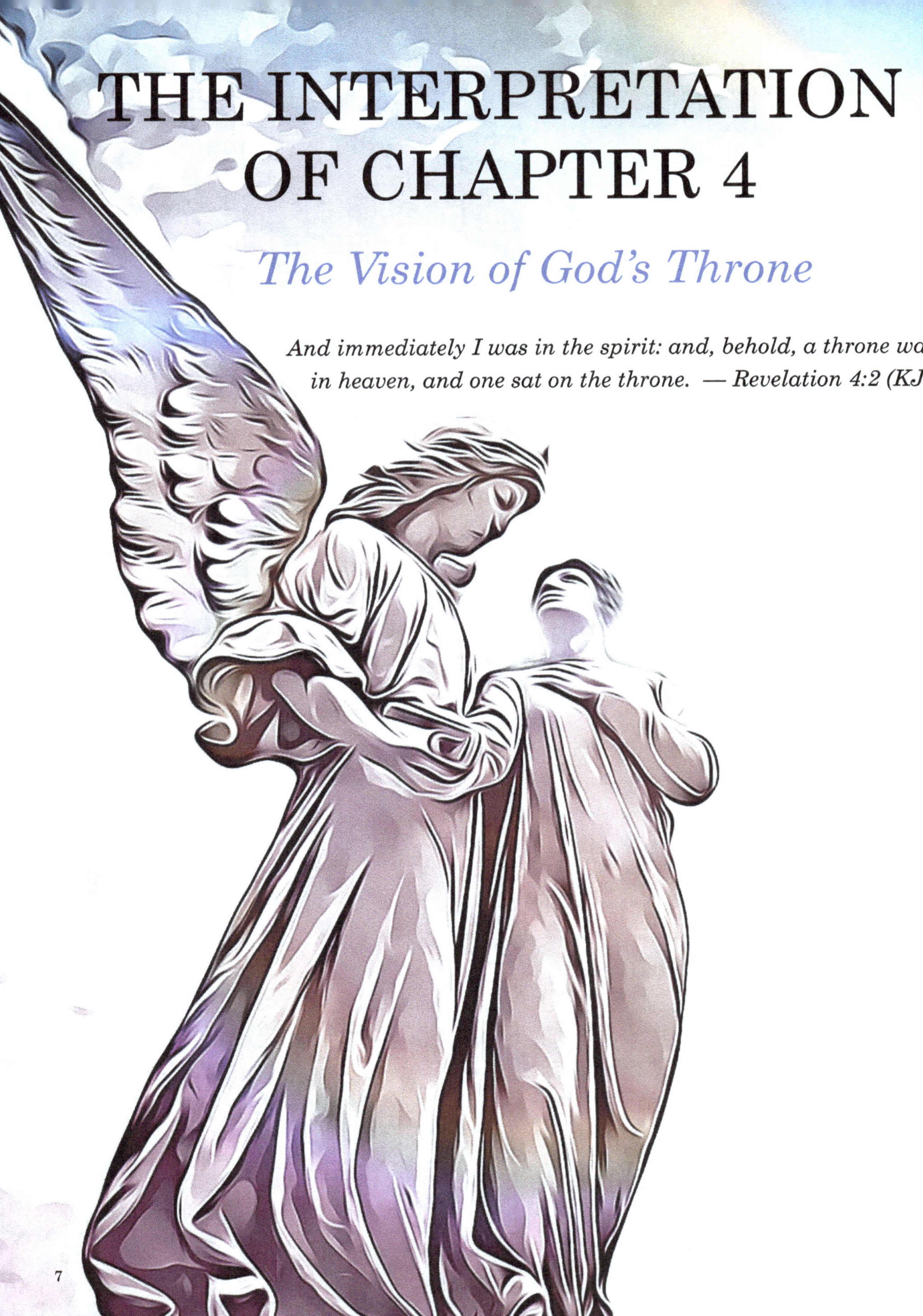

CHAPTER 4 is the vision of God's throne. Revelation 4 allows the Prophet John to see God's throne. God's Throne in Revelation 4 is described in the same manner as the Prophet Ezekiel's vision of God's throne as described in the Book of Ezekiel Chapter 1: 1-28 and Chapter 10:1-22. Chapter 4 basically shows John how a church service is conducted in heaven. Chapter 4 shows angelic beings giving praise and worship to God.

Revelation Chapter 4

1. After this I looked, and, behold, a door was opened in heaven: and the first voice which I heard was as it were of a trumpet talking with me; which said, Come up hither, and I will shew thee things which must be hereafter.

2. And immediately I was in the spirit: and, behold, a throne was set in heaven, and one sat on the throne.

3. And he that sat was to look upon like a jasper and a sardine stone: and there was a rainbow round about the throne, in sight like unto an emerald.

4. And round about the throne were four and twenty seats: and upon the seats I saw four and twenty elders sitting, clothed in white raiment; and they had on their heads crowns of gold.

5. And out of the throne proceeded lightnings and thunderings and voices: and there were seven lamps of fire burning before the throne, which are the seven Spirits of God.

6. And before the throne there was a sea of glass like unto crystal: and in the midst of the throne, and round about the throne, were four beasts full of eyes before and behind.

7. And the first beast was like a lion, and the second beast like a calf, and the third beast had a face as a man, and the fourth beast was like a flying eagle.

8. And the four beasts had each of them six wings about him; and they were full of eyes within: and they rest not day and night, saying, Holy, holy, holy, Lord God Almighty, which was, and is, and is to come.

9. And when those beasts give glory and honour and thanks to him that sat on the throne, who liveth for ever and ever,

10. The four and twenty elders fall down before him that sat on the throne, and worship him that liveth for ever and ever, and cast their crowns before the throne, saying,

11. Thou art worthy, O Lord, to receive glory and honour and power: for thou hast created all things, and for thy pleasure they are and were created.

THE INTERPRETATION OF CHAPTER 5

The Impact of the Cross on the Heavens

And one of the elders saith unto me, Weep not: behold, the Lion of the tribe of Judah, the Root of David, hath prevailed to open the book, and to loose the seven seals thereof.
— Revelation 5:5 (KJV)

CHAPTER 5 explains the impact of the cross on the heavens. Most Christians are familiar with the earthly events that occurred after Jesus death on the cross, and his subsequent resurrection. However, Revelation Chapter 5 explains what happened in heaven after Jesus death on the cross. If you read Revelation Chapter 5 immediately after reading the four Gospels account of Jesus' death (Matthew 27:50, Luke 23:46, Mark 15:37, John 19:30), you would see a continuation of the story as follows:

Luke Chapter 23:46 (KJV)

And when Jesus had cried with a loud voice, he said, Father, into thy hands I commend my spirit: and having said thus, he gave up the ghost.

Revelation Chapter 5:6 (KJV)

*6. And I beheld, and, lo, in the midst of the throne and of the four beasts, and in the midst of the elders, stood a Lamb as it had been slain, having seven horns and seven eyes, which are the seven Spirits of God * sent forth into all the earth.*

After Jesus died on the cross, Revelation Chapter 5 shows Jesus as the slain lamb who prevailed against Satan to open the scroll with the seven seals. In biblical days, a scroll was enclosed with a seal to allow the recipient to know who sent the message and to keep the message private. The scroll with the seven seals was authored by God Almighty. Before Jesus' death on the cross, no one was worthy to open the scroll, which contains plagues and unlocks the future events that will occur to bring about the end of the world.

**The Seven Spirits:*
1) *The spirit of the Lord shall rest upon him*
2) *The spirit of wisdom*
3) *The spirit of understanding,*
4) *The spirit of counsel*
5) *The spirit of might,*
6) *The spirit of knowledge and*
7) *The fear of the Lord.*

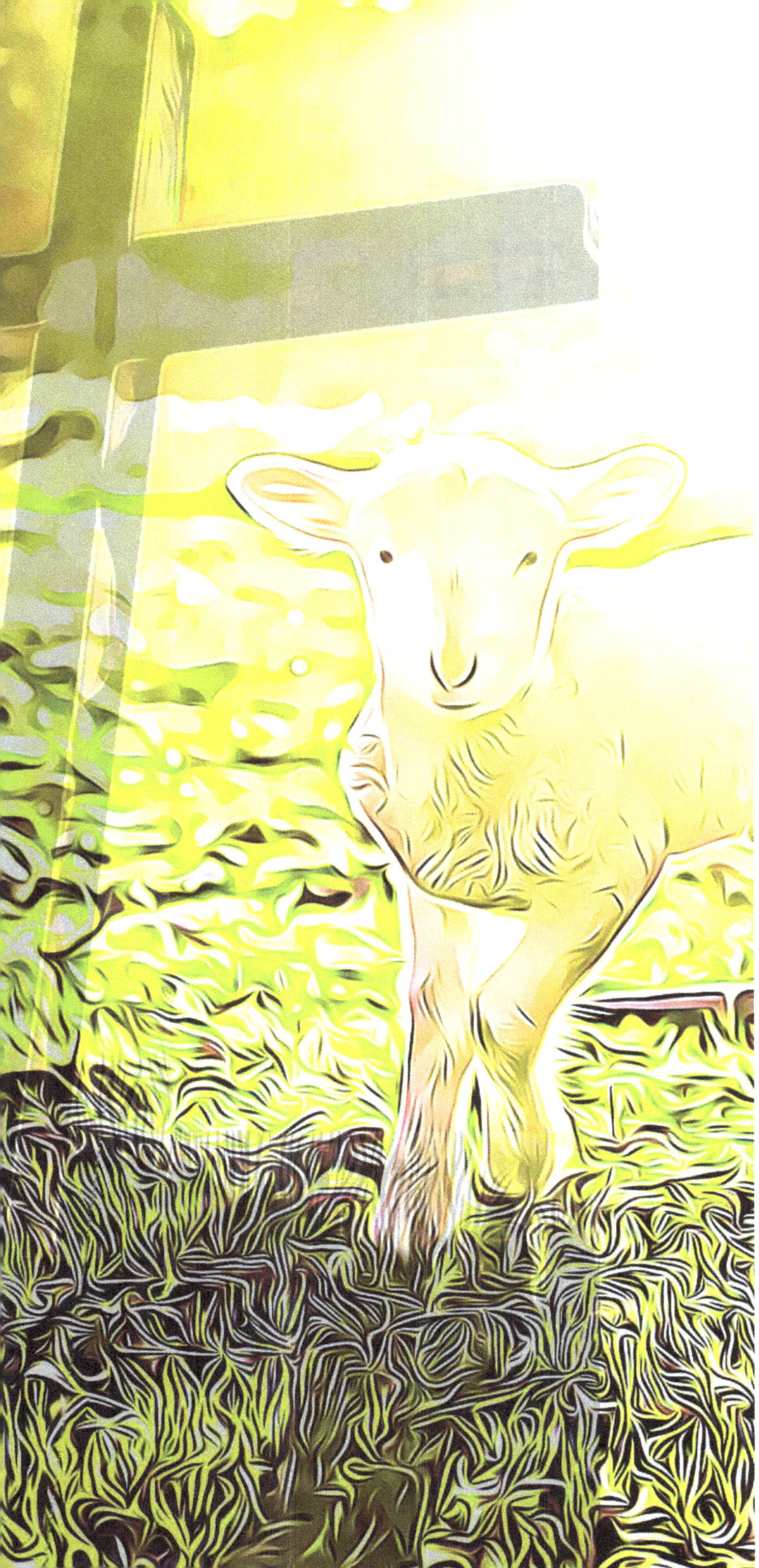

Revelation Chapter 5

1. And I saw in the right hand of him that sat on the throne a book written within and on the backside, sealed with seven seals.
2. And I saw a strong angel proclaiming with a loud voice, Who is worthy to open the book, and to loose the seals thereof?
3. And no man in heaven, nor in earth, neither under the earth, was able to open the book, neither to look thereon.
4. And I wept much, because no man was found worthy to open and to read the book, neither to look thereon.
5. And one of the elders saith unto me, Weep not: behold, the Lion of the tribe of Judah, the Root of David, hath prevailed to open the book, and to loose the seven seals thereof.
6. And I beheld, and, lo, in the midst of the throne and of the four beasts, and in the midst of the elders, stood a Lamb as it had been slain, having seven horns and seven eyes, which are the seven Spirits of God sent forth into all the earth.
7. And he came and took the book out of the right hand of him that sat upon the throne.
8. And when he had taken the book, the four beasts and four and twenty elders fell down before the Lamb, having every one of them harps, and golden vials full of odours, which are the prayers of saints.
9. And they sung a new song, saying, Thou art worthy to take the book, and to open the seals thereof: for thou wast slain, and hast redeemed us to God by thy blood out of every kindred, and tongue, and people, and nation;
10. And hast made us unto our God kings and priests: and we shall reign on the earth.
11. And I beheld, and I heard the voice of many angels round about the throne and the beasts and the elders: and the number of them was ten thousand times ten thousand, and thousands of thousands;
12. Saying with a loud voice, Worthy is the Lamb that was slain to receive power, and riches, and wisdom, and strength, and honour, and glory, and blessing.
13. And every creature which is in heaven, and on the earth, and under the earth, and such as are in the sea, and all that are in them, heard I saying, Blessing, and honour, and glory, and power, be unto him that sitteth upon the throne, and unto the Lamb for ever and ever.
14. And the four beasts said, Amen. And the four and twenty elders fell down and worshiped him that liveth for ever and ever.

THE INTERPRETATION OF CHAPTER 6

The Opening of the Seven Seals

And I saw when the Lamb opened one of the seals, and I heard, as it were the noise of thunder, one of the four beasts saying, Come and see. — Revelation 6:1 (KJV)

CHAPTER 6 explains to John the prophet the message contained within the scroll with the seven seals. In summary, the opening of seven seals set into motion the continuation of judgment on the earthly kingdoms and released the following events on earth that must occur before the end of earth will come:

1. False Prophet   Rev 6:1-2   Cross-reference: *Matthew 24:3-5*

2. No Peace   Rev 6:3-4   Cross-reference: *Matthew 24:6-7*

3. Famine   Rev 6:5-6   Cross-reference: *Matthew 24:7*

4. Death and Disease   Rev 6:7-8   Cross-reference: *Matthew 24:7*

5. Tribulation   Rev 6:9-11   Cross-reference: *Matthew 24:8-26*

6. Natural Disaster   Rev 6:12-17   Cross-reference: *Matthew 24:27-29*

7. Final Judgment   The Seventh Seal is explained in Revelation Chapter 8

Revelation Chapter 6 explains all the events that will occur on earth before the end will come. These events are also explained in Matthew Chapter 24:1-29, when Jesus answered the disciples' questions to explain what would happen before the end comes. Chapter 6 marks the beginning of the end and the closure of the church age. In the Book of Daniel, God communicated to the prophet Daniel through an angel that the earthly kingdoms were headed toward final judgment and eternal damnation because they were wicked, but a Messiah would come and interrupt this final judgment to give mankind space to get saved and repent. This was accomplished through Jesus' death, burial, and resurrection. With Jesus' resurrection, he ushered in the Church Age. However, Chapter 6 explains the events that will happen on earth that signals when the church age is nearing its end.

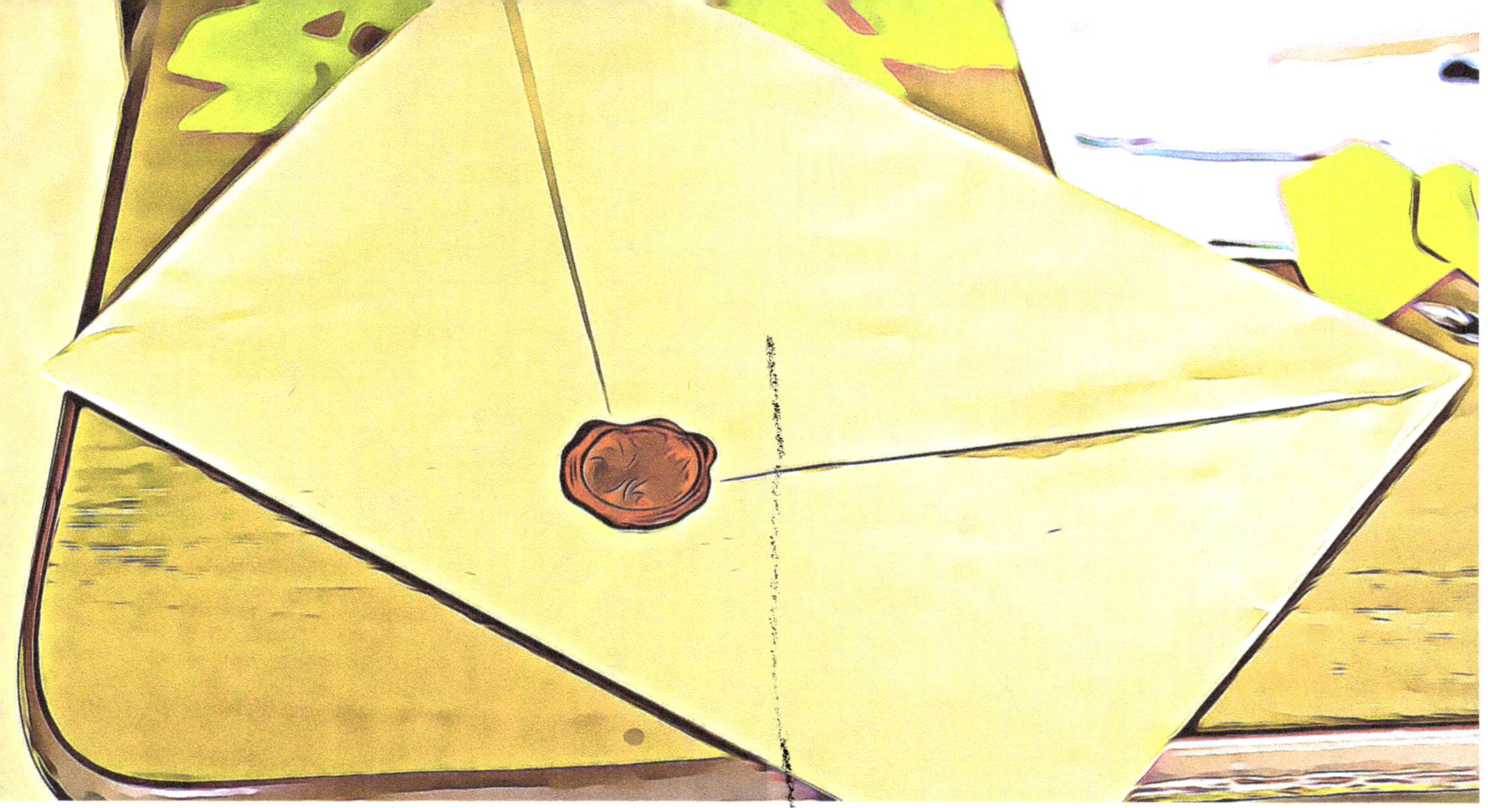

Revelation Chapter 6 King James Version (KJV) Public Domain

1. And I saw when the Lamb opened one of the seals, and I heard, as it were the noise of thunder, one of the four beasts saying, Come and see.

2. And I saw and behold a white horse: and he that sat on him had a bow; and a crown was given unto him: and he went forth conquering, and to conquer.

3. And when he had opened the second seal, I heard the second beast say, Come and see.

4. And there went out another horse that was red: and power was given to him that sat thereon to take peace from the earth, and that they should kill one another: and there was given unto him a great sword.

5. And when he had opened the third seal, I heard the third beast say, Come and see. And I beheld, and lo a black horse; and he that sat on him had a pair of balances in his hand.

6. And I heard a voice in the midst of the four beasts say, A measure of wheat for a penny, and three measures of barley for a penny; and see thou hurt not the oil and the wine.

7. And when he had opened the fourth seal, I heard the voice of the fourth beast say, Come and see.

8. And I looked and behold a pale horse: and his name that sat on him was Death, and Hell followed with him. And power was given unto them over the fourth part of the earth, to kill with sword, and with hunger, and with death, and with the beasts of the earth.

9. And when he had opened the fifth seal, I saw under the altar the souls of them that were slain for the word of God, and for the testimony which they held:

10. And they cried with a loud voice, saying, How long, O Lord, holy and true, dost thou not judge and avenge our blood on them that dwell on the earth?

11. And white robes were given unto every one of them; and it was said unto them, that they should rest yet for a little season, until their fellow servants also and their brethren, that should be killed as they were, should be fulfilled.

12. And I beheld when he had opened the sixth seal, and, lo, there was a great earthquake; and the sun became black as sackcloth of hair, and the moon became as blood;

13. And the stars of heaven fell unto the earth, even as a fig tree casteth her untimely figs, when she is shaken of a mighty wind.

14. And the heaven departed as a scroll when it is rolled together; and every mountain and island were moved out of their places.

15. And the kings of the earth, and the great men, and the rich men, and the chief captains, and the mighty men, and every bondman, and every free man, hid themselves in the dens and in the rocks of the mountains;

16. And said to the mountains and rocks, Fall on us, and hide us from the face of him that sitteth on the throne, and from the wrath of the Lamb:

17. For the great day of his wrath is come; and who shall be able to stand?

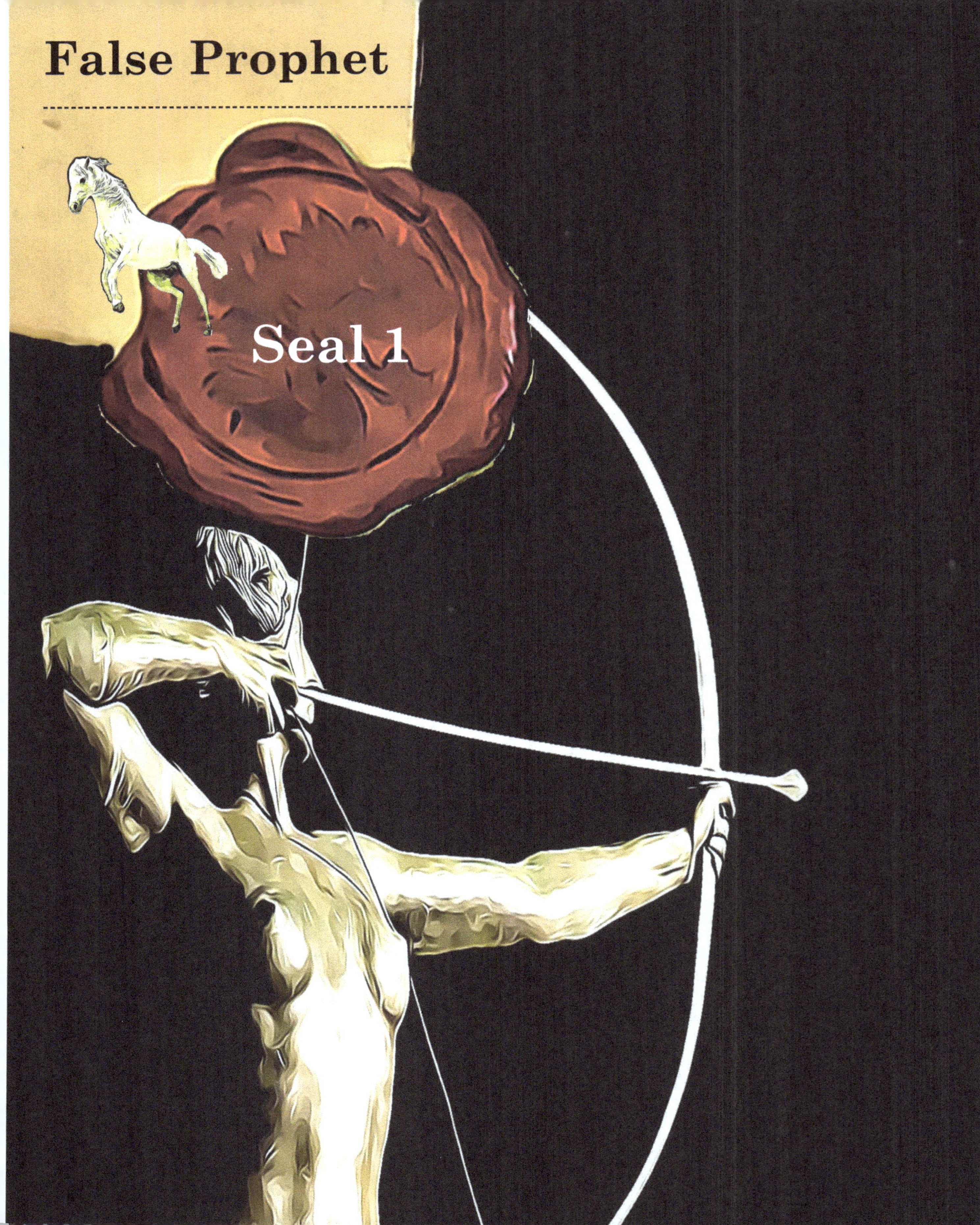

False Prophet
Seal 1

Revelation 6:2 King James Version (KJV) Public Domain

And I saw and behold a white horse: and he that sat on him had a bow; and a crown was given unto him: and he went forth conquering, and to conquer.

(Rev 6:1-2 cross-references to *Matthew 24:3-5 and Revelations 19:11-13*)

Revelations 19:11-13 reveals the real Jesus
This rider tries to mimic Jesus, but the False Prophet is coming to conquer instead of to save.

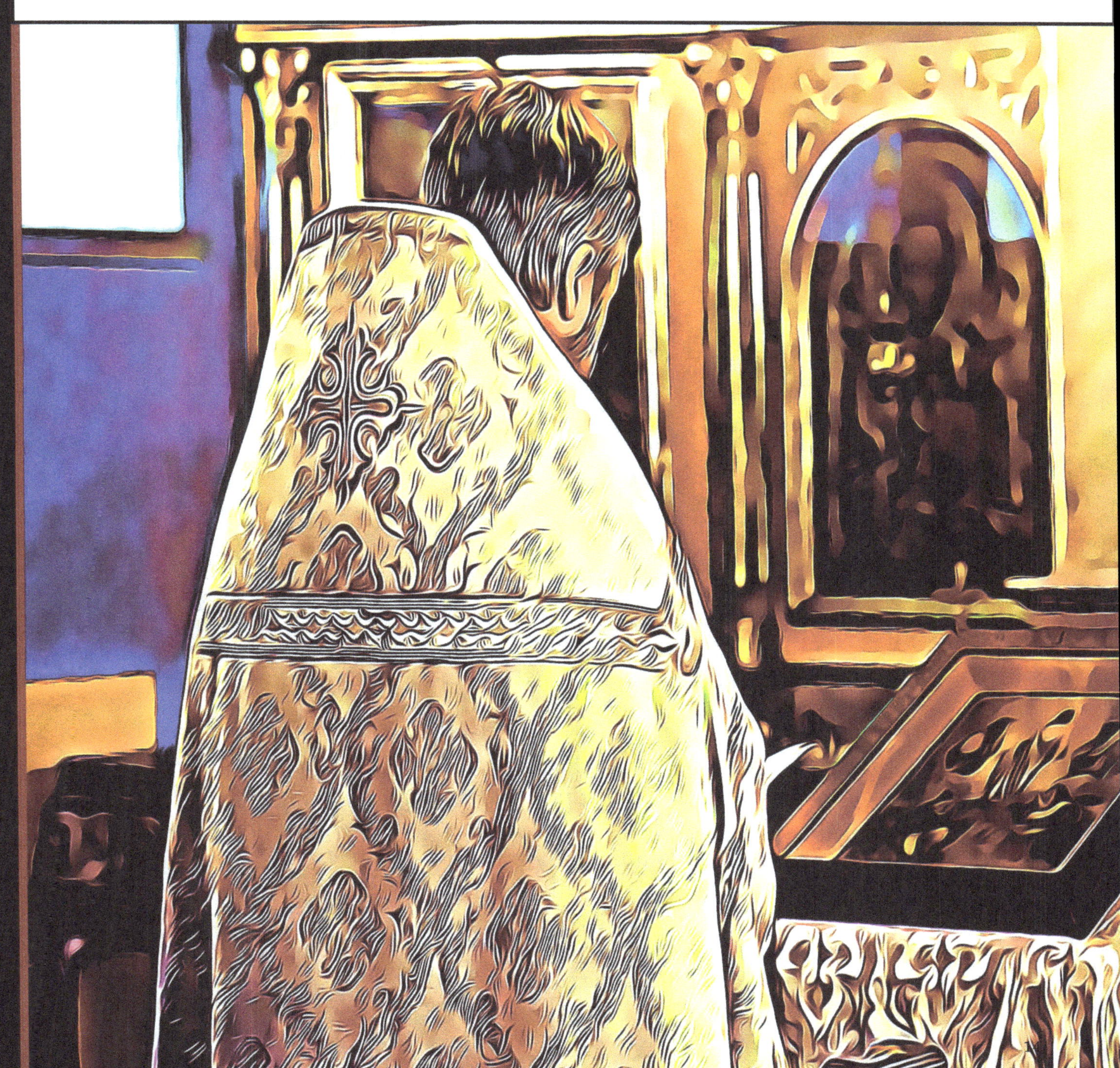

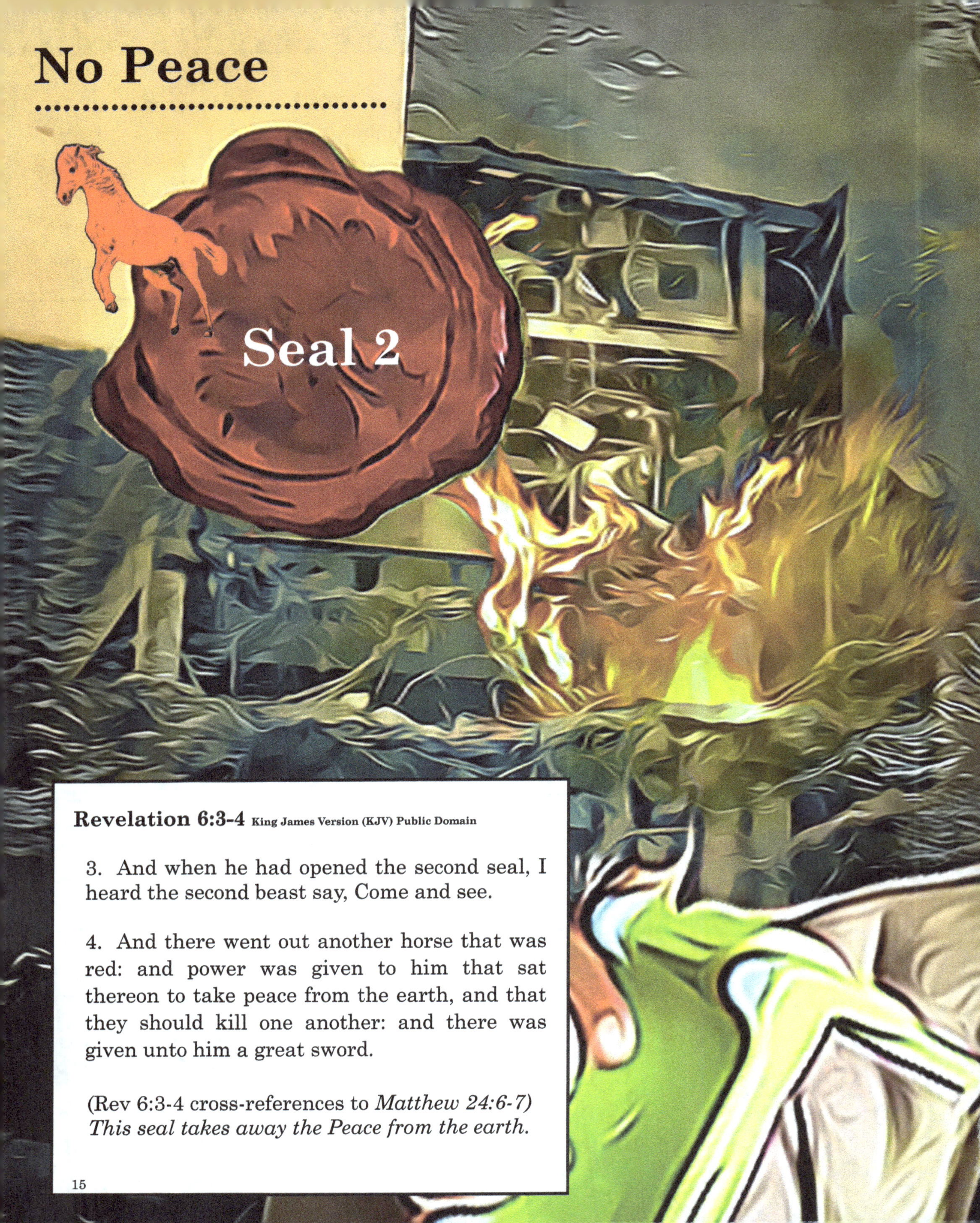

No Peace

Seal 2

Revelation 6:3-4 King James Version (KJV) Public Domain

3. And when he had opened the second seal, I heard the second beast say, Come and see.

4. And there went out another horse that was red: and power was given to him that sat thereon to take peace from the earth, and that they should kill one another: and there was given unto him a great sword.

(Rev 6:3-4 cross-references to *Matthew 24:6-7*) *This seal takes away the Peace from the earth.*

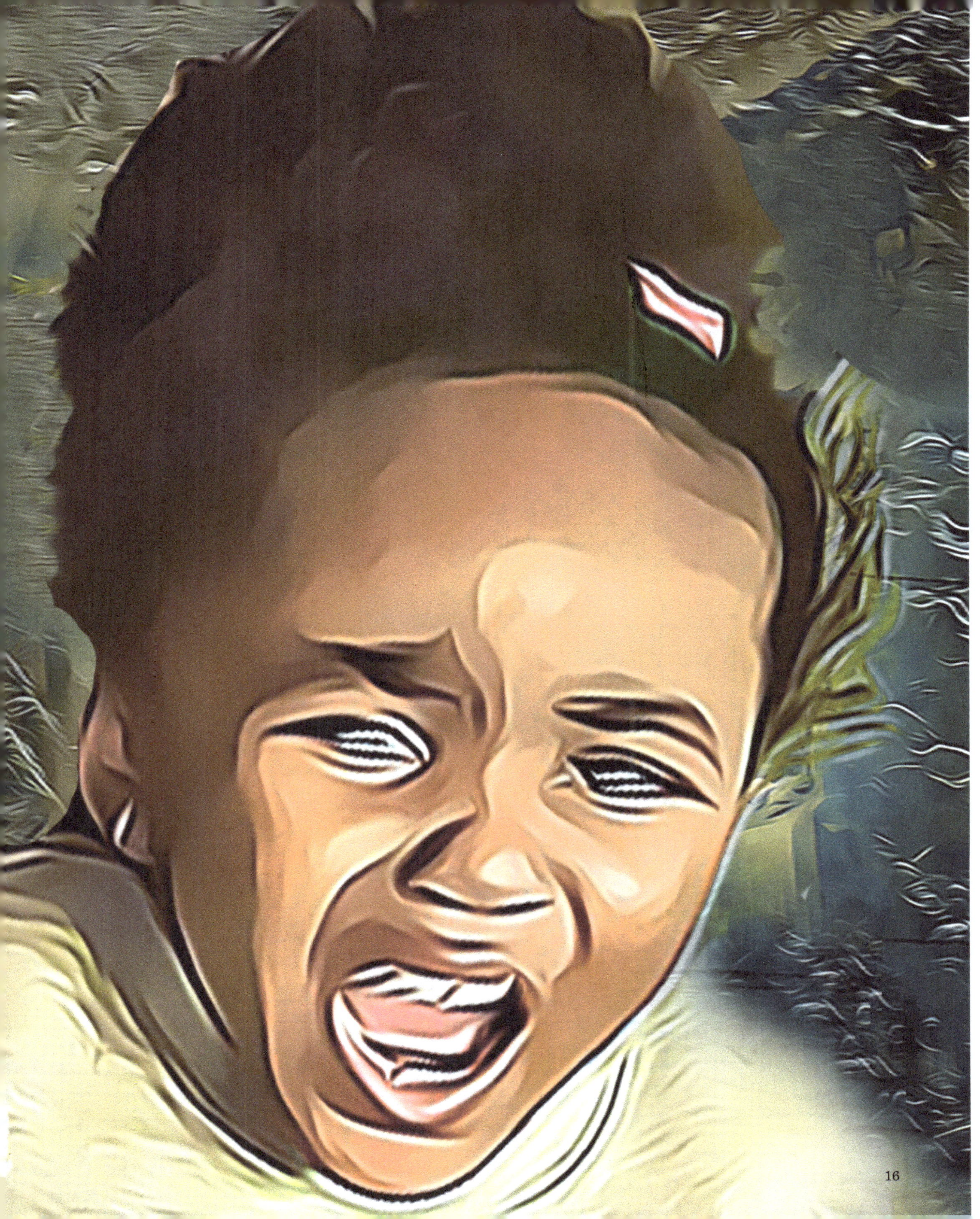

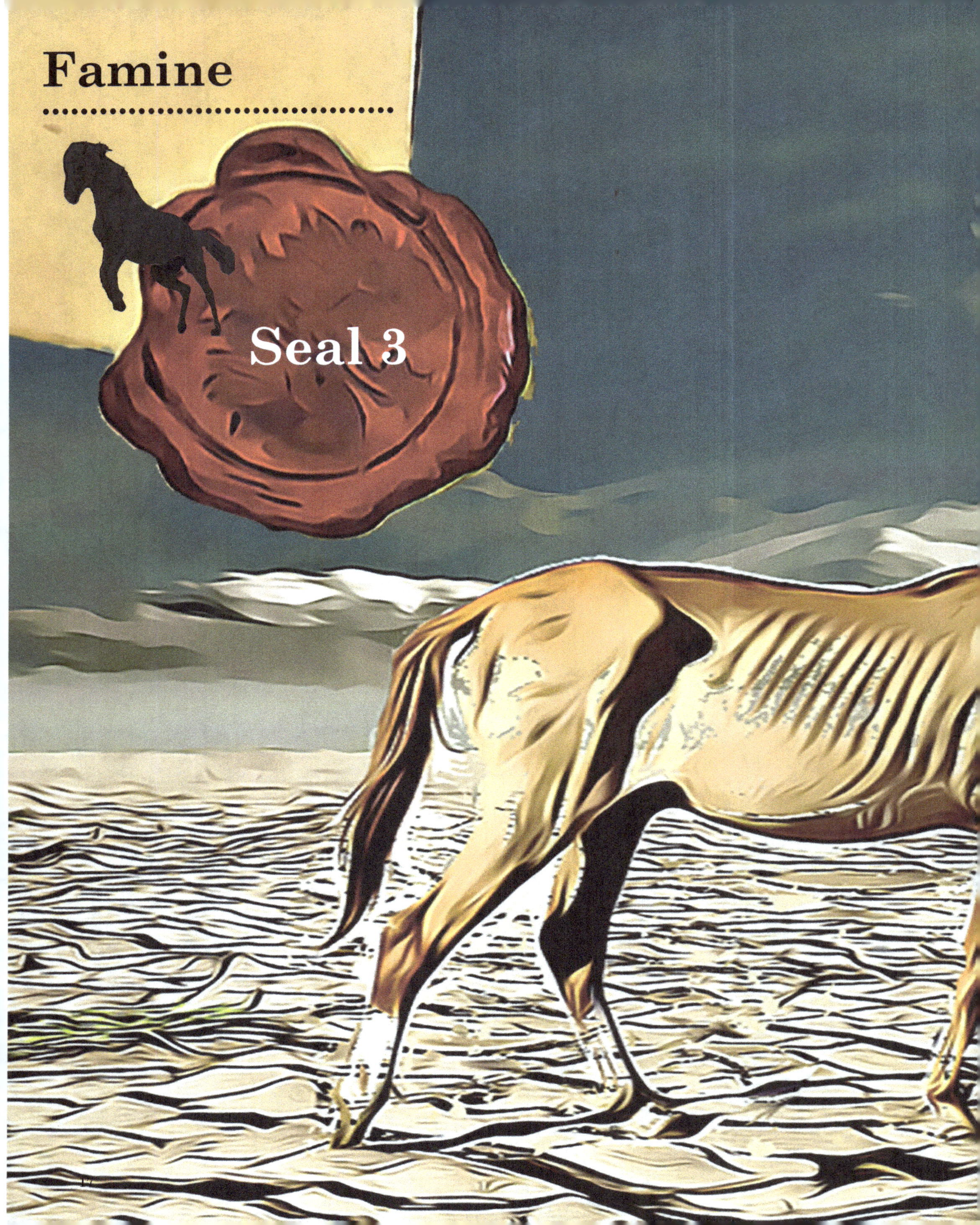
Famine
Seal 3

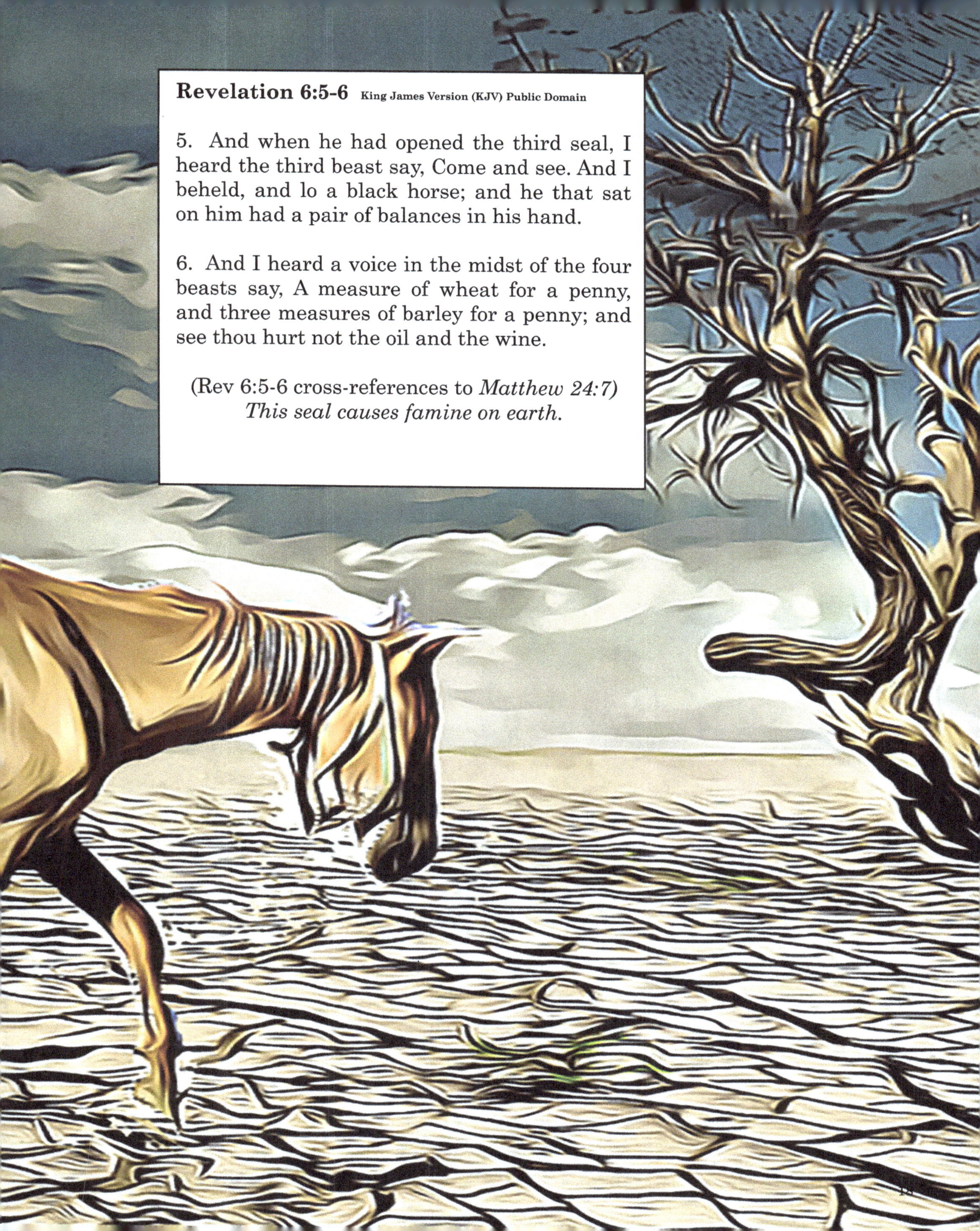

Revelation 6:5-6   King James Version (KJV) Public Domain

5.   And when he had opened the third seal, I heard the third beast say, Come and see. And I beheld, and lo a black horse; and he that sat on him had a pair of balances in his hand.

6.   And I heard a voice in the midst of the four beasts say, A measure of wheat for a penny, and three measures of barley for a penny; and see thou hurt not the oil and the wine.

(Rev 6:5-6 cross-references to Matthew 24:7)
This seal causes famine on earth.

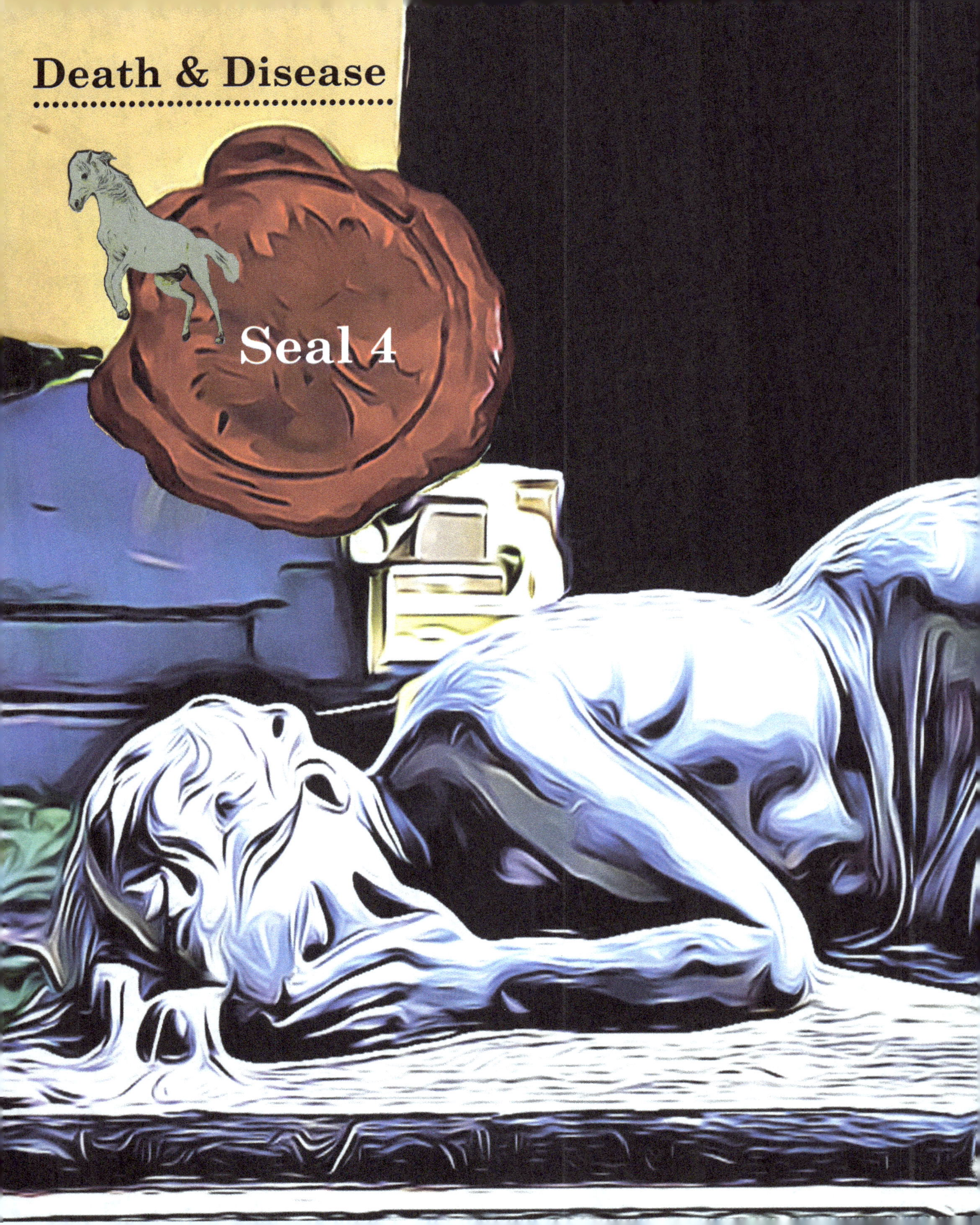

Death & Disease
Seal 4

7. And when he had opened the fourth seal, I heard the voice of the fourth beast say, Come and see.

8. And I looked and behold a pale horse: and his name that sat on him was Death, and Hell followed with him. And power was given unto them over the fourth part of the earth, to kill with sword, and with hunger, and with death, and with the beasts of the earth.

(Rev 6:7-8 cross-references to *Matthew 24:7*)
This seal causes War, Famine, Death and Disease on earth.

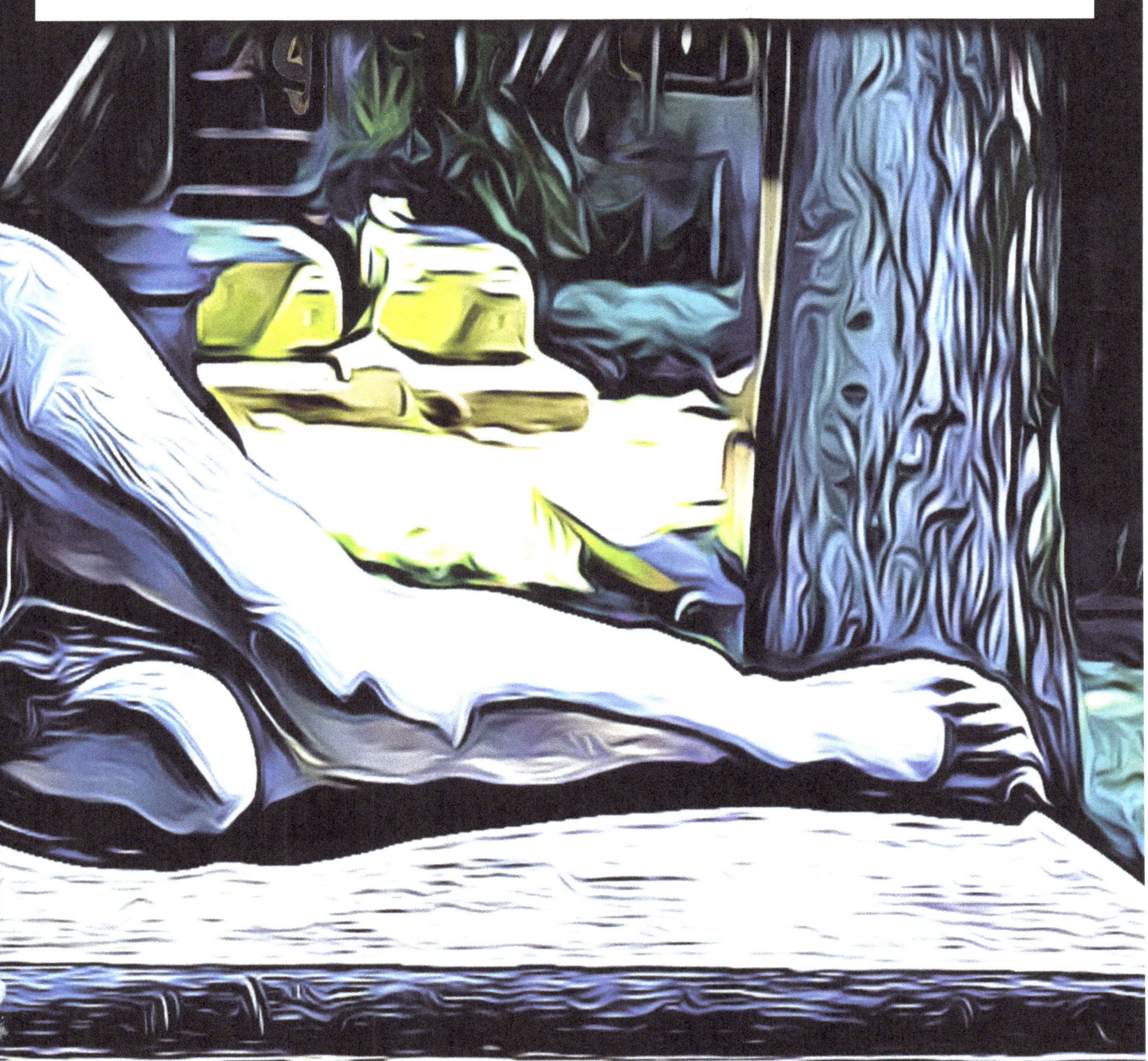

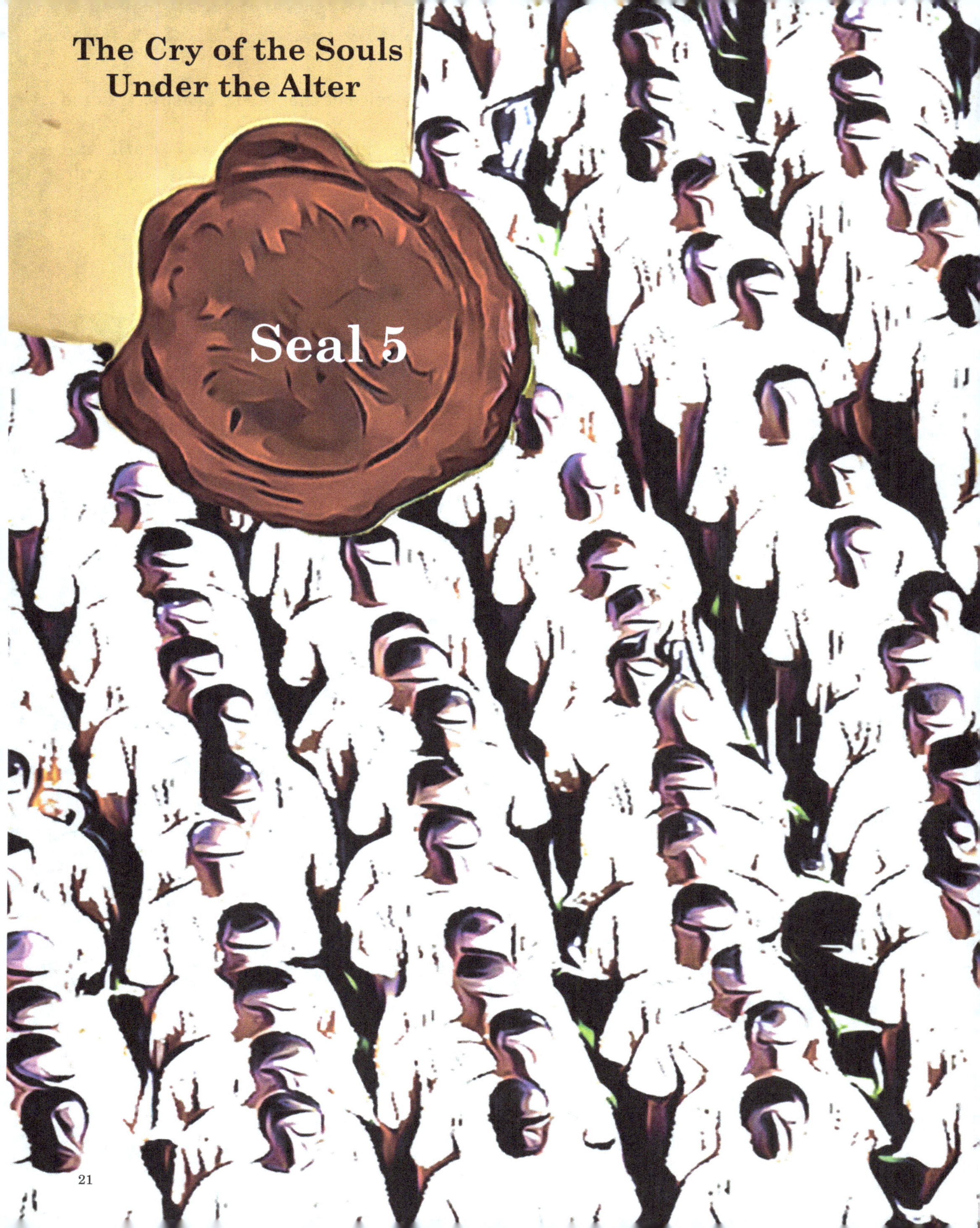
The Cry of the Souls
Under the Alter
Seal 5

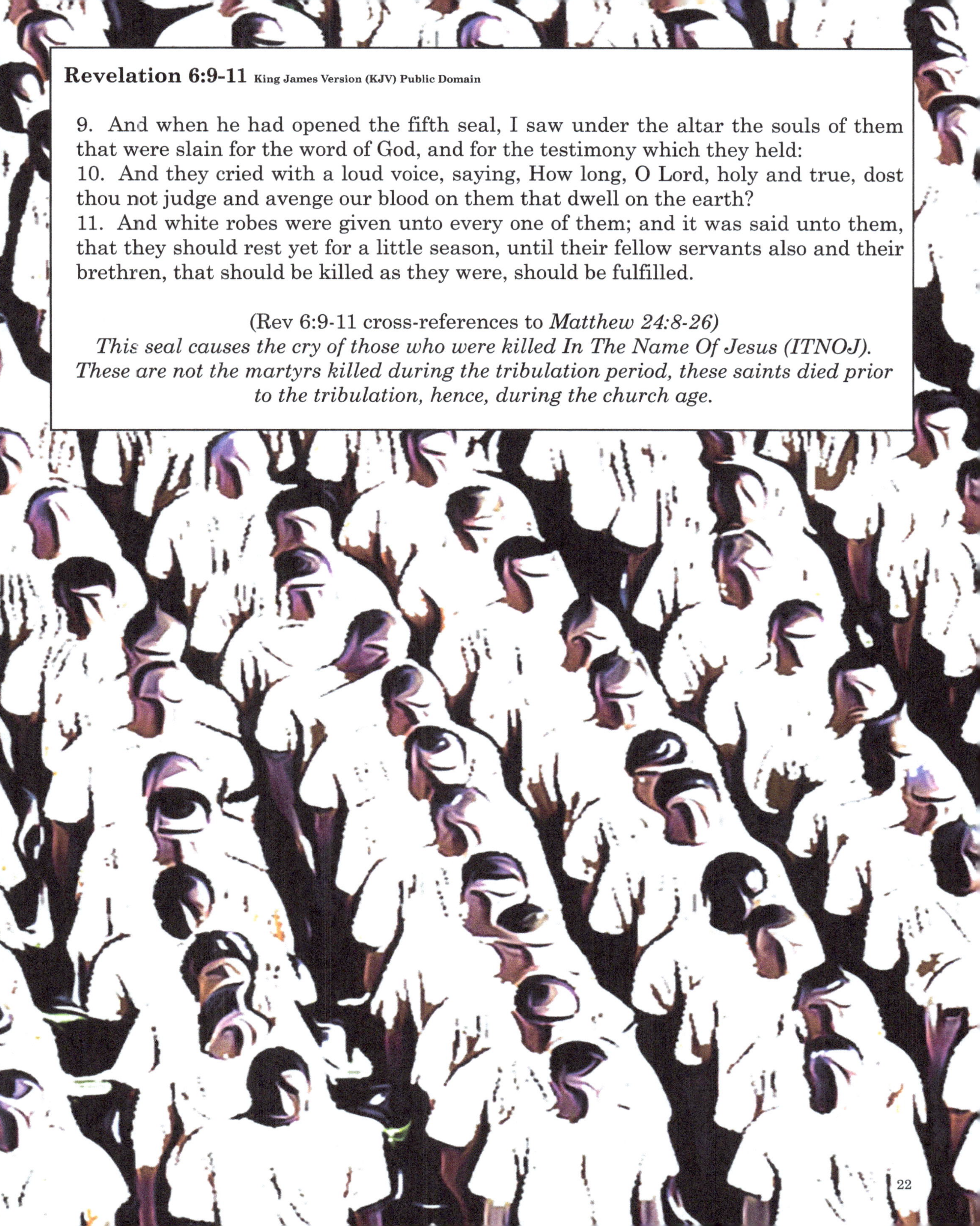

Revelation 6:9-11 King James Version (KJV) Public Domain

9. And when he had opened the fifth seal, I saw under the altar the souls of them that were slain for the word of God, and for the testimony which they held:
10. And they cried with a loud voice, saying, How long, O Lord, holy and true, dost thou not judge and avenge our blood on them that dwell on the earth?
11. And white robes were given unto every one of them; and it was said unto them, that they should rest yet for a little season, until their fellow servants also and their brethren, that should be killed as they were, should be fulfilled.

(Rev 6:9-11 cross-references to *Matthew 24:8-26*)
This seal causes the cry of those who were killed In The Name Of Jesus (ITNOJ).
These are not the martyrs killed during the tribulation period, these saints died prior
to the tribulation, hence, during the church age.

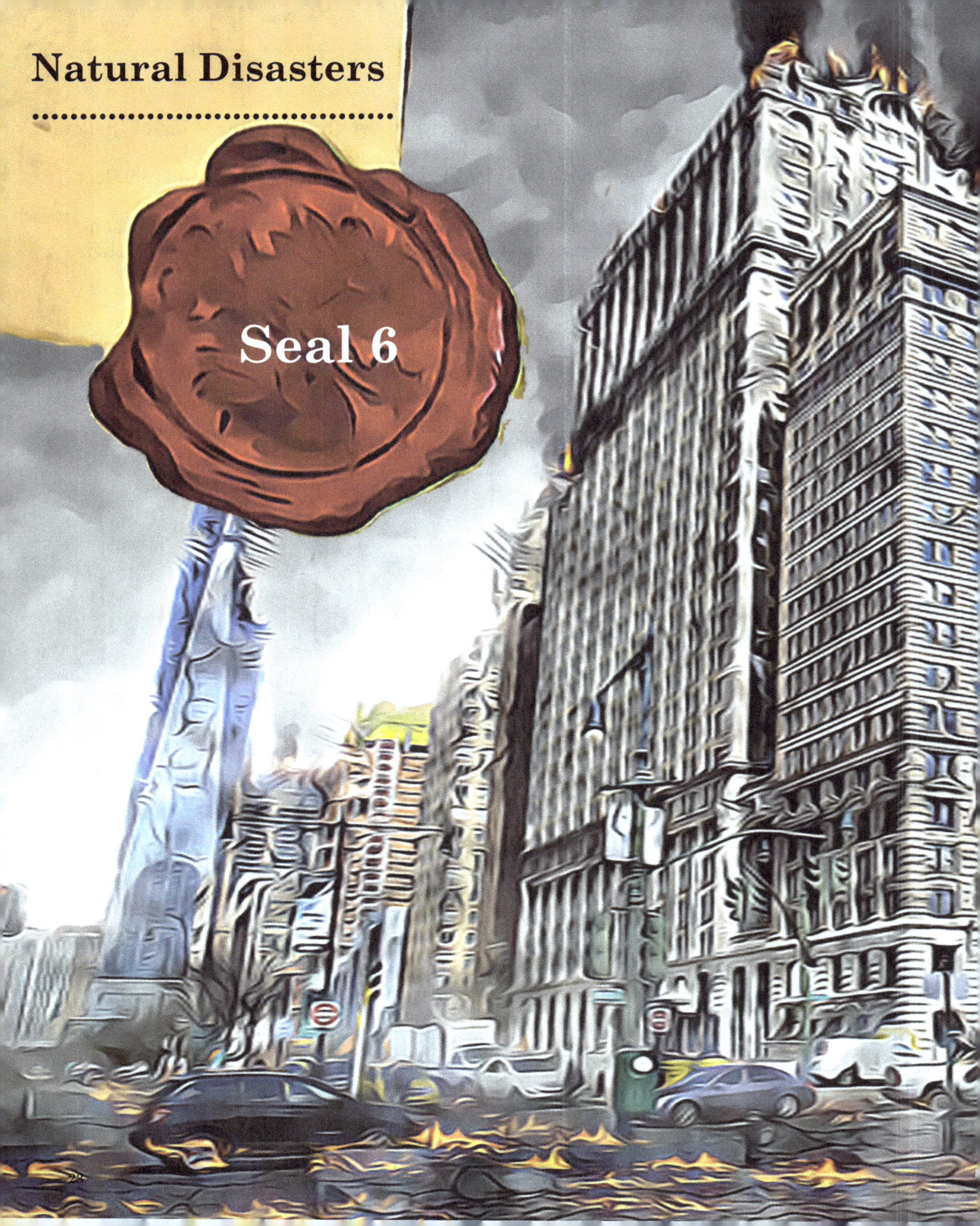
Natural Disasters
Seal 6

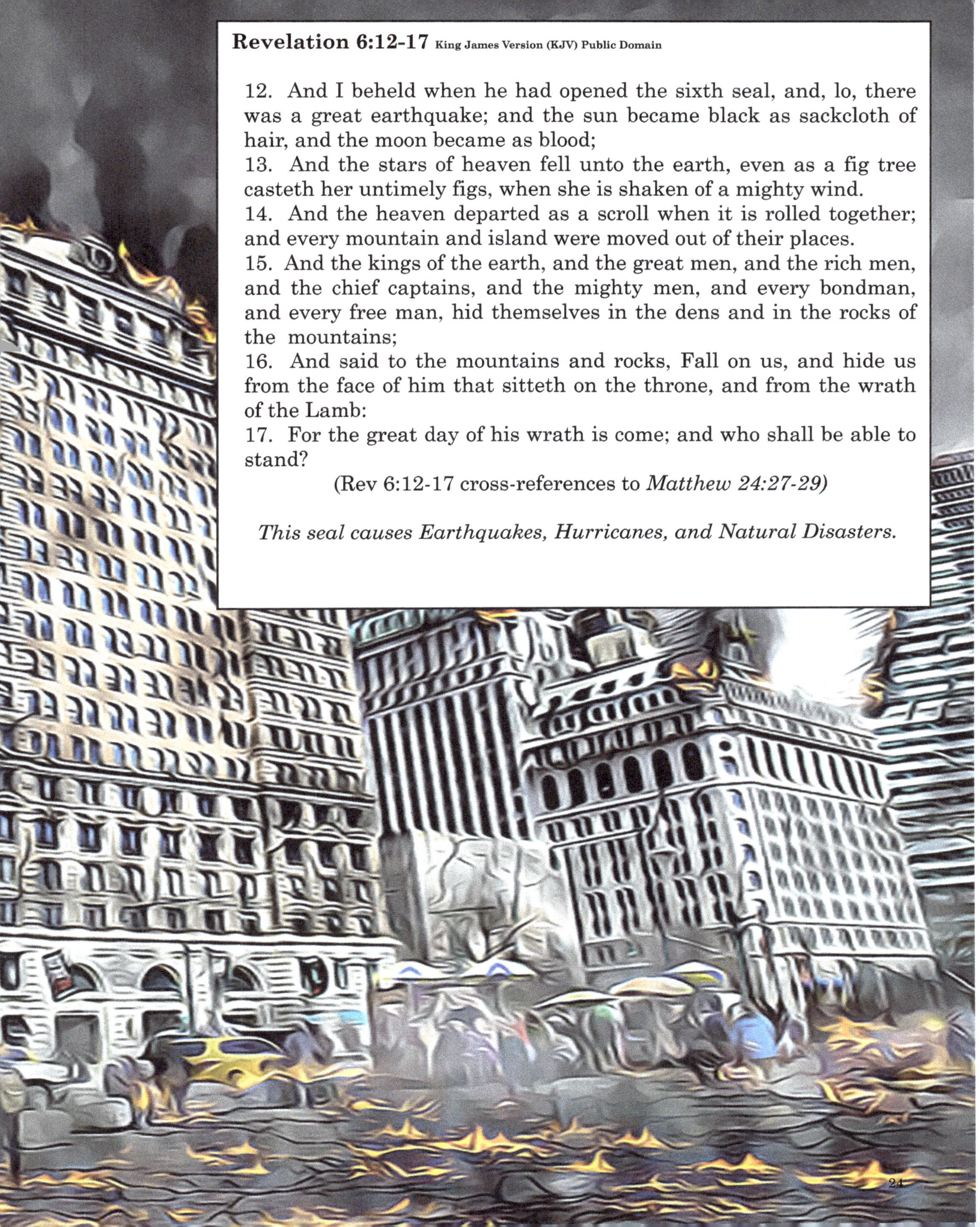

Revelation 6:12-17 King James Version (KJV) Public Domain

12.   And I beheld when he had opened the sixth seal, and, lo, there was a great earthquake; and the sun became black as sackcloth of hair, and the moon became as blood;
13.   And the stars of heaven fell unto the earth, even as a fig tree casteth her untimely figs, when she is shaken of a mighty wind.
14.   And the heaven departed as a scroll when it is rolled together; and every mountain and island were moved out of their places.
15.   And the kings of the earth, and the great men, and the rich men, and the chief captains, and the mighty men, and every bondman, and every free man, hid themselves in the dens and in the rocks of the mountains;
16.   And said to the mountains and rocks, Fall on us, and hide us from the face of him that sitteth on the throne, and from the wrath of the Lamb:
17.   For the great day of his wrath is come; and who shall be able to stand?

(Rev 6:12-17 cross-references to *Matthew 24:27-29*)

This seal causes Earthquakes, Hurricanes, and Natural Disasters.

THE INTERPRETATION OF CHAPTER 7

Selection of the 144,000 and the Church

Saying, Hurt not the earth, neither the sea, nor the trees, till we have sealed the servants of our God in their foreheads. — Revelation 7:3 (KJV)

CHAPTER 7 explains how God protected a portion of Israel and the church from the Great Tribulation. Chapter 7 describes the heavenly events that occurred to temporarily stop the natural disasters from occurring on the earth to give space for the sealing of God's servants, which means to be selected to be taken away from the earth. This chapter chronicles the end of the church age. The church age interrupted the final judgment of the earthly kingdoms to allow for salvation from eternal damnation. Jesus Christ's death on the cross and subsequent resurrection ushered in a heavenly kingdom on earth to allow all who would believe to gain eternal life. Since Jesus ushered in the church age, Jesus is the only one qualified to end the church age. Chapter 7 marks the official end of the church age with the sealing / selection of God's servants. God's servants were spared from participating in the following events:

Once the Church Age closes, the Tribulation period begins, and Daniel's prophecy of the 70 weeks resumes (Daniel 9:25-28). Daniel's prophecy states that 70 prophetic weeks (490 years) will be divided into three parts: seven weeks (49 years) Israel was exiled to Babylon; plus 62 weeks (434 years) Israel was held in captivity by the Persian, Grecian, and the Roman Empires; plus one week (7 years) will occur after the Messiah is "cut-off," hence after Jesus is crucified. The events explained in Revelation Chapters 6 and 7 occur within the final week of Daniel's 70 weeks prophecy. This week is also called the 70th week. The prophecy concludes by explaining that in the 70th week, following the death of the Messiah and the destruction of Jerusalem, "the prince who is to come" will make a treaty with 10 kings, which includes Israel. This treaty will allow the Anti-Christ to desecrate the third rebuilt temple of Jerusalem. The Anti-Christ (2 Thessalonian 2), will come from the same people who destroyed the second temple, which was the Romans.

Both scriptures, Daniel 9:27 and 2 Thessalonian 2, explain that in the middle of this 70th week (3 1/2 years), the Anti-Christ would break the covenant with Israel and declare himself to be God. He will stop the sacrifices and he will erect a statue of himself (an abomination of desolation). The book of Revelation continues that Jesus will return to the earth 3 1/2 years after this statue is erected in the new third temple in Jerusalem to lead the final end-time wars. The servants who have God's seal are spared from participating in these final events that bring about the end of the world.

Revelation Chapter 7

King James Version (KJV) Public Domain

1. And after these things I saw four angels standing on the four corners of the earth, holding the four winds of the earth, that the wind should not blow on the earth, nor on the sea, nor on any tree.

2. And I saw another angel ascending from the east, having the seal of the living God: and he cried with a loud voice to the four angels, to whom it was given to hurt the earth and the sea,

3. Saying, Hurt not the earth, neither the sea, nor the trees, till we have sealed the servants of our God in their foreheads.

4. And I heard the number of them which were sealed: and there were sealed an hundred and forty and four thousand of all the tribes of the children of Israel.

5. Of the tribe of Judah were sealed twelve thousand. Of the tribe of Reuben were sealed twelve thousand. Of the tribe of Gad were sealed twelve thousand.

6. Of the tribe of Aser were sealed twelve thousand. Of the tribe of Nephthalim were sealed twelve thousand. Of the tribe of Manasses were sealed twelve thousand.

7. Of the tribe of Simeon were sealed twelve thousand. Of the tribe of Levi were sealed twelve thousand. Of the tribe of Issachar were sealed twelve thousand.

8. Of the tribe of Zabulon were sealed twelve thousand. Of the tribe of Joseph were sealed twelve thousand. Of the tribe of Benjamin were sealed twelve thousand.

9. After this I beheld, and, lo, a great multitude, which no man could number, of all nations, and kindreds, and people, and tongues, stood before the throne, and before the Lamb, clothed with white robes, and palms in their hands;

10. And cried with a loud voice, saying, Salvation to our God which sitteth upon the throne, and unto the Lamb.

11. And all the angels stood round about the throne, and about the elders and the four beasts, and fell before the throne on their faces, and worshiped God,

12. Saying, Amen: Blessing, and glory, and wisdom, and thanksgiving, and honour, and power, and might, be unto our God for ever and ever. Amen.

13. And one of the elders answered, saying unto me, What are these which are arrayed in white robes? and whence came they?

14. And I said unto him, Sir, thou knowest. And he said to me, These are they which came out of great tribulation, and have washed their robes, and made them white in the blood of the Lamb.

15. Therefore, are they before the throne of God, and serve him day and night in his temple: and he that sitteth on the throne shall dwell among them.

16. They shall hunger no more, neither thirst any more; neither shall the sun light on them, nor any heat.

17. For the Lamb which is in the midst of the throne shall feed them, and shall lead them unto living fountains of waters: and God shall wipe away all tears from their eyes.

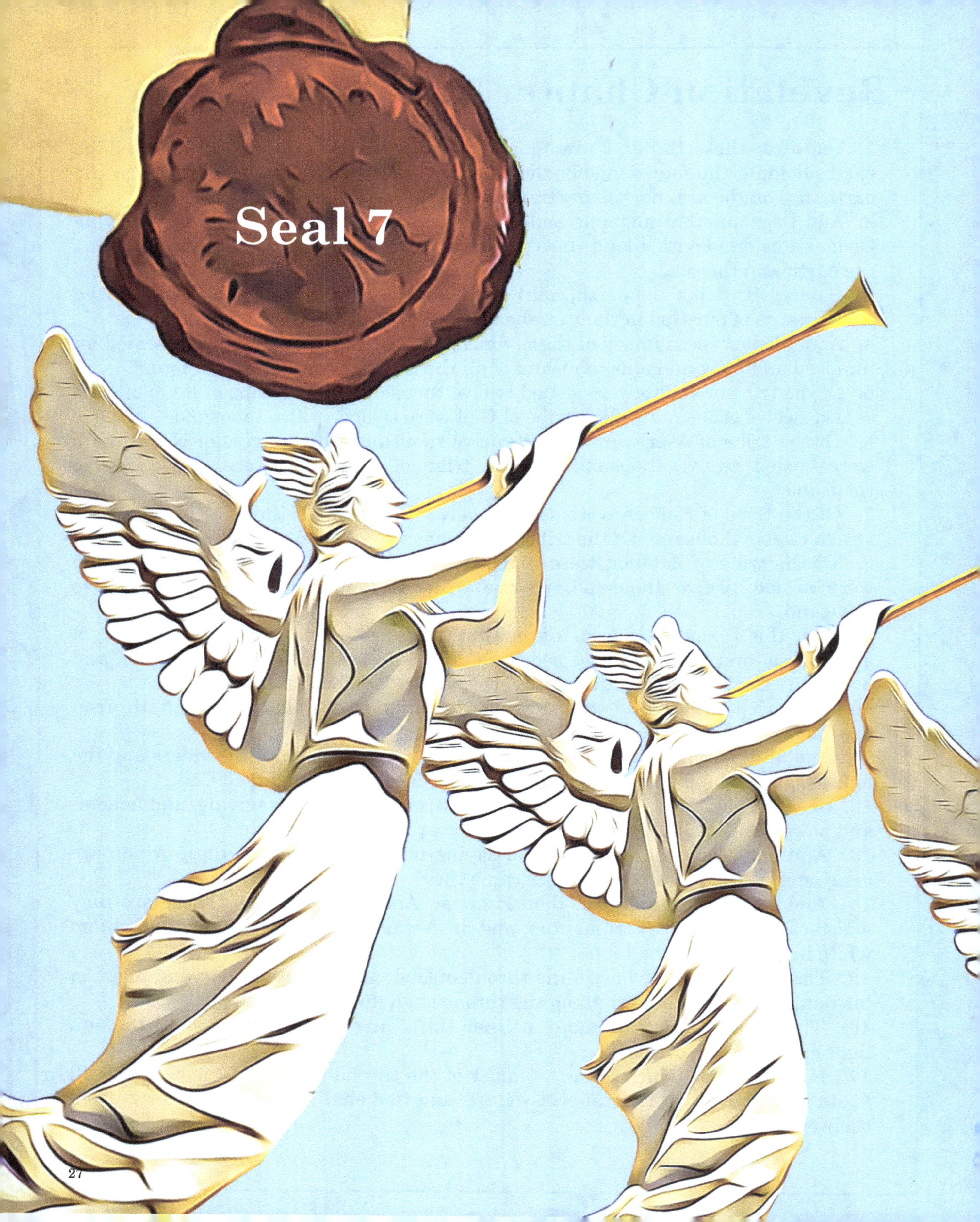
Seal 7

THE INTERPRETATION OF CHAPTER 8

The Sounding of 4 of the 7 Trumpets

And when he had opened the seventh seal, there was silence in heaven about the space of half an hour. And I saw the seven angels which stood before God; and to them were given seven trumpets. Revelation 8:1-2 (KJV)

CHAPTER 8 explains to John the prophetic message contained within the 7th seal. The seventh seal released 7 plagues on the earth using 7 trumpets. Each plague was released by the sounding of a trumpet. Chapter 8 only covers 4 of 7 trumpets as follows:

1. Hail and fire injures the earth and trees
2. The sea floods, blood poisons the sea, and sea life dies
3. A star falls from the sky and poisons the waters. This star is called Wormwood
4. 1/3 of the sun, 1/3 of the moon, and 1/3 of the stars are darkened

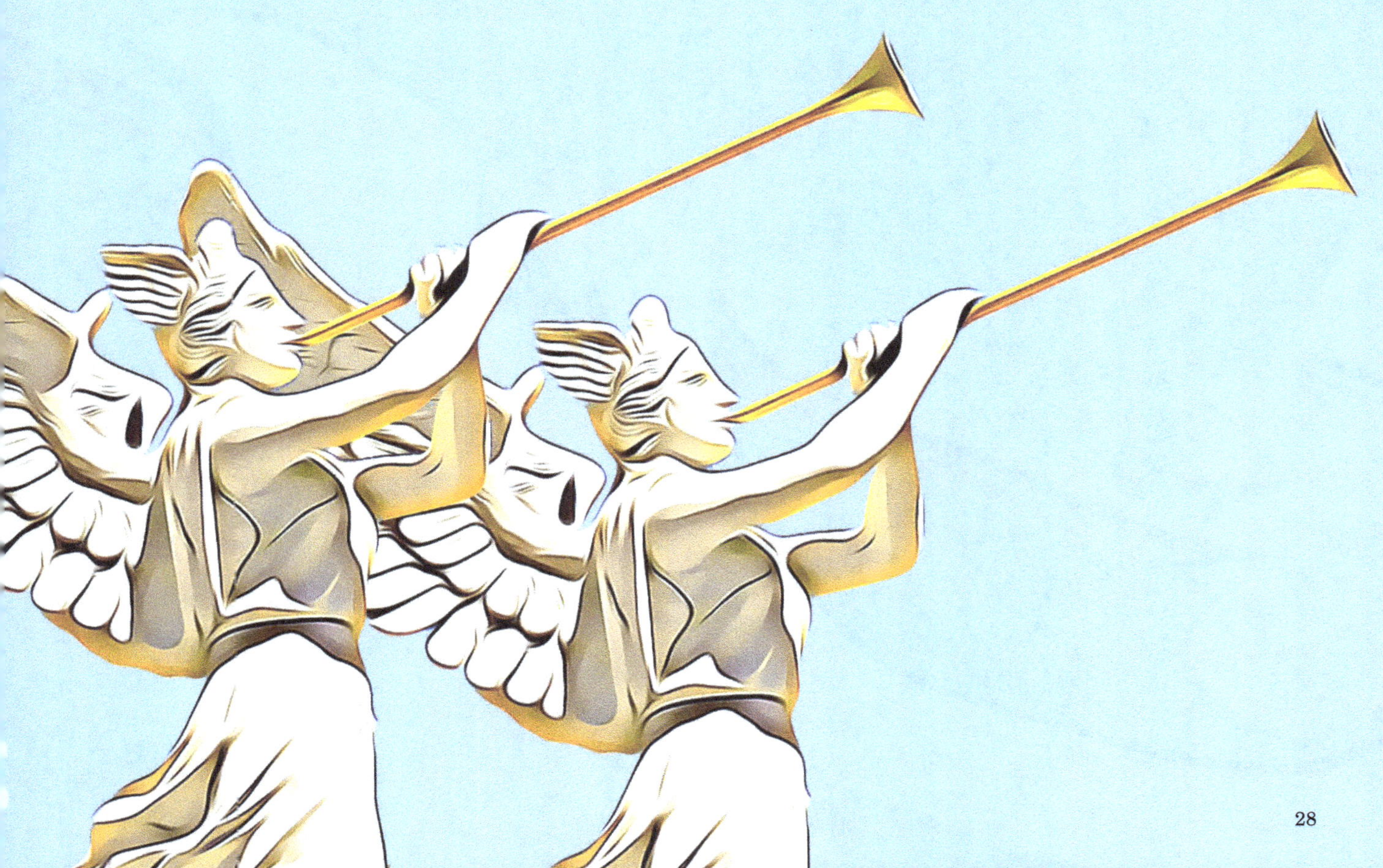

Trumpet 1 - *Injures the Earth*
Revelation Chapter 8:1-7 King James Version (KJV) Public Domain

1. And when he had opened the seventh seal, there was silence in heaven about the space of half an hour.
2. And I saw the seven angels which stood before God; and to them were given seven trumpets.
3. And another angel came and stood at the altar, having a golden censer; and there was given unto him much incense, that he should offer it with the prayers of all saints upon the golden altar which was before the throne.
4. And the smoke of the incense, which came with the prayers of the saints, ascended up before God out of the angel's hand.
5. And the angel took the censer, and filled it with fire of the altar, and cast it into the earth: and there were voices, and thunderings, and lightnings, and an earthquake.
6. And the seven angels which had the seven trumpets prepared themselves to sound.
7. The first angel sounded, and there followed hail and fire mingled with blood, and they were cast upon the earth: and the third part of trees was burnt up, and all green grass was burnt up.

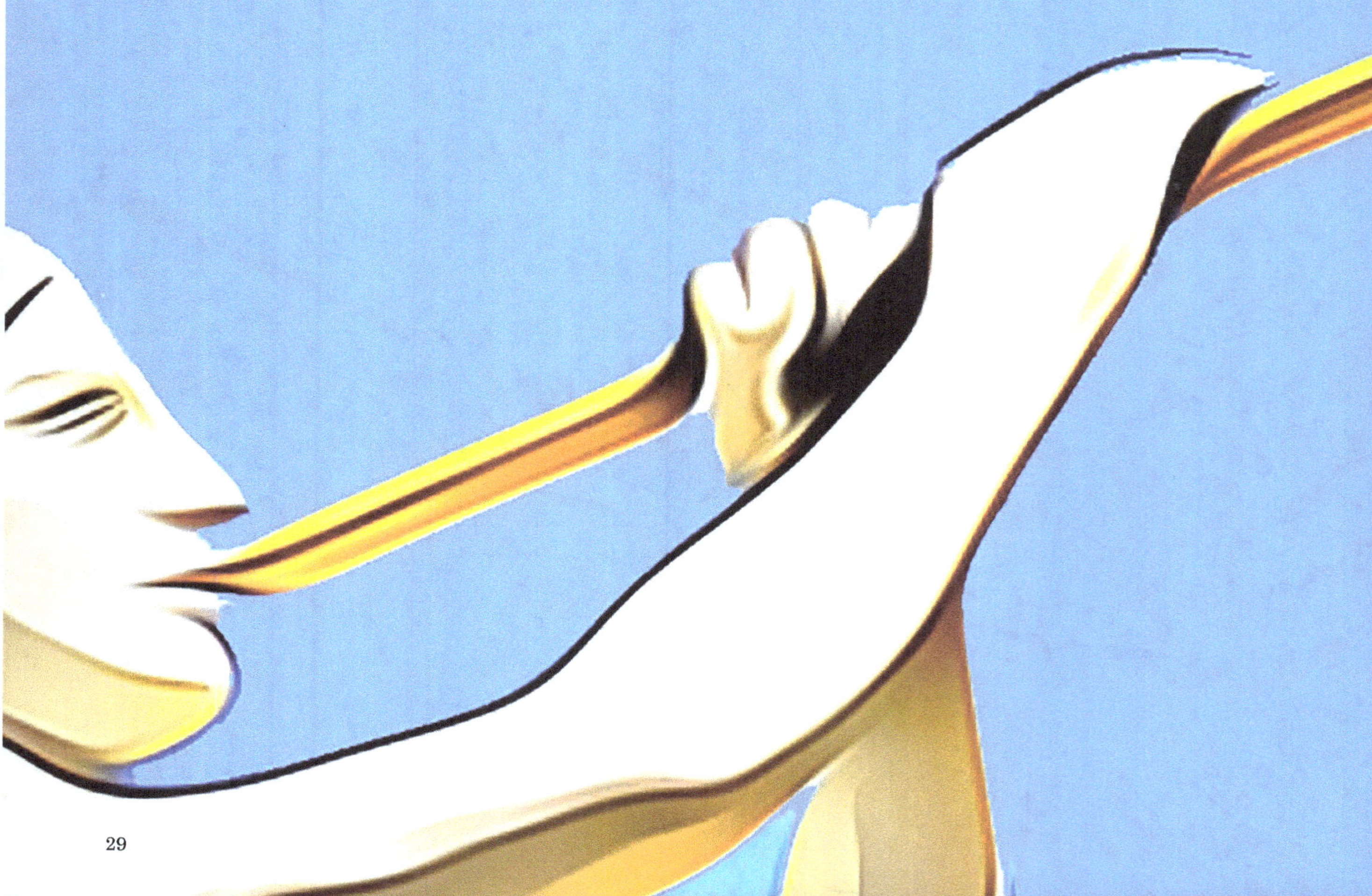

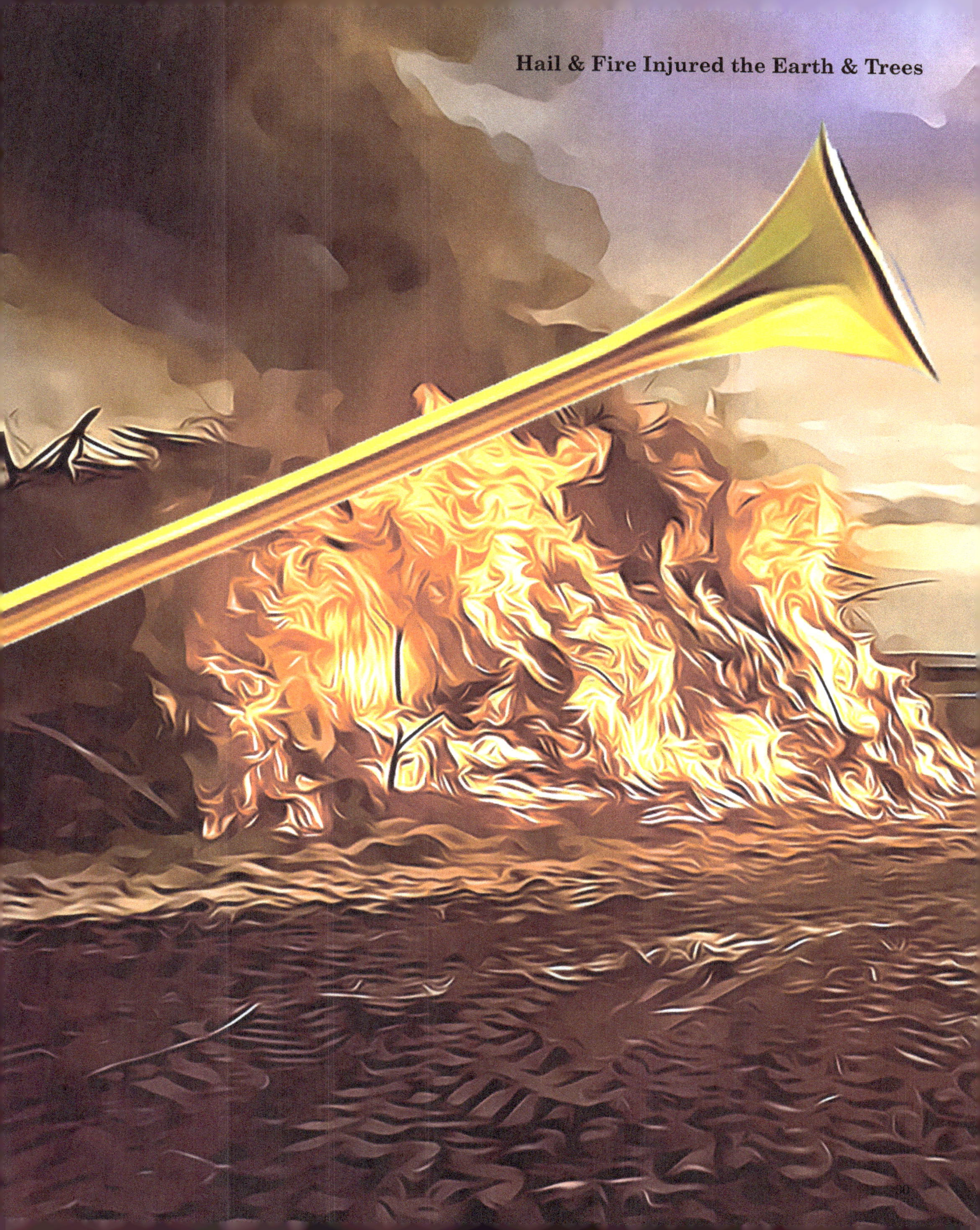

Trumpet 2 - *Injures the Earth*
Revelation Chapter 8:8-9 King James Version (KJV) Public Domain

8. And the second angel sounded, and as it were a great mountain burning with fire was cast into the sea: and the third part of the sea became blood;

9. And the third part of the creatures which were in the sea, and had life, died; and the third part of the ships were destroyed.

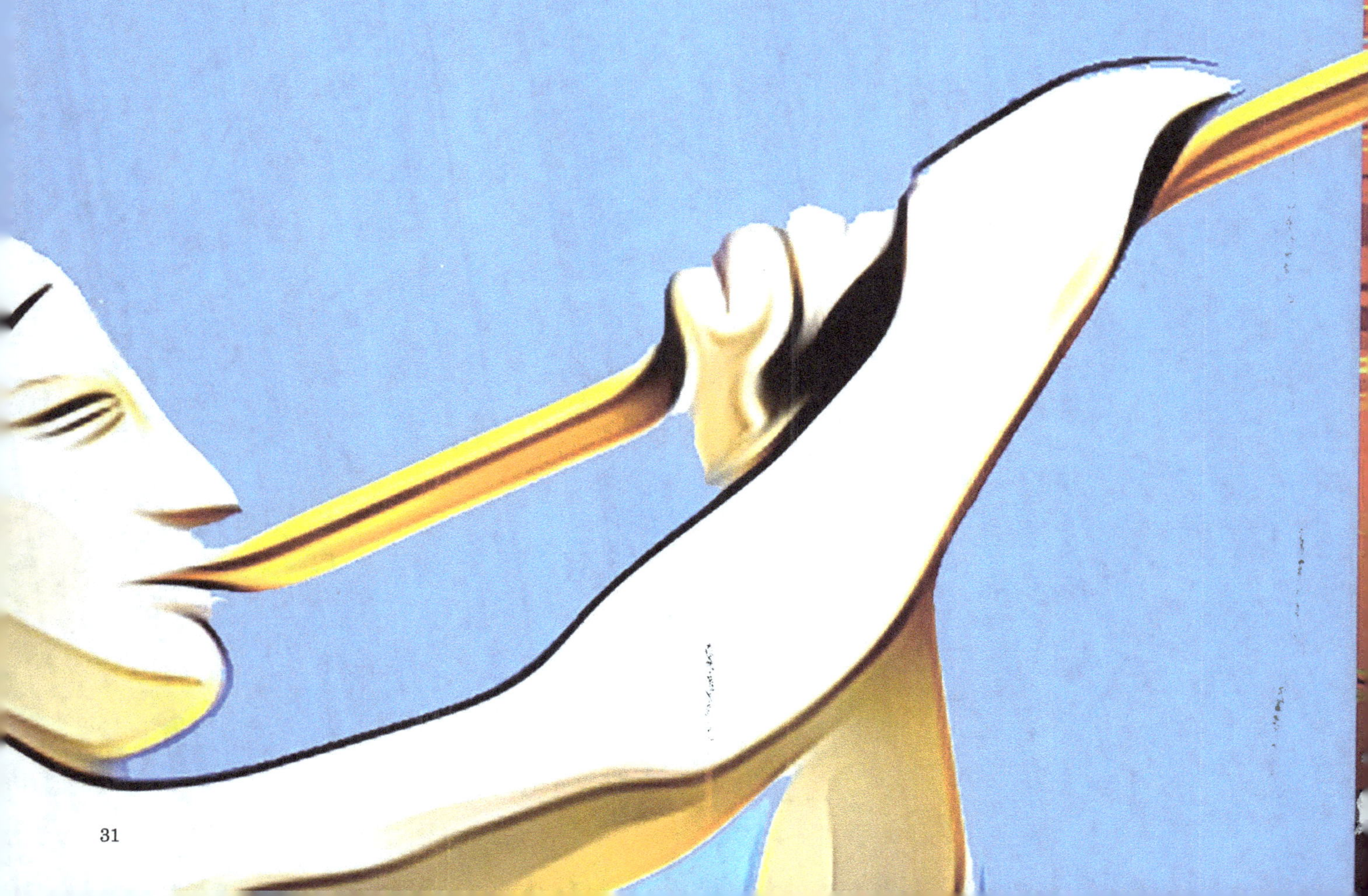

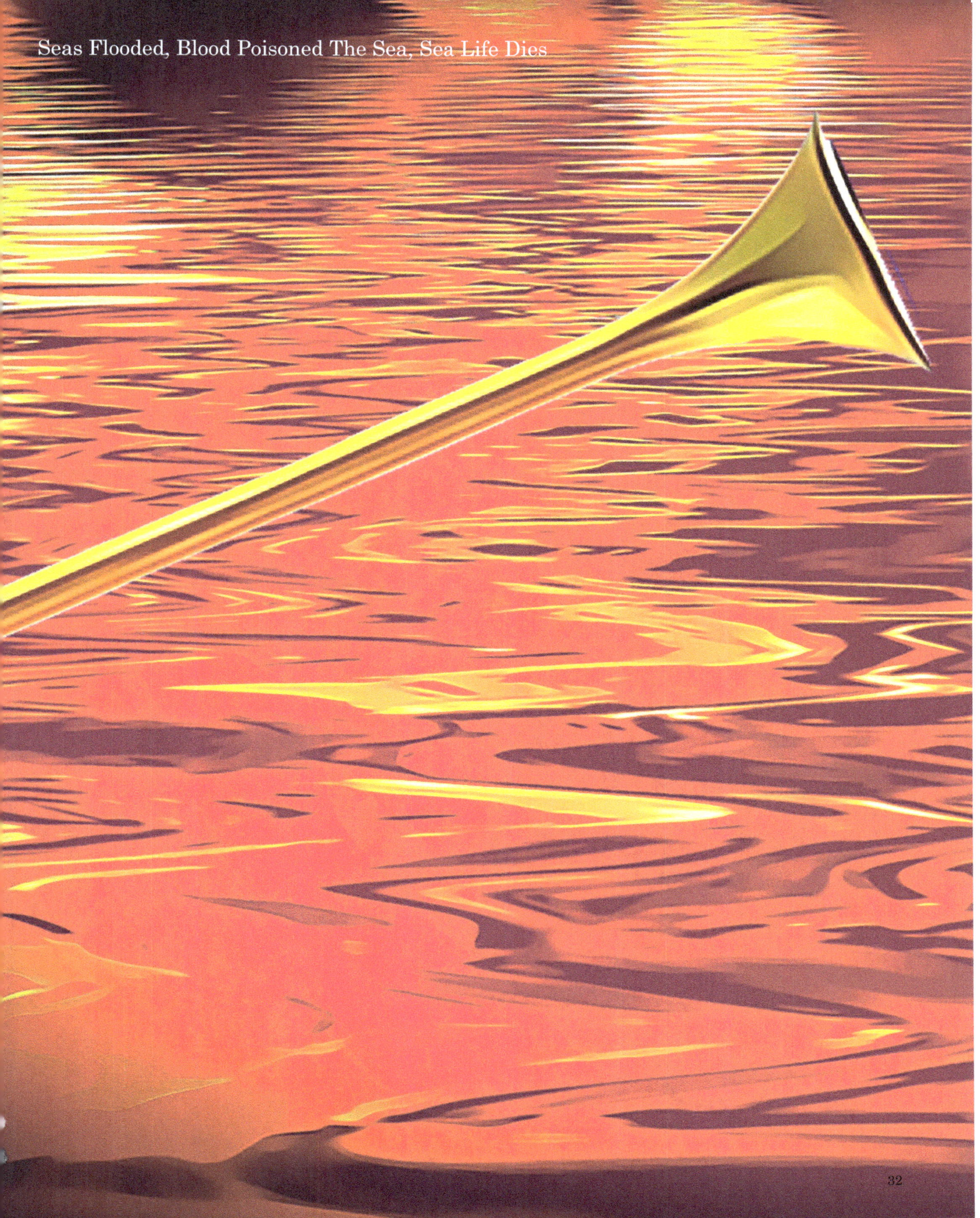

Trumpet 3 - *Injures the Earth*

Revelation Chapter 8:10-11 King James Version (KJV) Public Domain

10.   And the third angel sounded, and there fell a great star from heaven, burning as it were a lamp, and it fell upon the third part of the rivers, and upon the fountains of waters;

11.   And the name of the star is called Wormwood: and the third part of the waters became wormwood; and many men died of the waters, because they were made bitter.

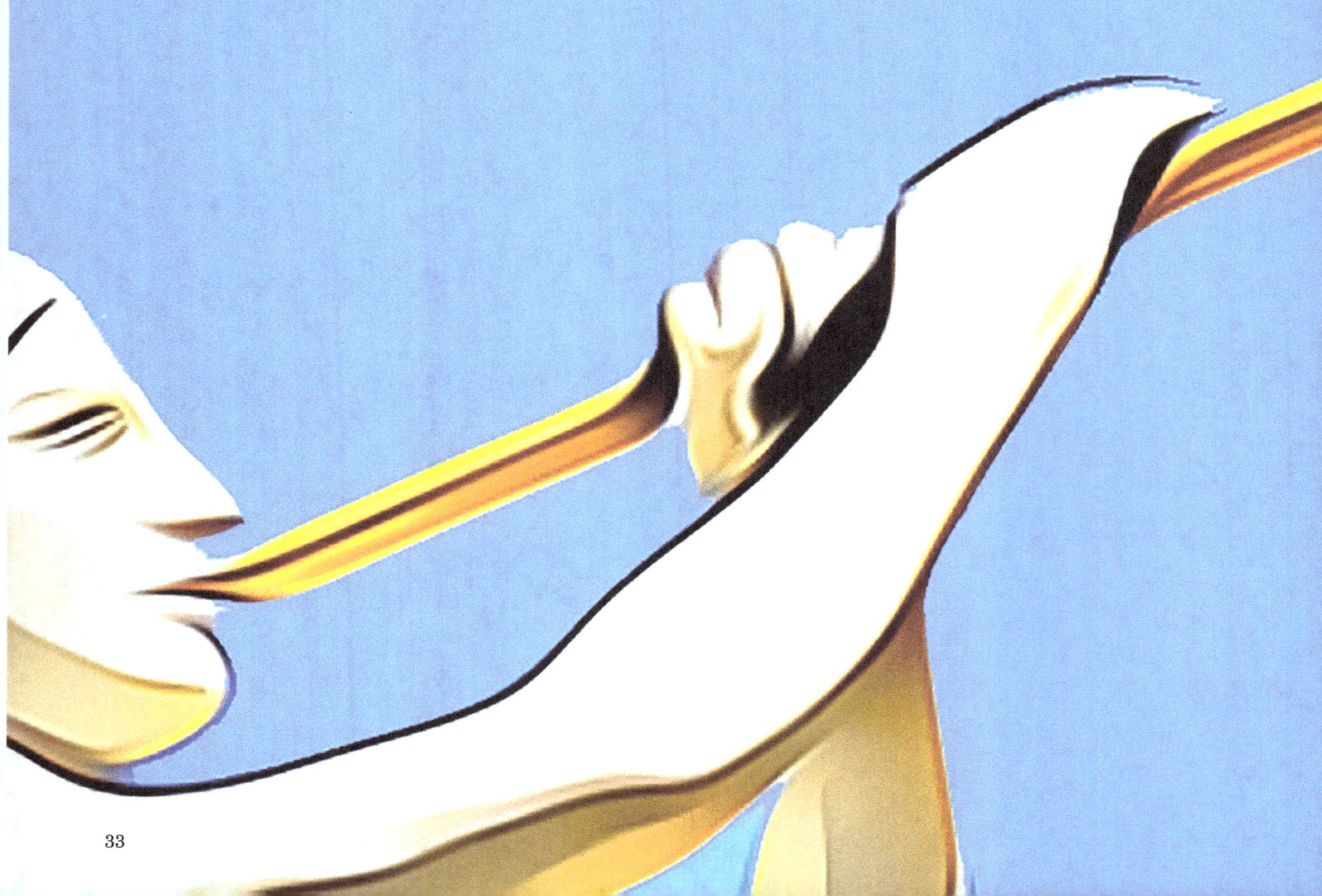

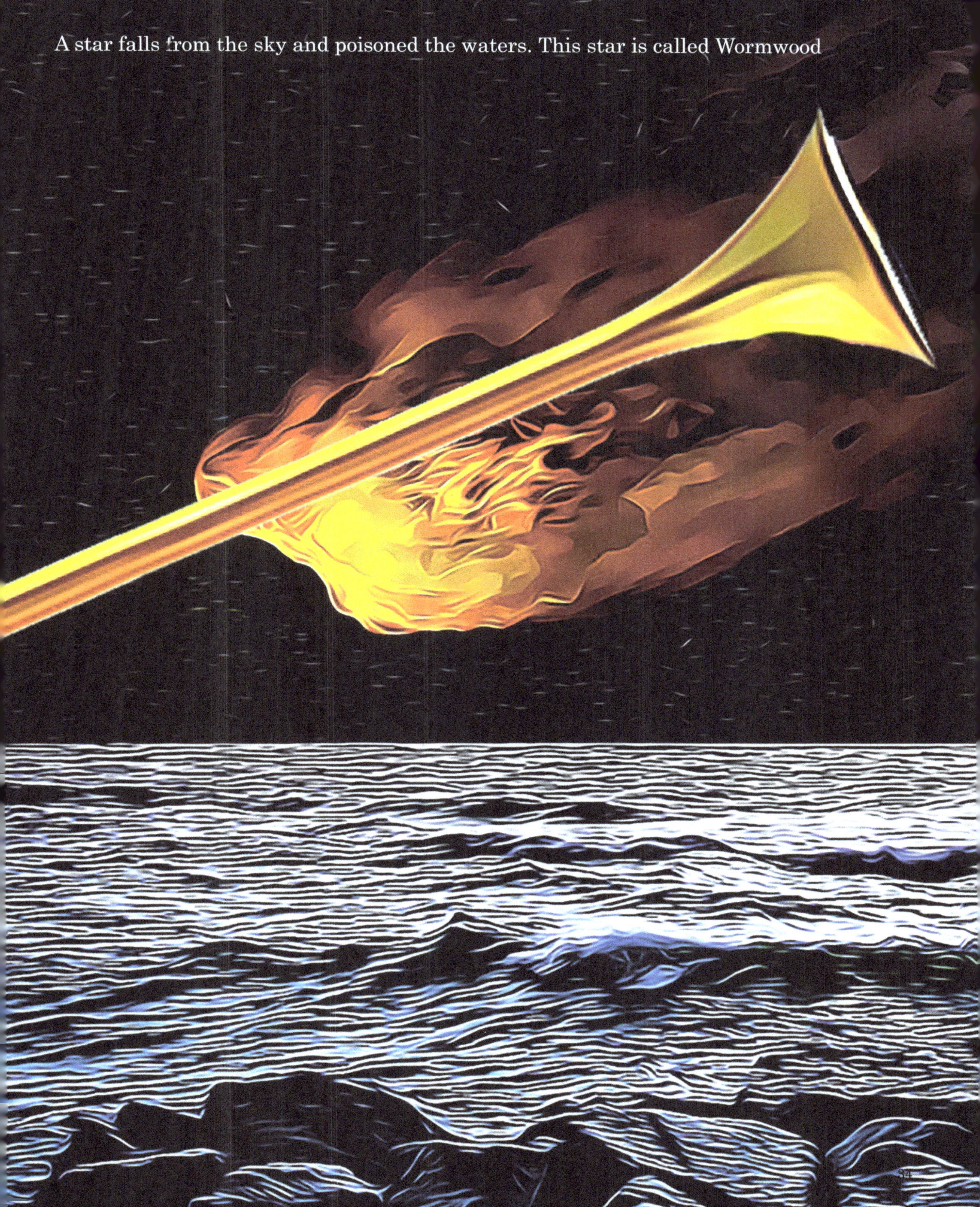
A star falls from the sky and poisoned the waters. This star is called Wormwood

Trumpet 4 - *Injures the Earth*
Revelation Chapter 8:12-13 King James Version (KJV) Public Domain

12. And the fourth angel sounded, and the third part of the sun was smitten, and the third part of the moon, and the third part of the stars; so as the third part of them was darkened, and the day shone not for a third part of it, and the night likewise.

13. And I beheld, and heard an angel flying through the midst of heaven, saying with a loud voice, Woe, woe, woe, to the inhabiters of the earth by reason of the other voices of the trumpet of the three angels, which are yet to sound!

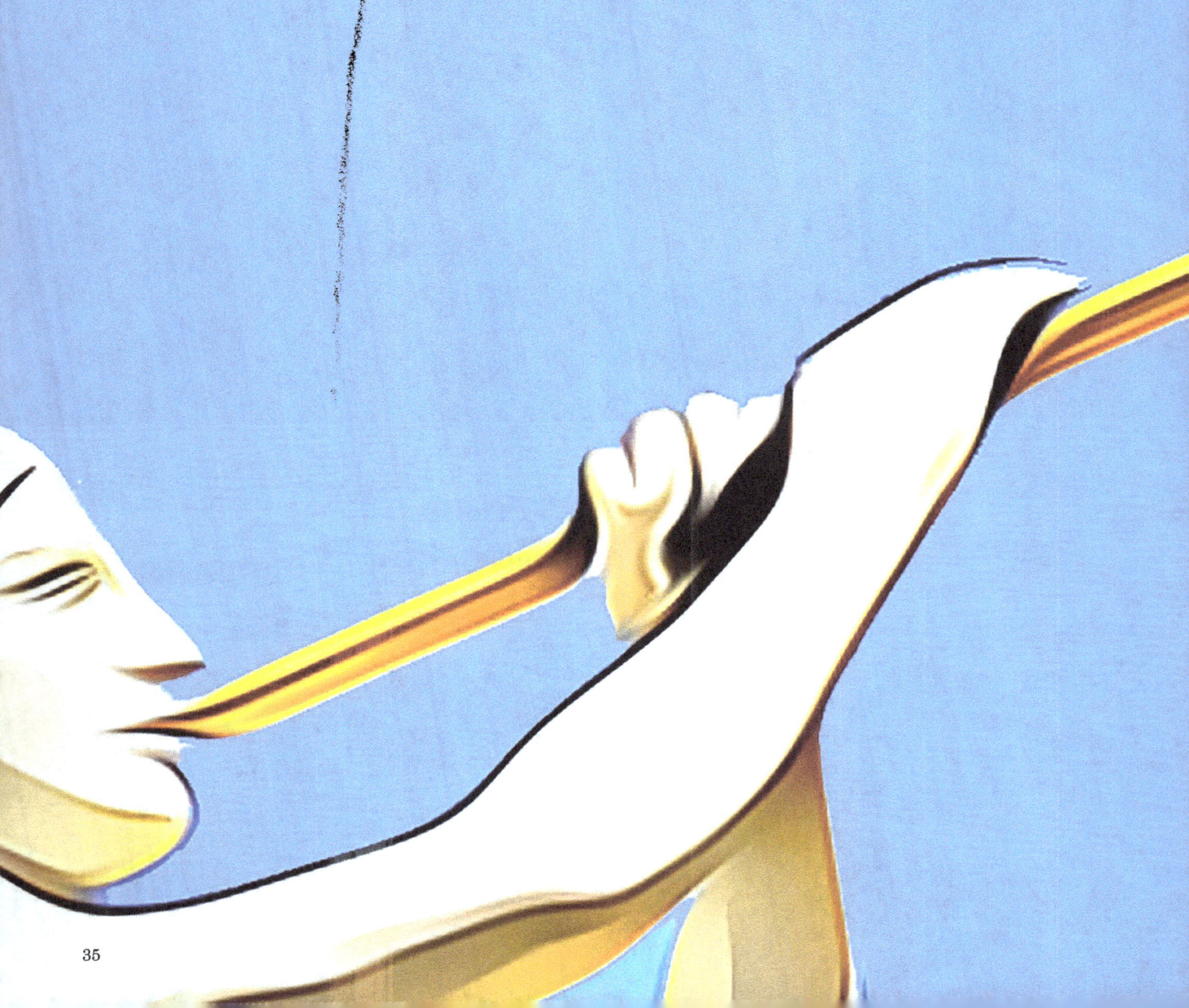

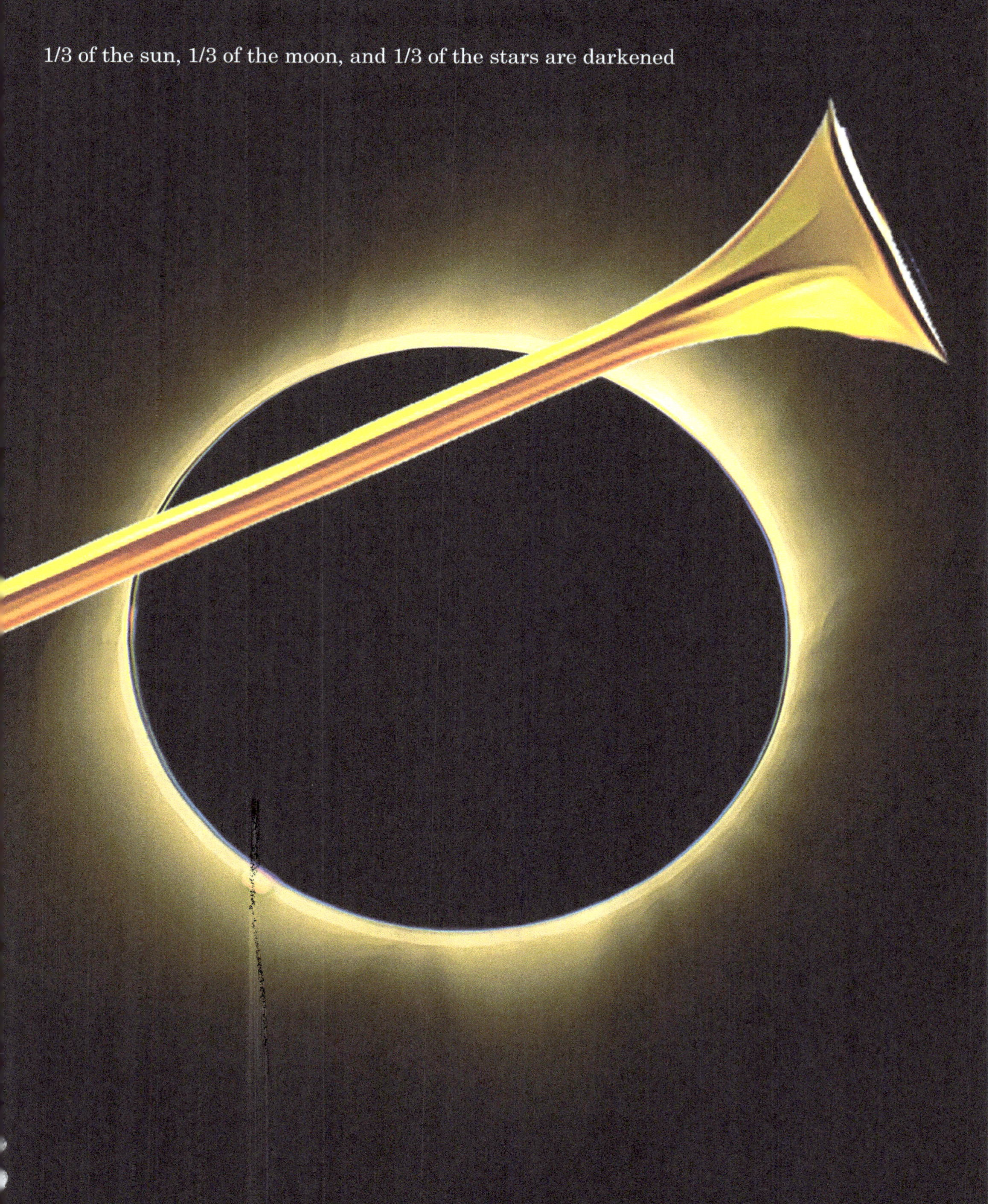
1/3 of the sun, 1/3 of the moon, and 1/3 of the stars are darkened

THE INTERPRETATION OF CHAPTER 9

The Sounding of the 5th and 6th Trumpets

And the fifth angel sounded, and I saw a star fall from heaven unto the earth: and to him was given the key of the bottomless pit. — *Revelation 9:1 (KJV)*

CHAPTER 9 releases the plagues by the sounding of the 5th and 6th trumpet. Chapter 9 also covers the first two, of three Woes as follows:

Woe 1-Unrepentant men tormented by poor sun and air quality and locust for 5 months.
Woe 2-A great army is allowed to kill 1/3 of the world.
Woe 3-*The two prophets preach and show signs and wonders for 3 ½ years (1260 days).*

This is the second half of the 70th week as prophesied by Daniel. The Prophets are killed and resurrected in the same location as Jesus, which ushers in the final judgment and end of the world.

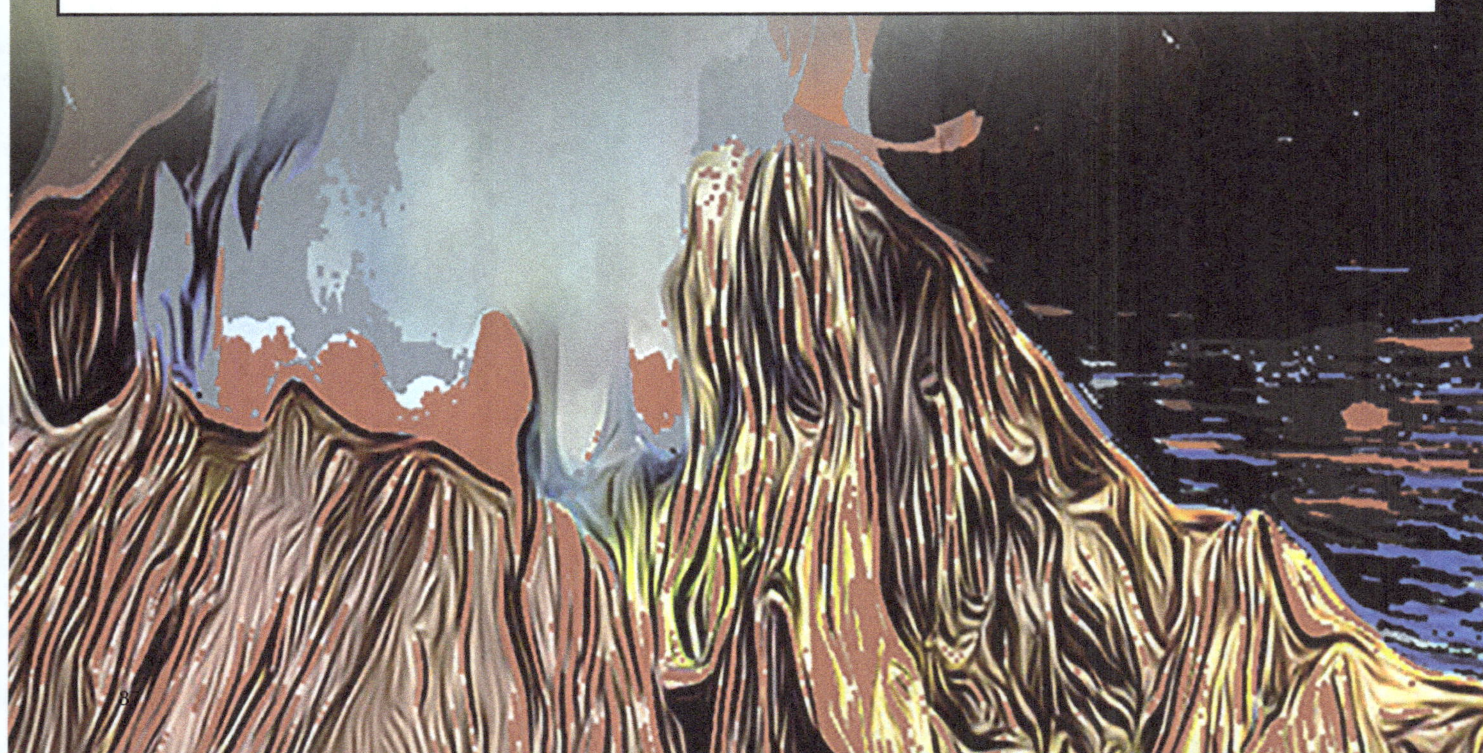

Revelation Chapter 9 King James Version (KJV) Public Domain

1. And the fifth angel sounded, and I saw a star fall from heaven unto the earth: and to him was given the key of the bottomless pit.

2. And he opened the bottomless pit; and there arose a smoke out of the pit, as the smoke of a great furnace; and the sun and the air were darkened by reason of the smoke of the pit.

3. And there came out of the smoke locusts upon the earth: and unto them was given power, as the scorpions of the earth have power.

4. And it was commanded them that they should not hurt the grass of the earth, neither any green thing, neither any tree; but only those men which have not the seal of God in their foreheads.

5. And to them it was given that they should not kill them, but that they should be tormented five months: and their torment was as the torment of a scorpion, when he striketh a man.

6. And in those days shall men seek death, and shall not find it; and shall desire to die, and death shall flee from them.

7. And the shapes of the locusts were like unto horses prepared unto battle; and on their heads were as it were crowns like gold, and their faces were as the faces of men.

8. And they had hair as the hair of women, and their teeth were as the teeth of lions.

9. And they had breastplates, as it were breastplates of iron; and the sound of their wings was as the sound of chariots of many horses running to battle.

10. And they had tails like unto scorpions, and there were stings in their tails: and their power was to hurt men five months.

11. And they had a king over them, which is the angel of the bottomless pit, whose name in the Hebrew tongue is Abaddon, but in the Greek tongue hath his name Apollyon.

12. One woe is past; and, behold, there come two woes more hereafter.

13. And the sixth angel sounded, and I heard a voice from the four horns of the golden altar which is before God,

14. Saying to the sixth angel which had the trumpet, Loose the four angels which are bound in the great river Euphrates.

15. And the four angels were loosed, which were prepared for an hour, and a day, and a month, and a year, for to slay the third part of men.

16. And the number of the army of the horsemen were two hundred thousand thousand: and I heard the number of them.

17. And thus I saw the horses in the vision, and them that sat on them, having breastplates of fire, and of jacinth, and brimstone: and the heads of the horses were as the heads of lions; and out of their mouths issued fire and smoke and brimstone.

18. By these three was the third part of men killed, by the fire, and by the smoke, and by the brimstone, which issued out of their mouths.

19. For their power is in their mouth, and in their tails: for their tails were like unto serpents, and had heads, and with them they do hurt.

20. And the rest of the men which were not killed by these plagues yet repented not of the works of their hands, that they should not worship devils, and idols of gold, and silver, and brass, and stone, and of wood: which neither can see, nor hear, nor walk:

21. Neither repented they of their murders, nor of their sorceries, nor of their fornication, nor of their thefts.

<u>Trumpet 5 - *Injures Humans (Woe 1)*</u>

Revelation Chapter 9:3-11 King James Version (KJV) Public Domain

3. And there came out of the smoke locusts upon the earth: and unto them was given power, as the scorpions of the earth have power.

4. And it was commanded them that they should not hurt the grass of the earth, neither any green thing, neither any tree; **but only those men which have not the seal of God in their foreheads.**

5. And to them it was given that they should not kill them, but that they should be tormented five months: and their torment was as the torment of a scorpion, when he striketh a man.

6. And in those days shall men seek death, and shall not find it; and shall desire to die, and death shall flee from them.

7. And the shapes of the locusts were like unto horses prepared unto battle; and on their heads were as it were crowns like gold, and their faces were as the faces of men.

8. And they had hair as the hair of women, and their teeth were as the teeth of lions.

9. And they had breastplates, as it were breastplates of iron; and the sound of their wings was as the sound of chariots of many horses running to battle.

10. And they had tails like unto scorpions, and there were stings in their tails: and their power was to hurt men five months.

11. And they had a king over them, which is the angel of the bottomless pit, whose name in the Hebrew tongue is Abaddon, but in the Greek tongue hath his name Apollyon.

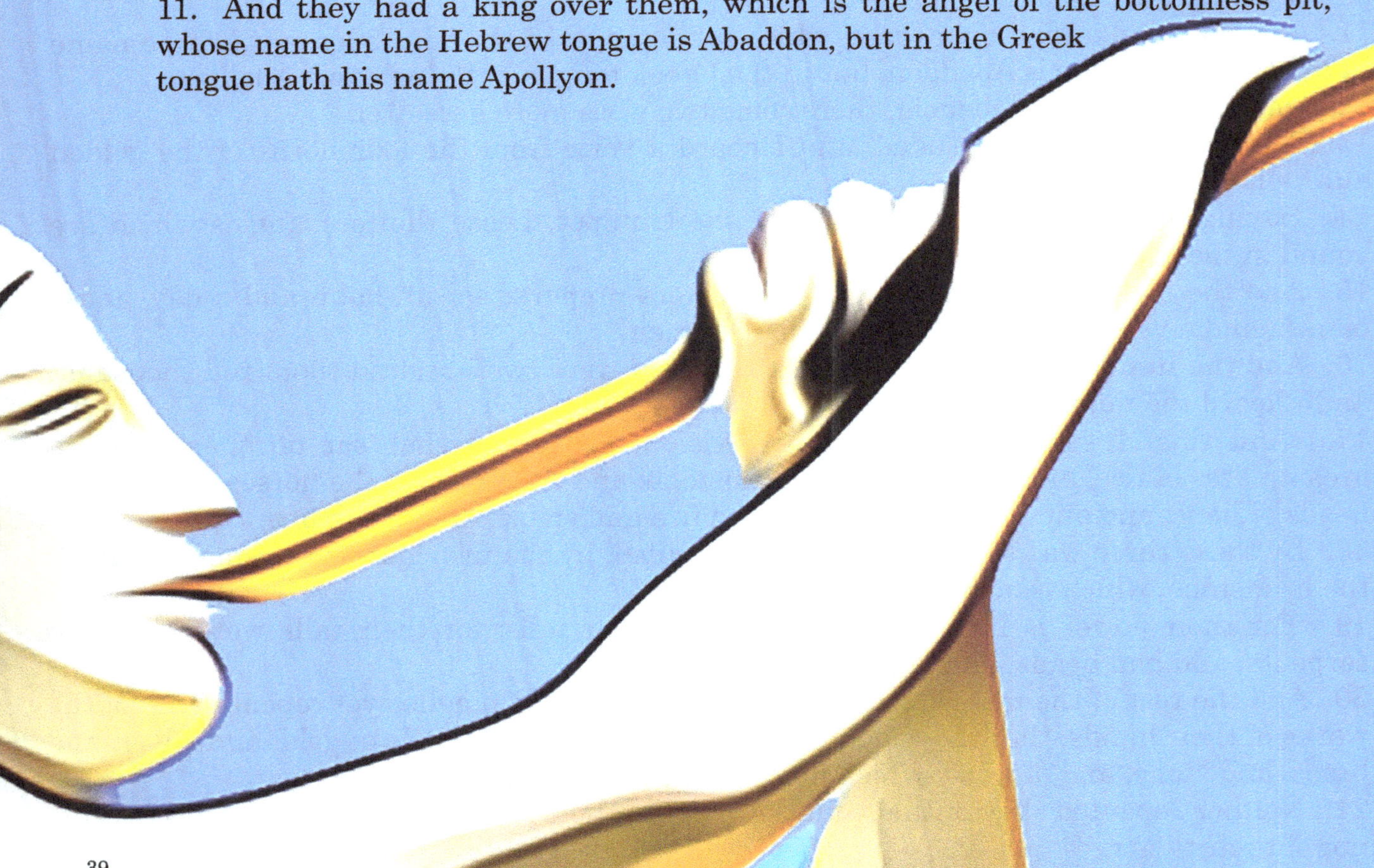

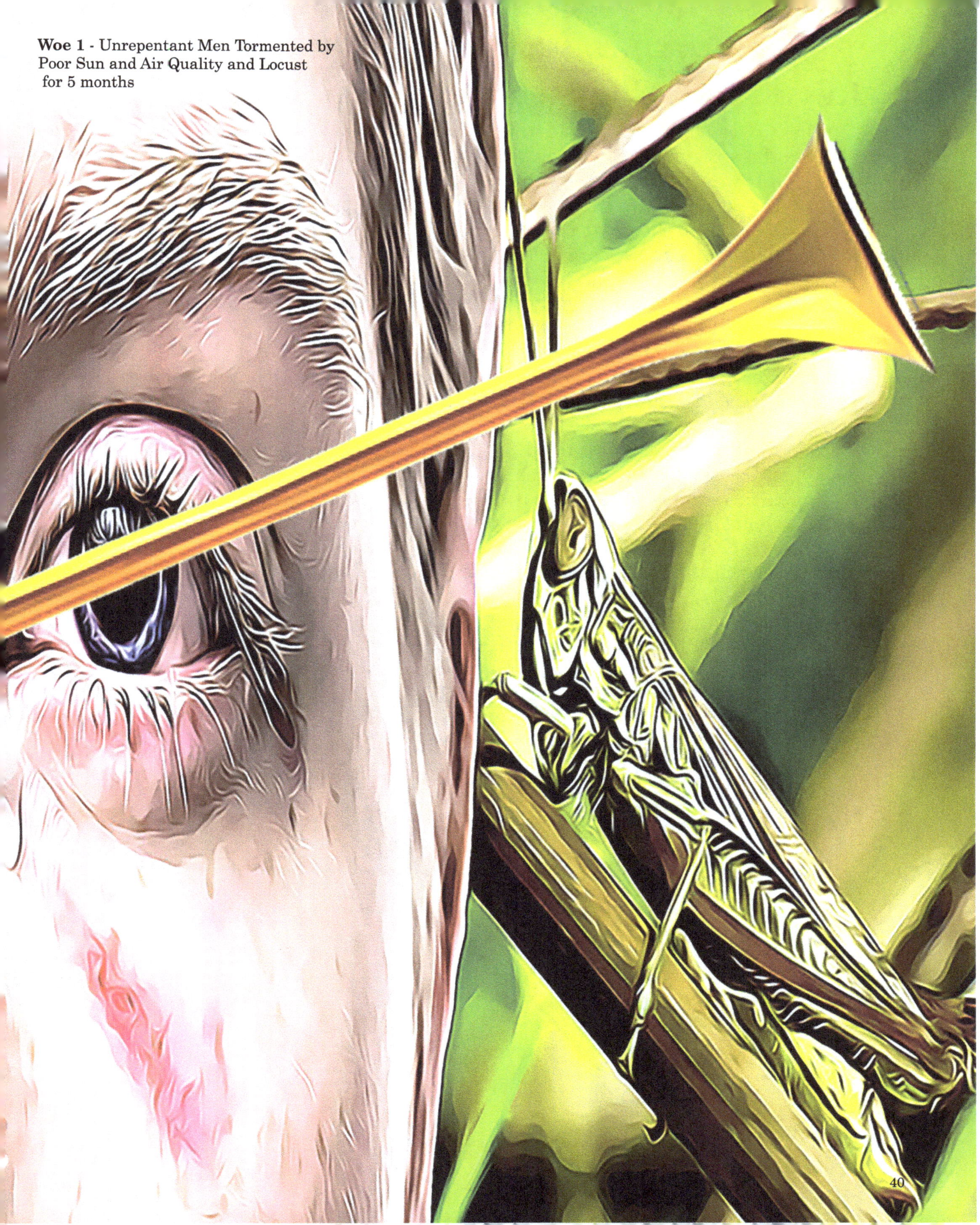

Woe 1 - Unrepentant Men Tormented by
Poor Sun and Air Quality and Locust
 for 5 months

Trumpet 6 - *Injures Humans (Woe 2)*
Revelation Chapter 9:12-21 King James Version (KJV) Public Domain

12. One woe is past; and, behold, there come two woes more hereafter.

13. And the sixth angel sounded, and I heard a voice from the four horns of the golden altar which is before God,

14. Saying to the sixth angel which had the trumpet, Loose the four angels which are bound in the great river Euphrates.

15. And the four angels were loosed, which were prepared for an hour, and a day, and a month, and a year, for to slay the third part of men.

16. And the number of the army of the horsemen were two hundred thousand thousand: and I heard the number of them.

17. And thus I saw the horses in the vision, and them that sat on them, having breastplates of fire, and of jacinth, and brimstone: and the heads of the horses were as the heads of lions; and out of their mouths issued fire and smoke and brimstone.

18. By these three was the third part of men killed, by the fire, and by the smoke, and by the brimstone, which issued out of their mouths.

19. For their power is in their mouth, and in their tails: for their tails were like unto serpents, and had heads, and with them they do hurt.

20. And the rest of the men which were not killed by these plagues yet repented not of the works of their hands, that they should not worship devils, and idols of gold, and silver, and brass, and stone, and of wood: which neither can see, nor hear, nor walk:

21. Neither repented they of their murders, nor of their sorceries, nor of their fornication, nor of their thefts.

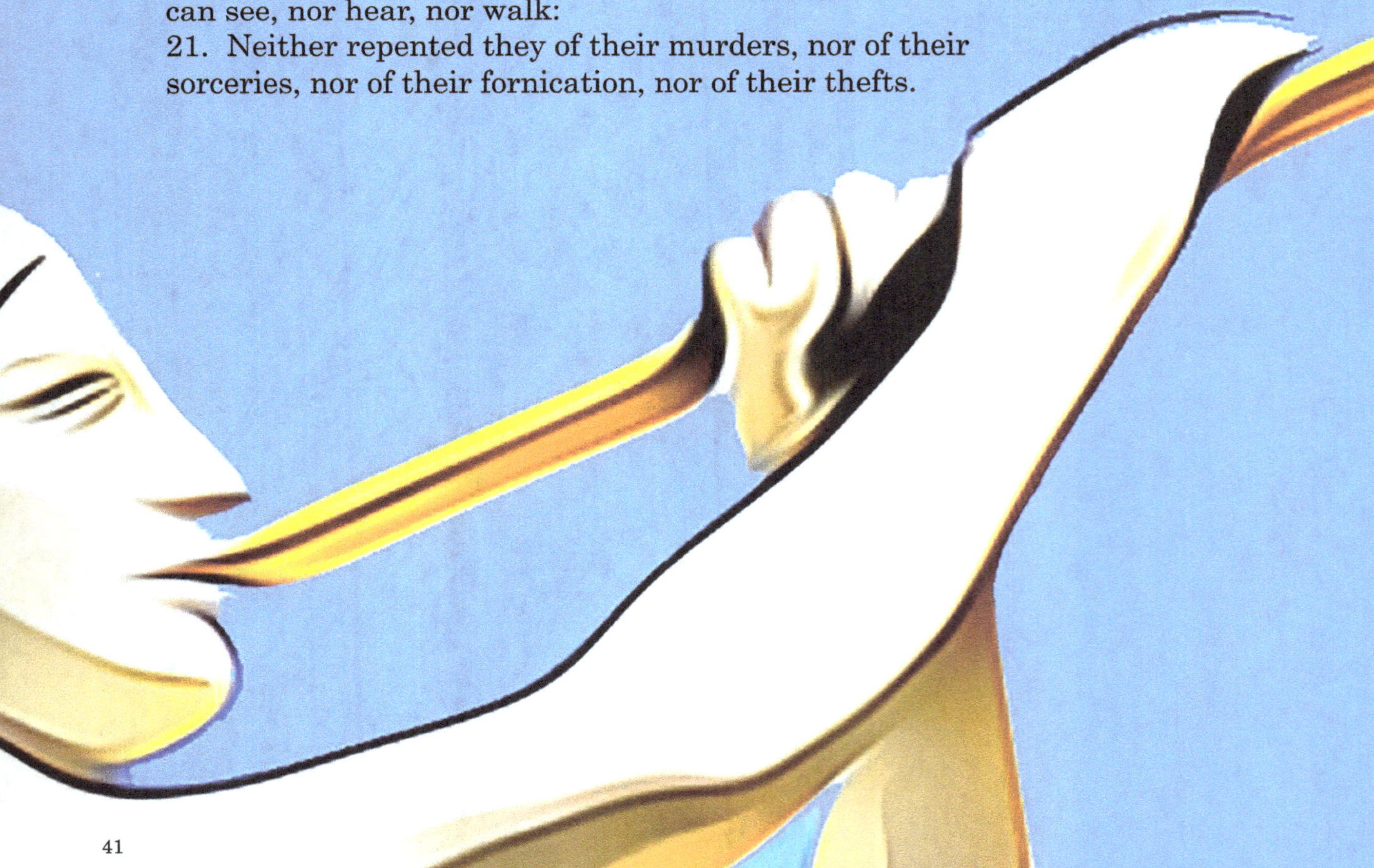

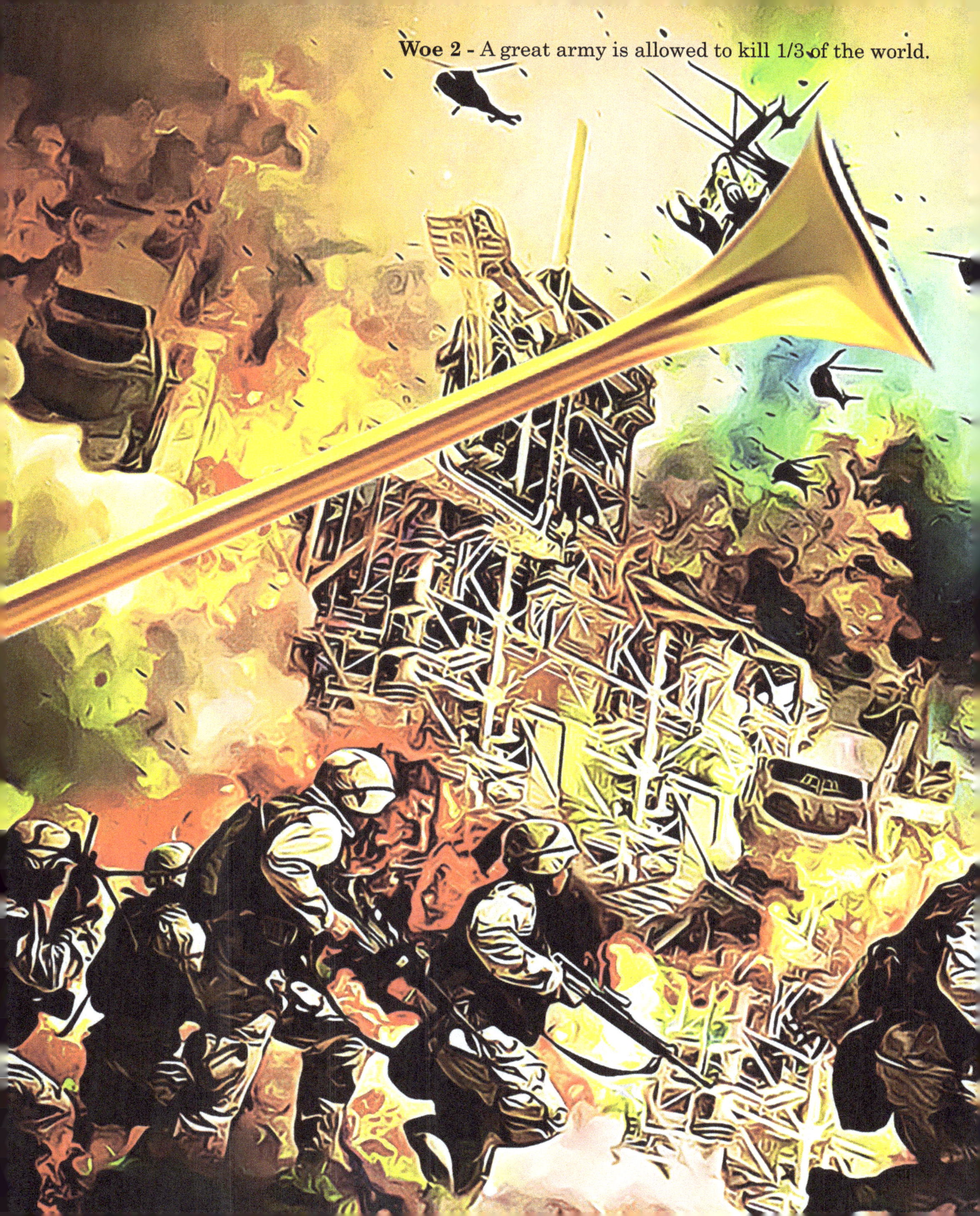
Woe 2 - A great army is allowed to kill 1/3 of the world.

THE INTERPRETATION OF CHAPTER 10

Seven Thunders Uttered

And when the seven thunders had uttered their voices, I was about to write: and I heard a voice from heaven saying unto me, Seal up those things which the seven thunders uttered, and write them not. — *Revelation 10:4 (KJV)*

CHAPTER 10 explains the events that happened when God determined the earth's time is up. God used an angel to cause John to eat a book, which symbolized that John received the prophesy of the end times to speak to the nations. John did as commissioned. Because of John's obedience, we have the Book of Revelation to help us prepare for God's judgment of the earth during the end times. Chapter 10 also chronicles what happened in the heavens at the end of the first 3 1/2 years, immediately prior to the tribulation period.

Revelation Chapter 10 King James Version (KJV) Public Domain

1. And I saw another mighty angel come down from heaven, clothed with a cloud: and a rainbow was upon his head, and his face was as it were the sun, and his feet as pillars of fire:
2. And he had in his hand a little book open: and he set his right foot upon the sea, and his left foot on the earth,
3. And cried with a loud voice, as when a lion roareth: and when he had cried, seven thunders uttered their voices.
4. And when the seven thunders had uttered their voices, I was about to write: and I heard a voice from heaven saying unto me, Seal up those things which the seven thunders uttered, and write them not.
5. And the angel which I saw stand upon the sea and upon the earth lifted up his hand to heaven,
6. And sware by him that liveth for ever and ever, who created heaven, and the things that therein are, and the earth, and the things that therein are, and the sea, and the things which are therein, that there should be time no longer:
7. But in the days of the voice of the seventh angel, when he shall begin to sound, the mystery of God should be finished, as he hath declared to his servants the prophets.
8. And the voice which I heard from heaven spake unto me again, and said, Go and take the little book which is open in the hand of the angel which standeth upon the sea and upon the earth.
9. And I went unto the angel, and said unto him, Give me the little book. And he said unto me, Take it, and eat it up; and it shall make thy belly bitter, but it shall be in thy mouth sweet as honey.
10. And I took the little book out of the angel's hand, and ate it up; and it was in my mouth sweet as honey: and as soon as I had eaten it, my belly was bitter.
11. And he said unto me, Thou must prophesy again before many peoples, and nations, and tongues, and kings.

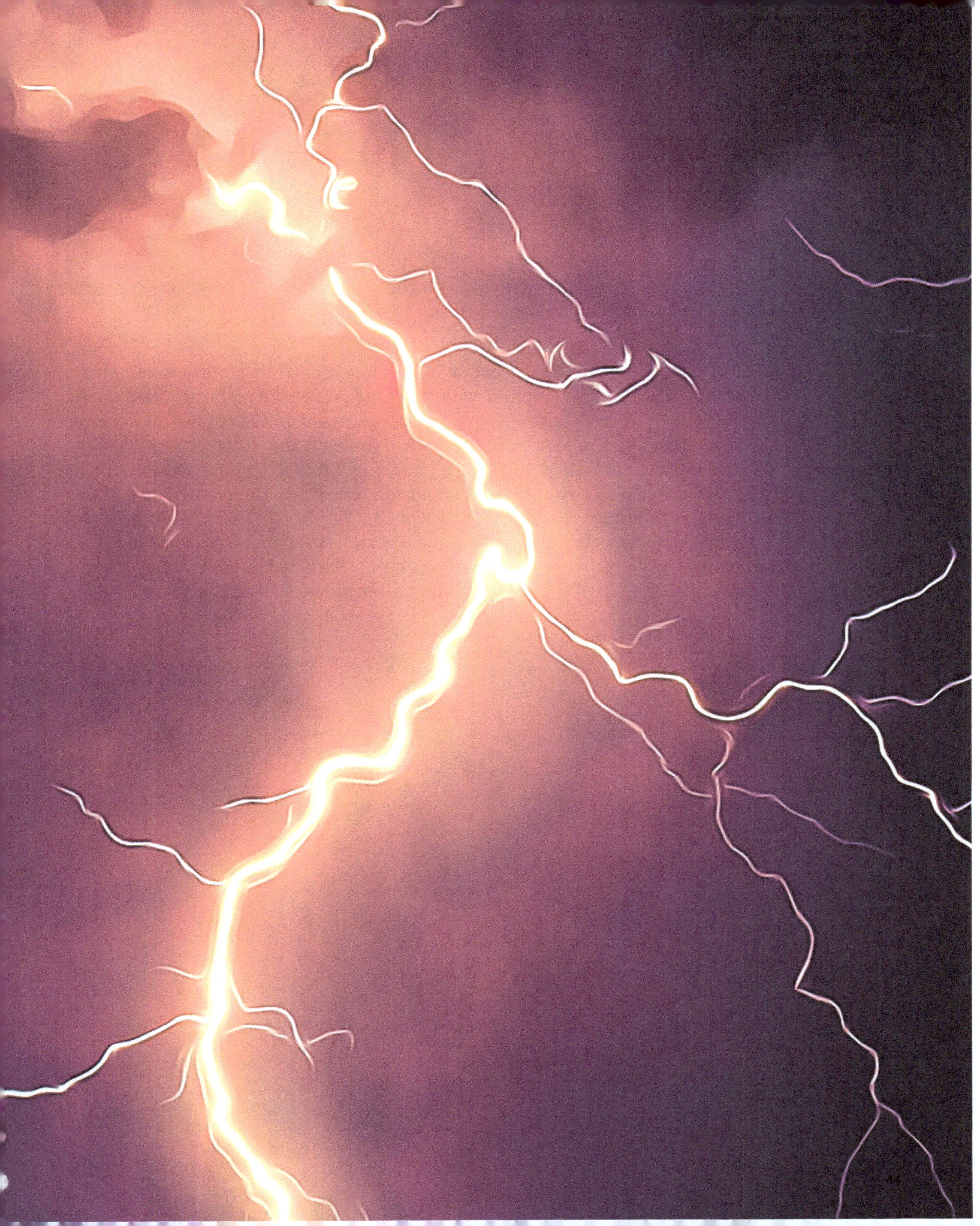

THE INTERPRETATION OF CHAPTER 11

The Two Prophets

And I will give power unto my two witnesses, and they shall prophesy a thousand two hundred and threescore days, clothed in sackcloth. *Revelation 11:3 (KJV)*

CHAPTER 11 chronicles the events that occur after the Anti-Christ defiled the third temple. In this Chapter, John is given a ruler to measure the rebuilt Jerusalem temple, but he is told not to measure the outer-courts because the Gentiles will destroy this area for 42 months (3 1/2 years). This is the time of the Anti-Christ's reign. During this time, two prophets will emerge and prophesy for 3 1/2 years, which is the second half of the 70th week as prophesied by Daniel. The Anti-Christ will kill them and their dead bodies will lay in the streets for 3 1/2 days. Then they will be resurrected, just like Jesus, in the same place where He was crucified. After the two prophets' resurrection, God will begin the final judgment. This is the end of the second woe and the beginning of the third woe, which will usher in the end of the world.

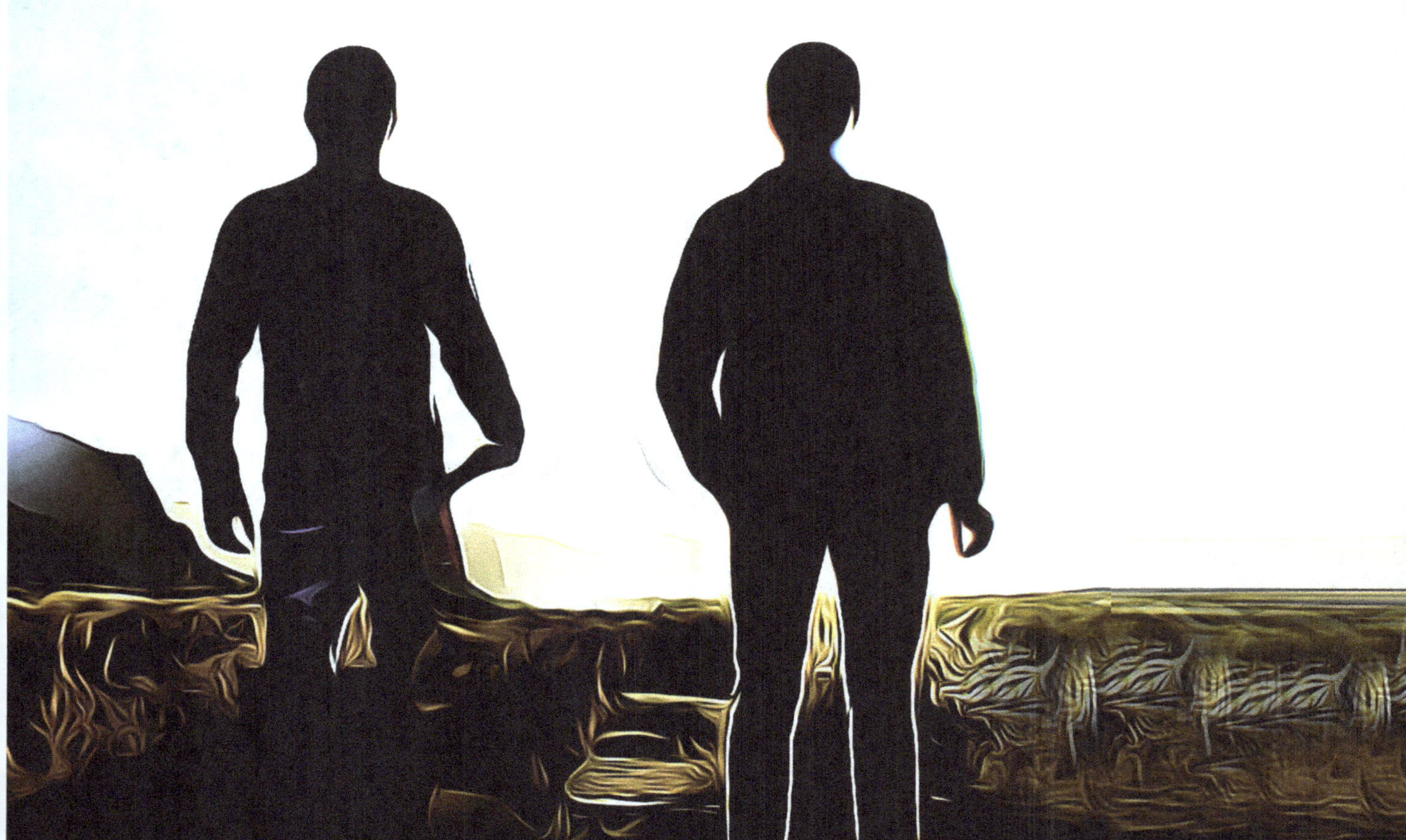

Revelation Chapter 11 King James Version (KJV) Public Domain

1. And there was given me a reed like unto a rod: and the angel stood, saying, Rise, and measure the temple of God, and the altar, and them that worship therein.

2. But the court which is without the temple leave out, and measure it not; for it is given unto the Gentiles: and the holy city shall they tread under foot forty and two months.

3. And I will give power unto my two witnesses, and they shall prophesy a thousand two hundred and threescore days, clothed in sackcloth.

4. These are the two olive trees, and the two candlesticks standing before the God of the earth.

5. And if any man will hurt them, fire proceedeth out of their mouth, and devoureth their enemies: and if any man will hurt them, he must in this manner be killed.

6. These have power to shut heaven, that it rain not in the days of their prophecy: and have power over waters to turn them to blood, and to smite the earth with all plagues, as often as they will.

7. And when they shall have finished their testimony, the beast that ascendeth out of the bottomless pit shall make war against them, and shall overcome them, and kill them.

8. And their dead bodies shall lie in the street of the great city, which spiritually is called Sodom and Egypt, where also our Lord was crucified.

9. And they of the people and kindreds and tongues and nations shall see their dead bodies three days and an half, and shall not suffer their dead bodies to be put in graves.

10. And they that dwell upon the earth shall rejoice over them, and make merry, and shall send gifts one to another; because these two prophets tormented them that dwelt on the earth.

11. And after three days and an half the spirit of life from God entered into them, and they stood upon their feet; and great fear fell upon them which saw them.

12. And they heard a great voice from heaven saying unto them, Come up hither. And they ascended up to heaven in a cloud; and their enemies beheld them.

13. And the same hour was there a great earthquake, and the tenth part of the city fell, and in the earthquake were slain of men seven thousand: and the remnant were affrighted, and gave glory to the God of heaven.

14. The second woe is past; and, behold, the third woe cometh quickly.

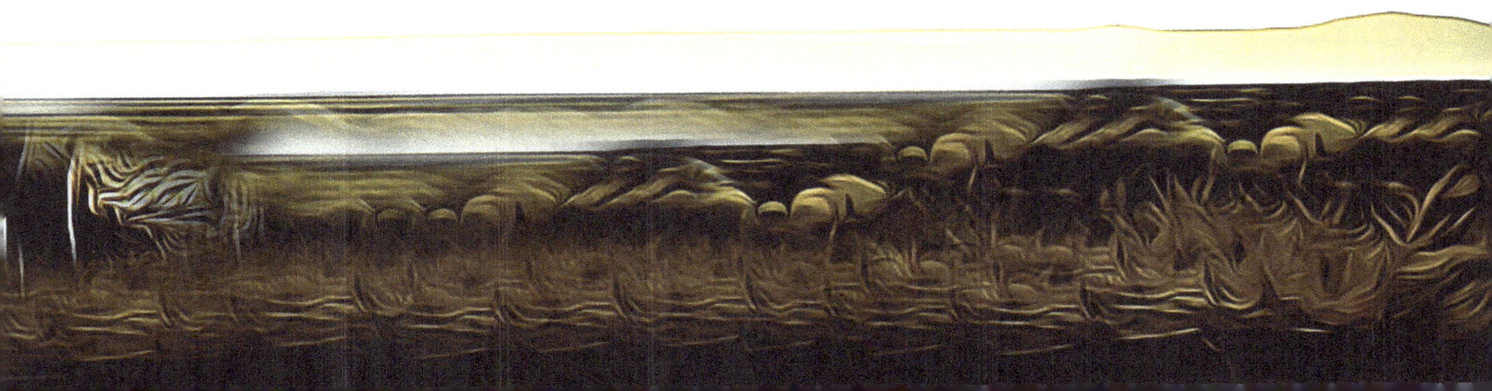

Trumpet 7 - Final Judgment *(Woe 3)*
Revelation Chapter 11:15-19 King James Version (KJV) Public Domain

15. And the seventh angel sounded; and there were great voices in heaven, saying, The kingdoms of this world are become the kingdoms of our Lord, and of his Christ; and he shall reign for ever and ever.

16. And the four and twenty elders, which sat before God on their seats, fell upon their faces, and worshiped God,

17. Saying, We give thee thanks, O Lord God Almighty, which art, and wast, and art to come; because thou hast taken to thee thy great power, and hast reigned.

18. And the nations were angry, and thy wrath is come, and the time of the dead, that they should be judged, and that thou shouldest give reward unto thy servants the prophets, and to the saints, and them that fear thy name, small and great; and shouldest destroy them which destroy the earth.

19. And the temple of God was opened in heaven, and there was seen in his temple the ark of his testament: and there were lightnings, and voices, and thunderings, and an earthquake, and great hail.

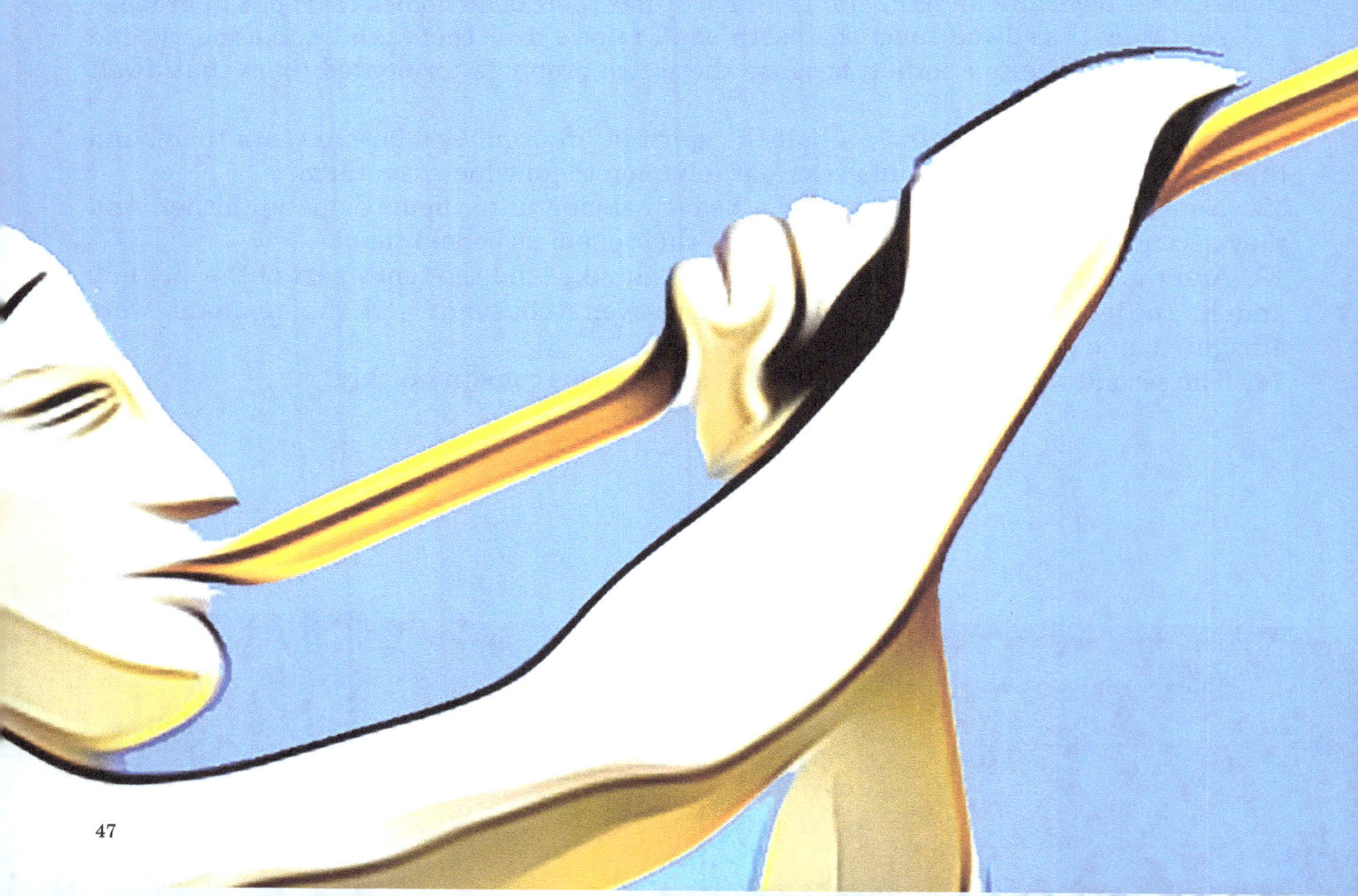

Final Judgment - The end of the world; Judgment of the living and the dead.

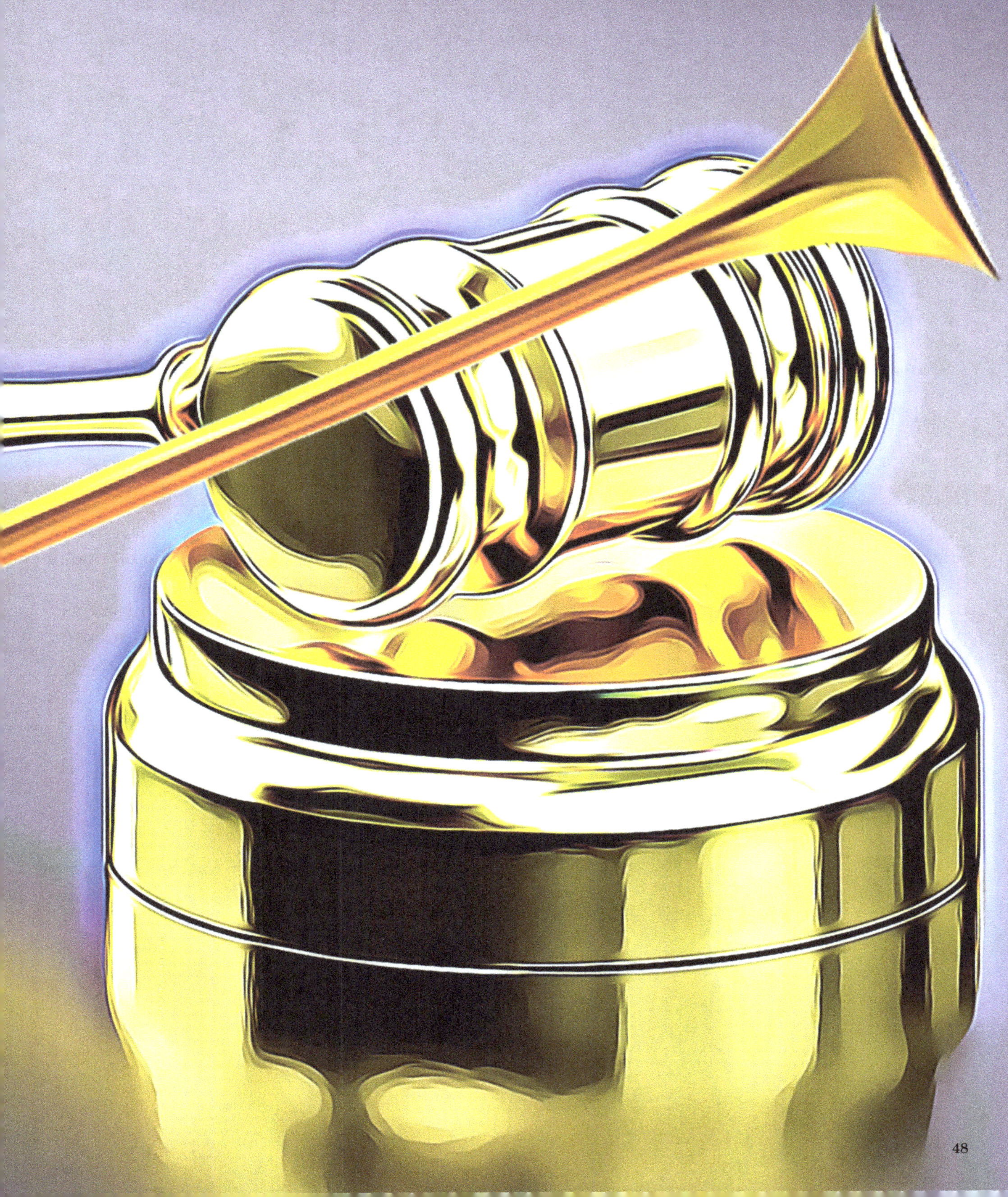

Revelation Time Line
Chapters 1 -11

Selection of the Prophet to prophesy of the end-times	The Prophetic Letters to 4 Churches	The Prophetic Letters to 3 Churches	Prophet given a Vision of God's Throne	Prophet sees the impact of Jesus death on the Heavens	Jesus opens the 7 seals to resume judgment of the earth.

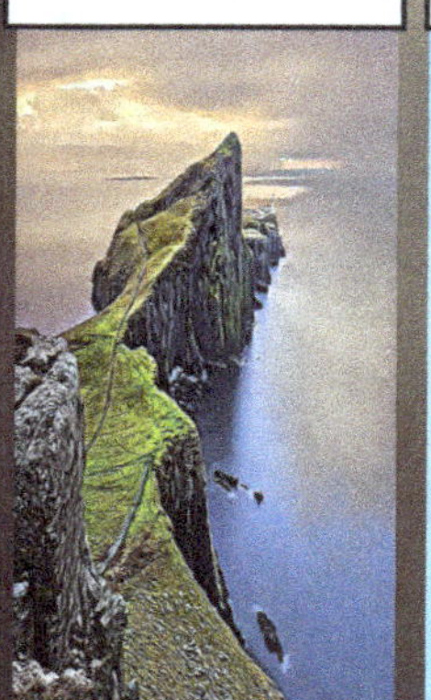
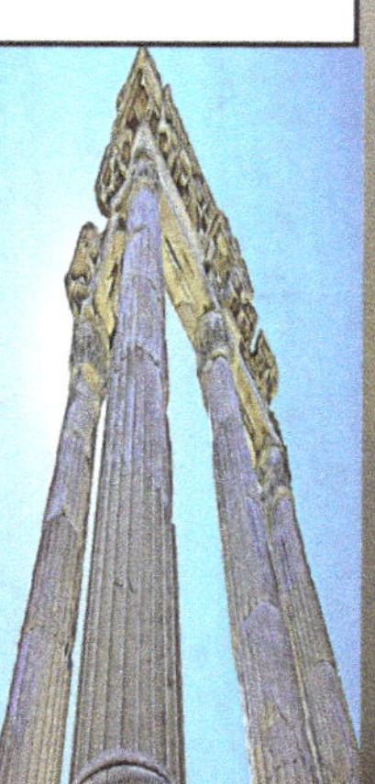
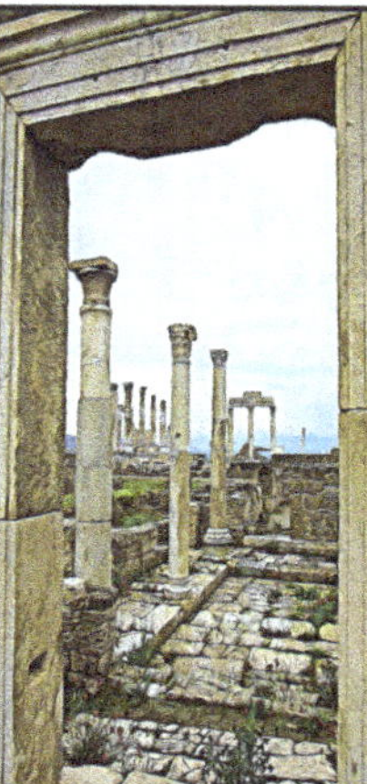
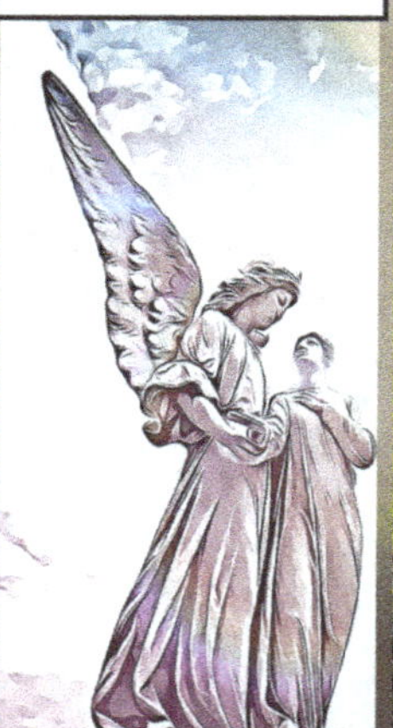
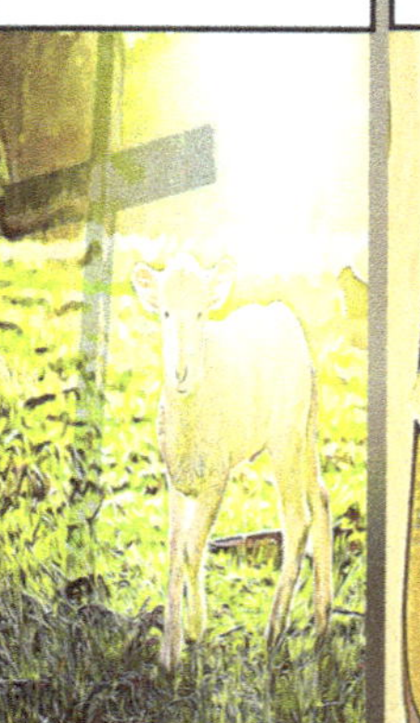
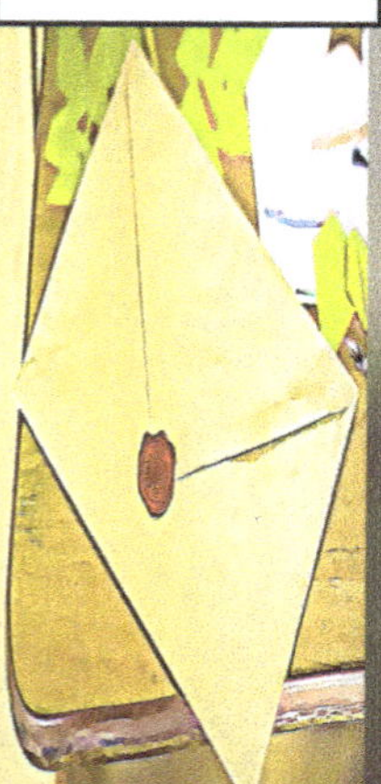

The Book of Revelation covers the events that shall happen during the 70th week as mentioned in the **Book of Daniel.**

The 70th week is equivalent to one prophetic week or a period of seven years. Chapters 1-6 focuses on the first 3 ½ years of the seven year period, which is the end of the Church Age. Chapters 7 - 11 briefly summarizes the second 3 ½ years, which is the Tribulation Period. These chapters explain the events that signal the end of the Church age, by explaining the release of plagues that injure the earth and humans. However, most importantly, these chapters explain the coming of the final judgment and the second coming of Jesus.

The Tribulation Period

Selection of the 144,000 Israelites and God's servants from the churches	The sounding of 4 of the 7 trumpets, which injures the earth.	The sounding of 5th & 6th of the 7 trumpets, which injures humans.	Prophet sees God determine earth's time is up.	The sounding of 7th trumpet, which brings about the end of the world and final judgment.

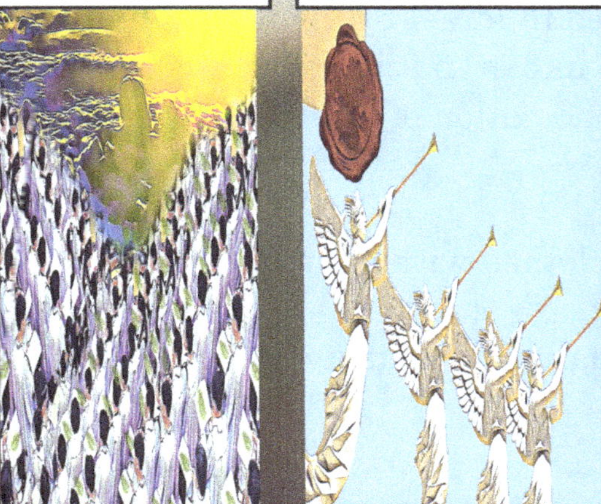
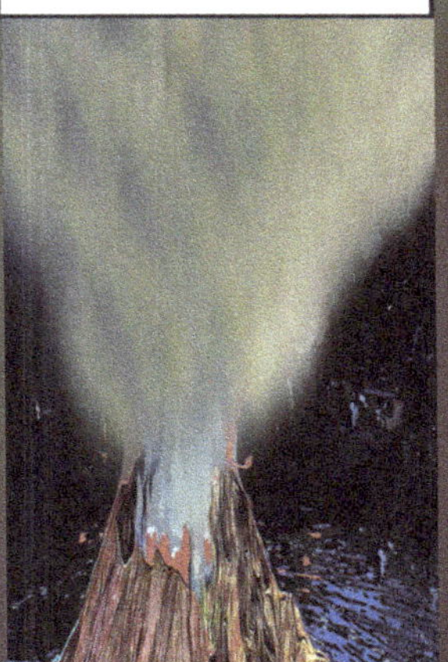
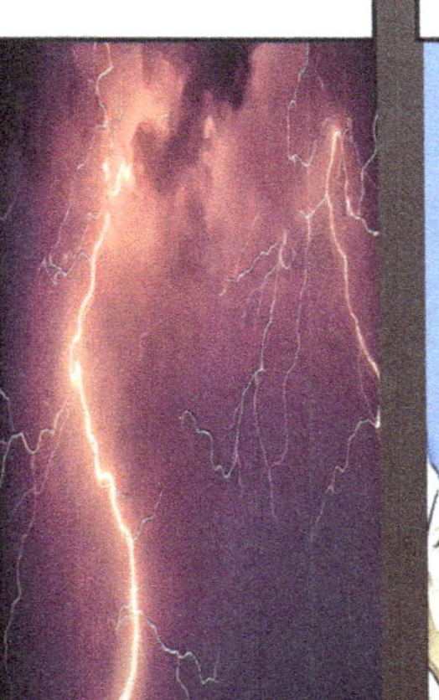
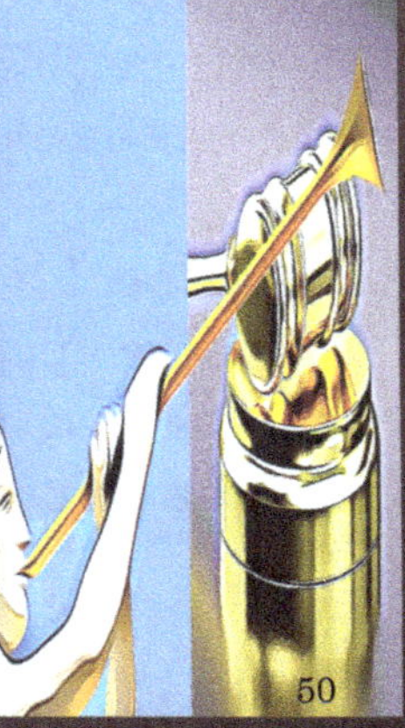

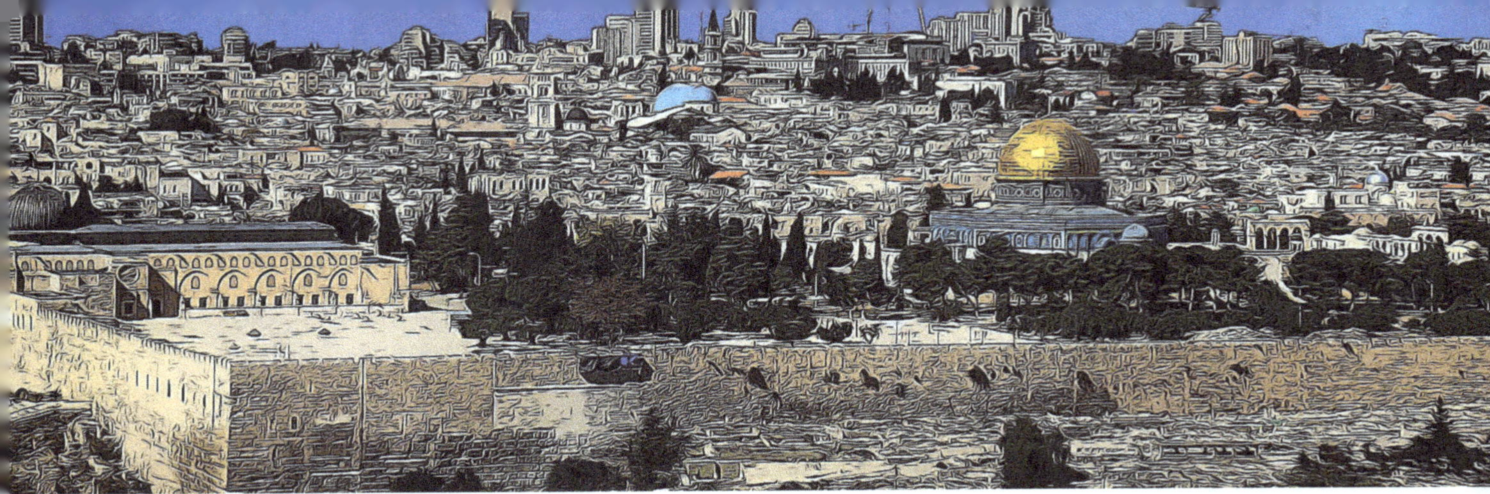

THE INTERPRETATION OF CHAPTER 12

The Pregnant Woman (Israel)

And there appeared a great wonder in heaven; woman clothed with the sun, and the moon
under her feet, and upon her head a crown of twelve stars: .
— *Revelation 12:1 (KJV)*

CHAPTER 12 introduces the nation that God used to fulfill the end time prophecy. Unlike
Chapters 1-11, Chapters 12-22 uses symbols to continue the end-time prophecy. In Chapter
12:1-2, God used a symbol of a pregnant woman who was clothed with the sun, had the
moon at her feet, and a crown of 12 stars to symbolize the Nation of Israel. The Nation of
Israel was the nation God selected to fulfill this end time prophecy.

We know that the pregnant woman symbolizes Israel because God gave Joseph these same
symbols to represent his family in Genesis 37:8-10. Joseph's family became the nation of
Israel. The sun described Jacob, the moon described Rachel, which was Jacob's wife, and the
stars represented Joseph's 11 brothers. Jacob was renamed to Israel by an angel, and it was
through Jacob's sons that Israel grew from a family into a nation. The unborn baby
represents Jesus and Christianity, which was birth from the nation of Israel.

Revelation 12:1-2 King James Version (KJV) Public Domain
1 And there appeared a great wonder in heaven; woman clothed with the sun, and the moon
under her feet, and upon her head a crown of twelve stars:
2 And she being with child cried, travailing in birth, and pained to be delivered.

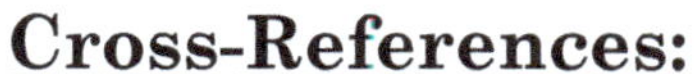

Genesis Chapter 37:8-10

9 And he dreamed yet another dream, and told it his brethren, and said, Behold, I have dreamed a dream more; and, behold, the sun and the moon and the eleven stars made obeisance to me.

10 And he told it to his father, and to his brethren: and his father rebuked him, and said unto him, What is this dream that thou hast dreamed? Shall I and thy mother and thy brethren indeed come to bow down ourselves to thee to the earth?

THE INTERPRETATION OF CHAPTER 12:3-4

The Dragon
(Seven Earthly Kingdoms Backed by Satan)

And there appeared another wonder in heaven; and behold a great red dragon, having seven heads and ten horns, and seven crowns upon his heads. — Revelation 12:3 (KJV)

CHAPTER 12:3-4 introduces the earthly kingdoms Satan used to hinder the fulfillment of this end time prophecy. Revelation Chapter 12:3-4 continues with another symbol, the dragon. This dragon had seven heads, seven crowns, and 10 horns. This dragon symbolizes 7 kingdoms and 10 kings. Satan influenced six earthly kingdoms to persecute Israel (the pregnant women) with the ultimate goal of preventing the coming of Jesus the Messiah and Christianity (the baby). Despite this, Jesus was born and prevailed. Jesus ushered in a heavenly kingdom on earth (Christianity). However, when Christianity (the church age) ends, Satan, through the 7th Kingdom (The Anti-Christ Kingdom), will war with Jesus before the end of the world comes.

The Old Testament speaks of these kingdoms as follows:

Persecuted Israel (The Pregnant Women):

1 Egypt	(Modern Day: Egypt)	(Ref: Exodus)
2 Assyrian Empire	(Modern Day: Syria, Iraq, Iran, Turkey)	(Ref: Isaiah)
3 Babylon	(Modern Day: Iraq)	(Ref: Daniel)
4 Persian Empire	(Modern Day: Iran)	(Ref: Daniel)
5 Grecian Empire	(Modern Day: Egypt, Syria, Iraq, Iran, Turkey, Greece, Lebanon, Jordan, Israel)	(Ref: Daniel)

Persecuted Israel, Jesus, and Christians (The Baby):

6 Roman Empire	(Modern Day: Same as Grecian Empire, European and North African Coastal Countries)	(Ref: Daniel)
7 Anti-Christ Kingdom	(10 Kings with the Anti-Christ)	(Ref: Daniel)

Revelation 12:3-4 King James Version (KJV) Public Domain

3 And there appeared another wonder in heaven; and behold a great red dragon, having seven heads and ten horns, and seven crowns upon his heads.

4 And his tail drew the third part of the stars of heaven, and did cast them to the earth: and the dragon stood before the woman which was ready to be delivered, for to devour her child as soon as it was born.

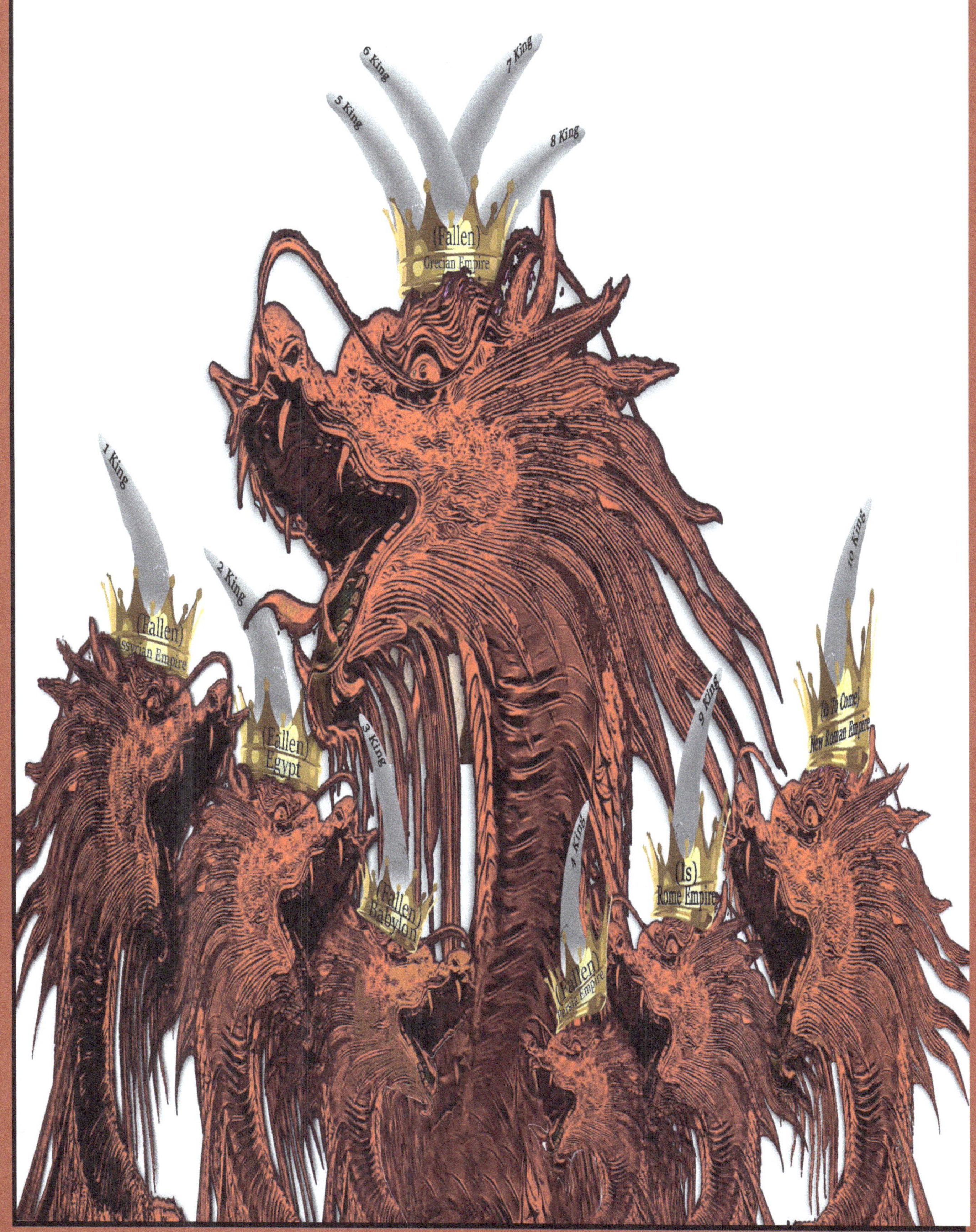

5 King
6 King
7 King
8 King
(Fallen)
Grecian Empire
1 King
(Fallen)
Assyrian Empire
2 King
(Fallen)
Egypt
3 King
(Fallen)
Babylon
4 King
(Fallen)
Persia Empire
9 King
(Is)
Rome Empire
10 King
(To To Come)
New Roman Empire

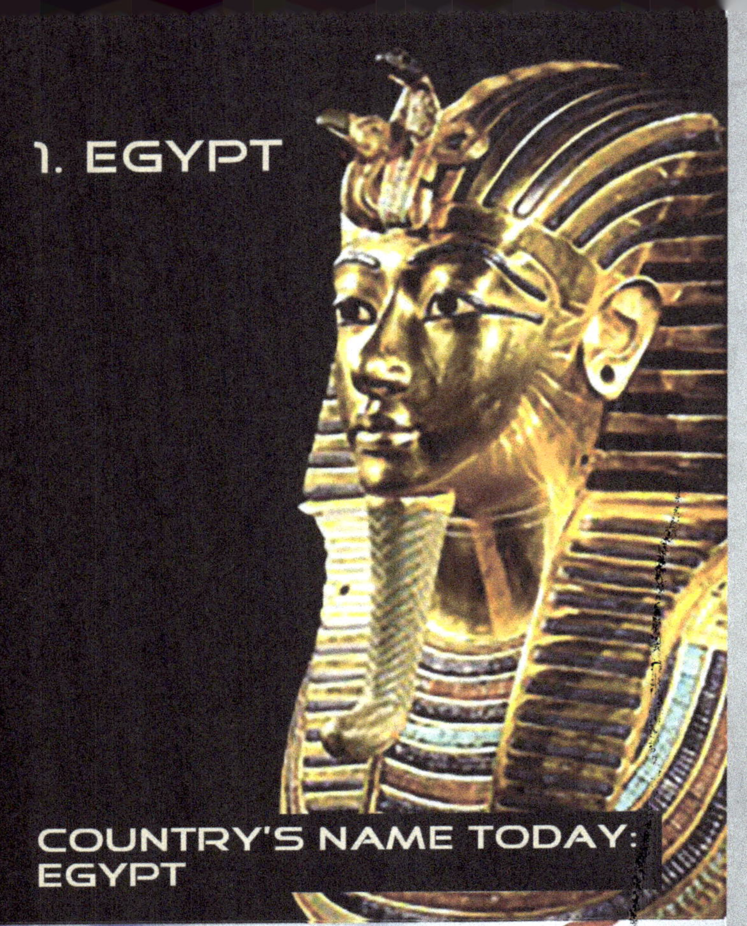

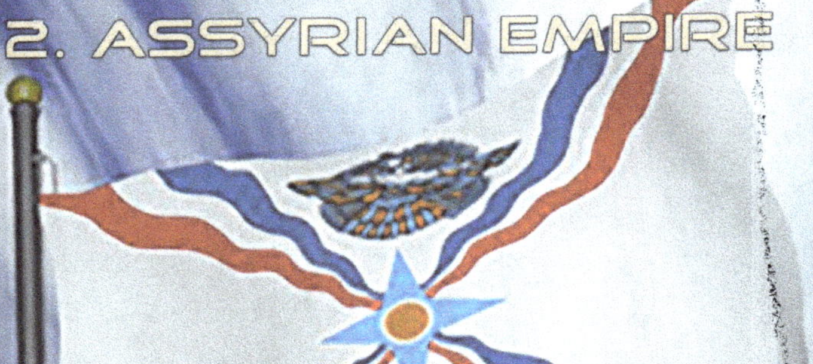

3. BABYLON

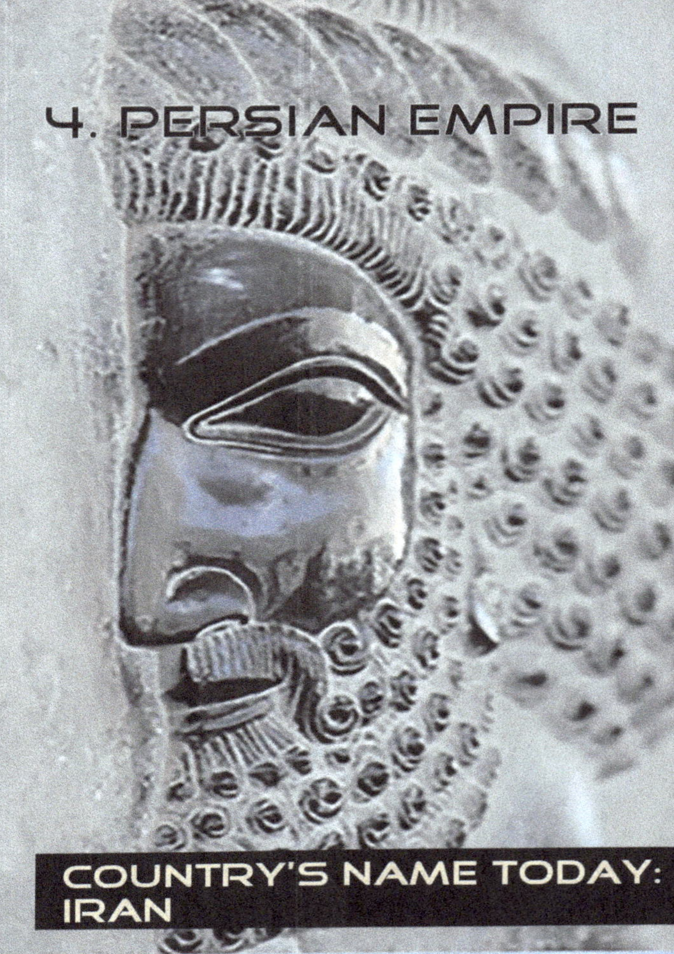

5. GRECIAN EMPIRE

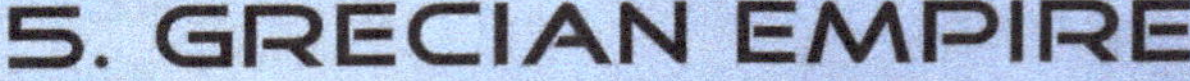

6. ROMAN EMPIRE

Interpretation:
Jesus Ushers in the Heavenly Kingdom

Israel (the pregnant woman) through the line of Judah birthed Jesus. Jesus, the Messiah, ushered in a heavenly kingdom. Through this heavenly kingdom, all nations have the ability to join the Kingdom of God and receive salvation that was paid for by Jesus Christ. Jesus provided this opportunity for all mankind by his crucifixion on the cross and his resurrection on the 3rd day. Since the resurrection of Jesus, the judgment of the earthly kingdoms has been delayed to give mankind a chance to become followers of Jesus Christ and a part of the heavenly kingdom on earth. Until the end of the Church Age, Israel is being kept hidden until the tribulation period. Afterward, the judgment of the earthly kingdoms will resume.

Jesus' sacrifice also permanently barred Satan from heaven. Jesus took away Satan's reason for entering into heaven, which was to be the accuser of mankind to God. Since mankind now has the ability to repent from sins through Jesus Christ, Satan and his demons, the fallen angels, also called 1/3 of the stars, have no more reason to enter into heaven. Satan can no longer persecute Israel, Jesus, and Christians before God.

7. The Anti-Christ Kingdom

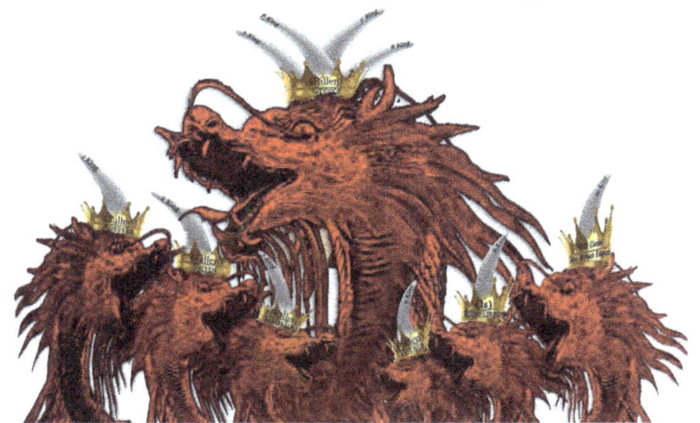

Revelation 12:5-13
King James Version (KJV) Public Domain

5 And she brought forth a man child, who was to rule all nations with a rod of iron: and her child was caught up unto God, and to his throne.

6 And the woman fled into the wilderness, where she hath a place prepared of God, that they should feed her there a thousand two hundred and threescore days.

7 And there was war in heaven: Michael and his angels fought against the dragon; and the dragon fought and his angels,

8 And prevailed not; neither was their place found any more in heaven.

9 And the great dragon was cast out, that old serpent, called the Devil, and Satan, which deceiveth the whole world: he was cast out into the earth, and his angels were cast out with him.

10 And I heard a loud voice saying in heaven, Now is come salvation, and strength, and the kingdom of our God, and the power of his Christ: for the accuser of our brethren is cast down, which accused them before our God day and night.

11 And they overcame him by the blood of the Lamb, and by the word of their testimony; and they loved not their lives unto the death.

12 Therefore rejoice, ye heavens, and ye that dwell in them. Woe to the inhabiters of the earth and of the sea! for the devil is come down unto you, having great wrath, because he knoweth that he hath but a short time.

13 And when the dragon saw that he was cast unto the earth, he persecuted the woman which brought forth the man child.

Interpretation: Israel's Hiding Place

Israel escaped Satan's attacks by fleeing into the wilderness into her designated land between the two eagles' wings, which is a symbol that represents Egypt and the Assyrian Empire. In the book of Daniel, Daniel had a dream of a lion with two eagle's wings. In this dream, eagle's wings symbolized Babylon's conquering of Egypt and the Assyrian Empire. The land where the Assyrian Empire occupied is all of the land northeast of Israel. God utilizes these same symbols to explain Israel's land location in the Book of Revelation. During the Church Age and 3 1/2 years prior to the tribulation period, God is keeping Israel from harm. Satan has even attempted to flood Israel several times, but God will not allow Israel to be destroyed. Therefore, Satan makes war with a remnant of Israel's descendants during the tribulation period.

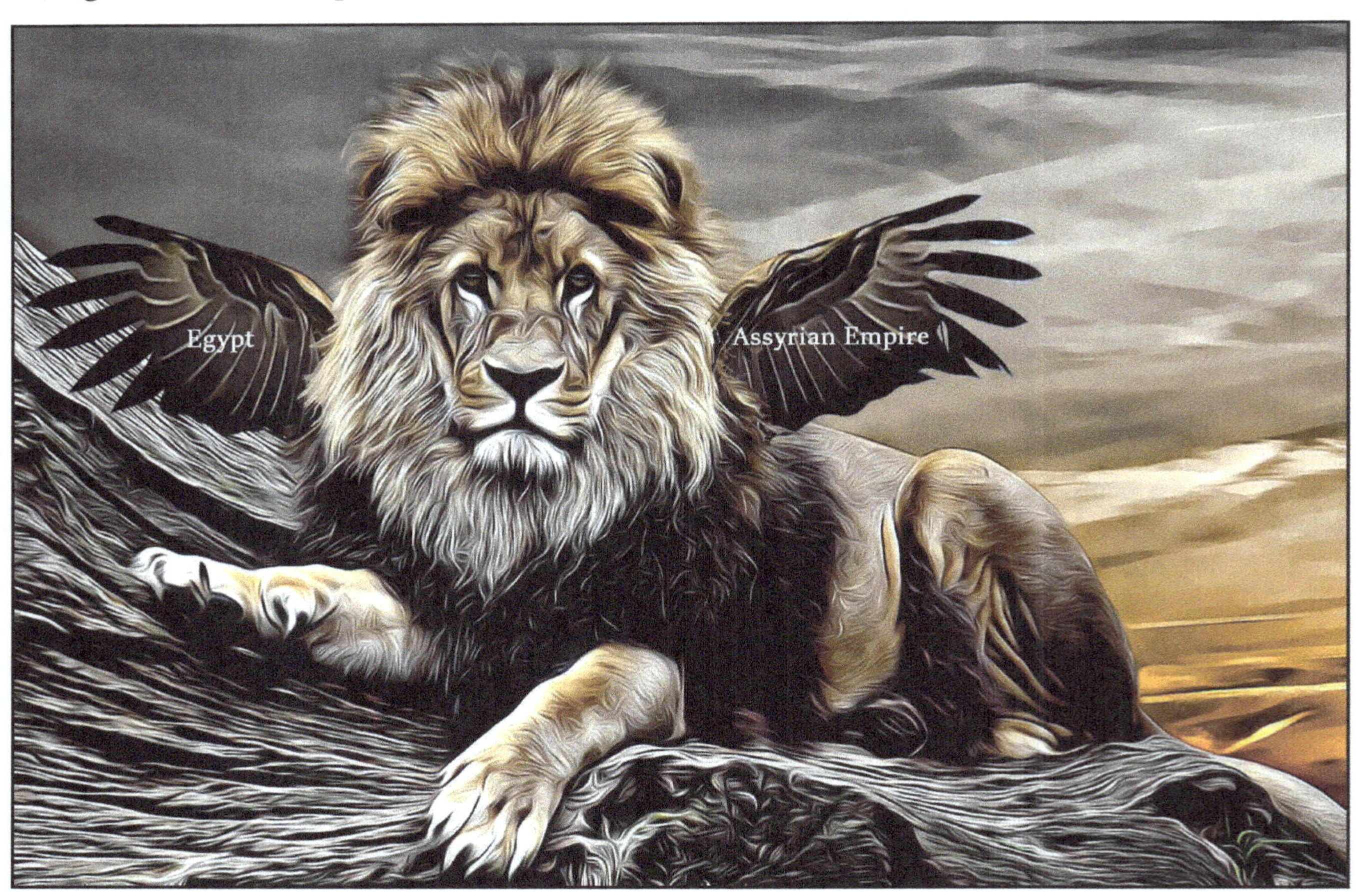

Revelation 12:14-17   King James Version (KJV) Public Domain

14 And to the woman were given two wings of a great eagle, that she might fly into the wilderness, into her place, where she is nourished for a time, and times, and half a time, from the face of the serpent.

15 And the serpent cast out of his mouth water as a flood after the woman, that he might cause her to be carried away of the flood.

16 And the earth helped the woman, and the earth opened her mouth, and swallowed up the flood which the dragon cast out of his mouth.

17 And the dragon was wroth with the woman, and went to make war with the remnant of her seed, which keep the commandments of God, and have the testimony of Jesus Christ.

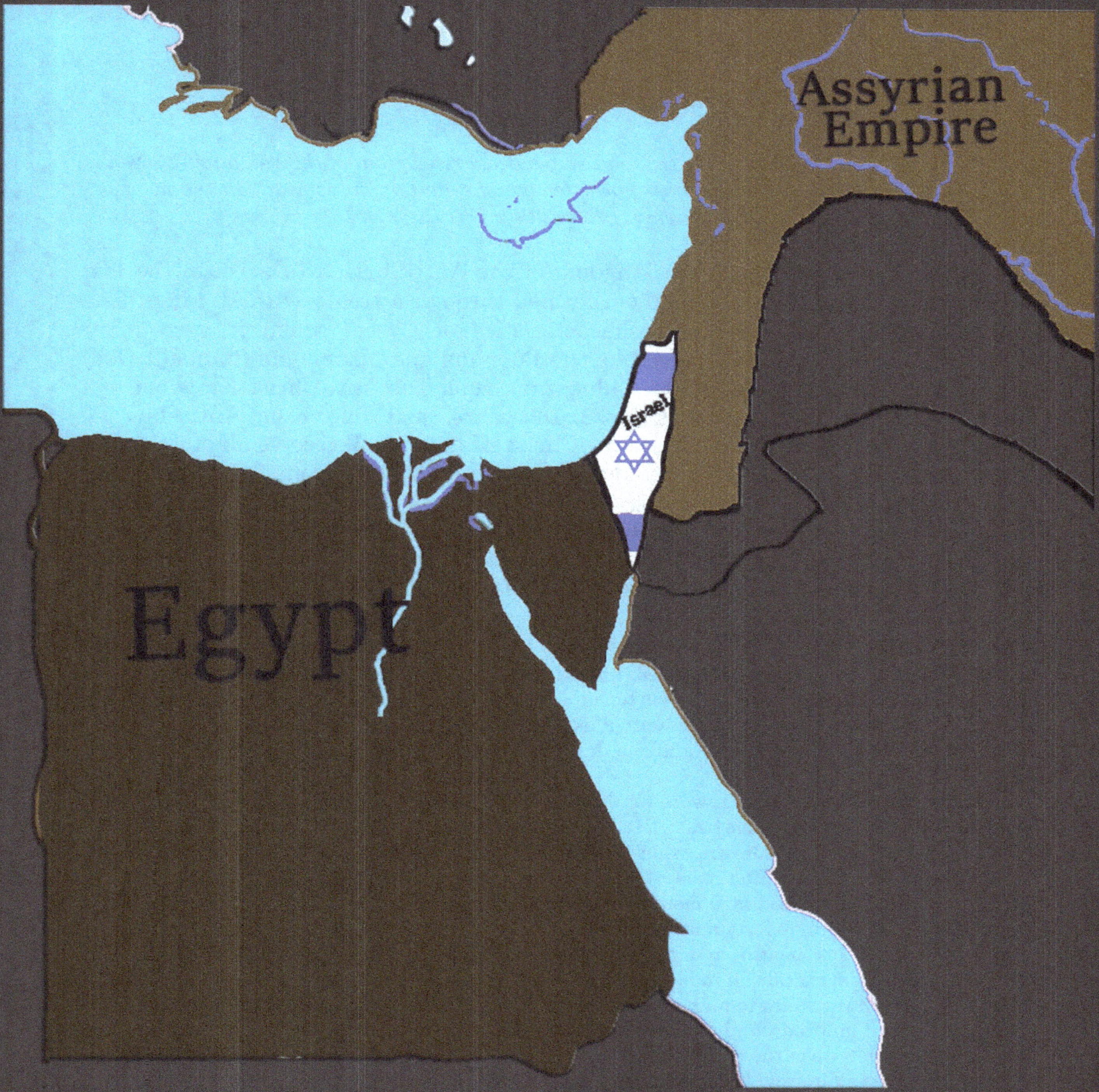

Assyrian
Empire
Israel
Egypt

THE INTERPRETATION OF CHAPTER 13

The Anti-Christ Kingdom

And I stood upon the sand of the sea, and saw a beast rise up out of the sea, having seven heads and ten horns, and upon his horns ten crowns, and upon his heads the name of blasphemy.   Revelation 13:1 (KJV)

CHAPTER 13 explains that the kingdom of the Anti-Christ will arise in the last day and become a combined kingdom formed through a treaty with 10 kings. The Anti-Christ Kingdom will have characteristics of Greece when it was under Alexander the Great. It will move like the Persians and blaspheme (to insult God) like the Babylonians under Nebuchadnezzar's rule. The Anti-Christ Kingdom will make war with God's servants for 3 1/2 years, just like King Antiochus IV Epiphanies did against Israel. The Anti-Christ Kingdom will receive all of its power from Satan. The Anti-Christ Kingdom is a treaty of 10 kings from 7 kingdoms that have already come on earth: Egypt, the Assyrian Empire, Babylon, Persian Empire, Grecian Empire and the Roman Empire. The coming of this kingdom was prophesied by Daniel as the 10 toes in Daniel Chapter 2. Note: When the Bible describes a beast coming out of the sea, this beast symbolizes a Kingdom.

Revelation 13 King James Version (KJV) Public Domain

13 And I stood upon the sand of the sea, and saw a beast rise up out of the sea, having seven heads and ten horns, and upon his horns ten crowns, and upon his heads the name of blasphemy.
2 And the beast which I saw was like unto a leopard, and his feet were as the feet of a bear, and his mouth as the mouth of a lion: and the dragon gave him his power, and his seat, and great authority.
3 And I saw one of his heads as it were wounded to death; and his deadly wound was healed: and all the world wondered after the beast.
4 And they worshiped the dragon which gave power unto the beast: and they worshiped the beast, saying, Who is like unto the beast? who is able to make war with him?
5 And there was given unto him a mouth speaking great things and blasphemies; and power was given unto him to continue forty and two months.
6 And he opened his mouth in blasphemy against God, to blaspheme his name, and his tabernacle, and them that dwell in heaven.
7 And it was given unto him to make war with the saints, and to overcome them: and power was given him over all kindreds, and tongues, and nations.
8 And all that dwell upon the earth shall worship him, whose names are not written in the book of life of the Lamb slain from the foundation of the world.
9 If any man have an ear, let him hear.
10 He that leadeth into captivity shall go into captivity: he that killeth with the sword must be killed with the sword. Here is the patience and the faith of the saints.

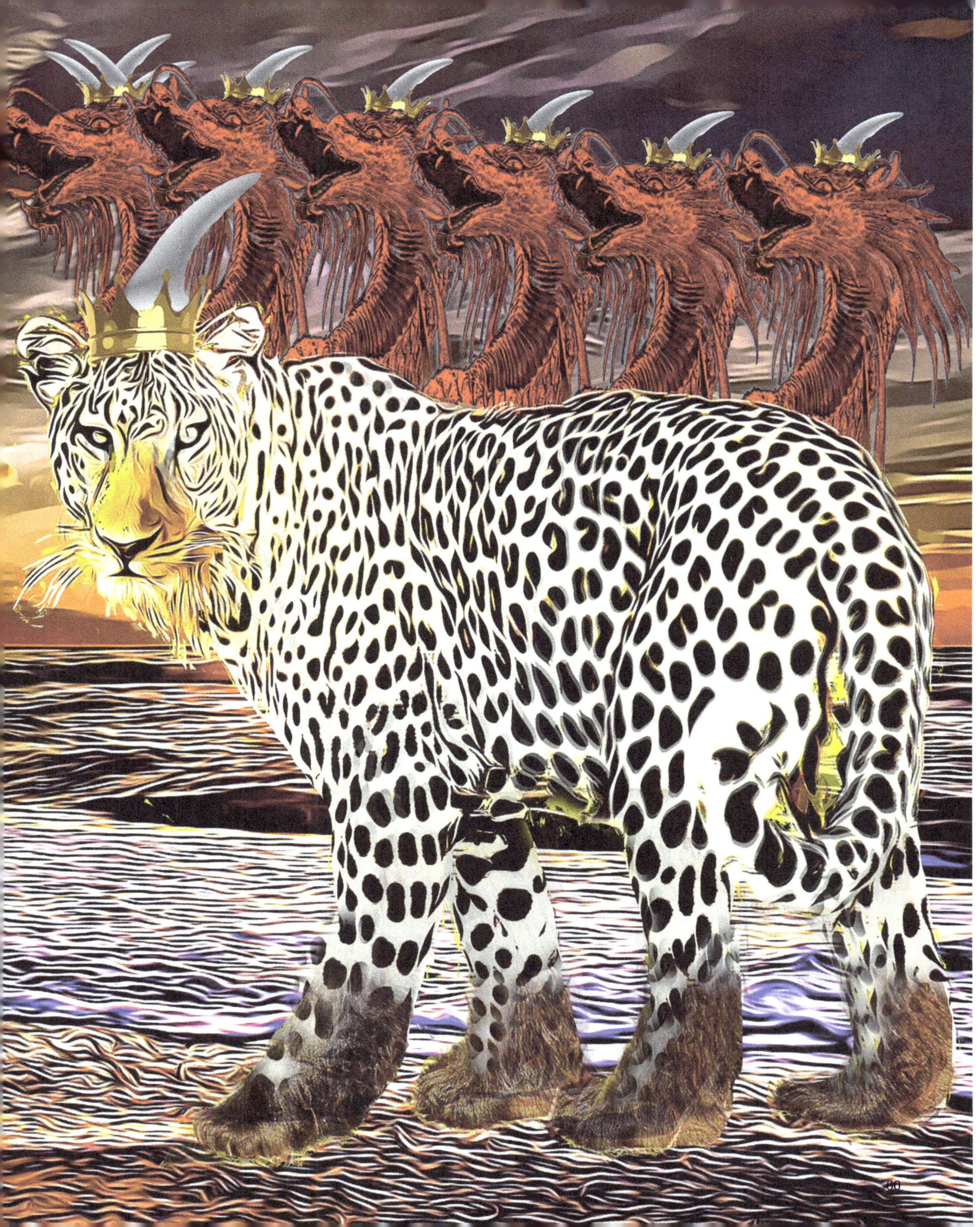

THE INTERPRETATION OF CHAPTER 13:11-18

The Anti-Christ and the False Prophet

And I beheld another beast coming up out of the earth; and he had two horns like a lamb, and he spake as a dragon. Revelations 13:11 (KJV)

The False Prophet causes all who are not identified as God's servants to worship the Anti-Christ, which is the first beast who was wounded, yet remained alive. The two horns on the lamb represents the False Prophet and the Anti-Christ. The False Prophet uses signs and wonders to deceive all of mankind. This False Prophet had the power to give life to the idol created to symbolize the Anti-Christ. The False Prophet caused all unrepentant men to receive the mark of the Anti-Christ in their hands and foreheads to be able to buy or sell food and goods. The number of the Anti-Christ is "666". Note: When the Bible describes a beast coming out of the earth, this beast symbolizes a man, which is similar to the beast that comes out of the sea (a Kingdom).

Revelation 13 King James Version (KJV) Public Domain

11 And I beheld another beast coming up out of the earth; and he had two horns like a lamb, and he spake as a dragon.

12 And he exerciseth all the power of the first beast before him, and causeth the earth and them which dwell therein to worship the first beast, whose deadly wound was healed.

13 And he doeth great wonders, so that he maketh fire come down from heaven on the earth in the sight of men,

14 And deceiveth them that dwell on the earth by the means of those miracles which he had power to do in the sight of the beast; saying to them that dwell on the earth, that they should make an image to the beast, which had the wound by a sword, and did live.

15 And he had power to give life unto the image of the beast, that the image of the beast should both speak, and cause that as many as would not worship the image of the beast should be killed.

16 And he causeth all, both small and great, rich and poor, free and bond, to receive a mark in their right hand, or in their foreheads:

17 And that no man might buy or sell, save he that had the mark, or the name of the beast, or the number of his name.

18 Here is wisdom. Let him that hath understanding count the number of the beast: for it is the number of a man; and his number is Six hundred threescore and six.

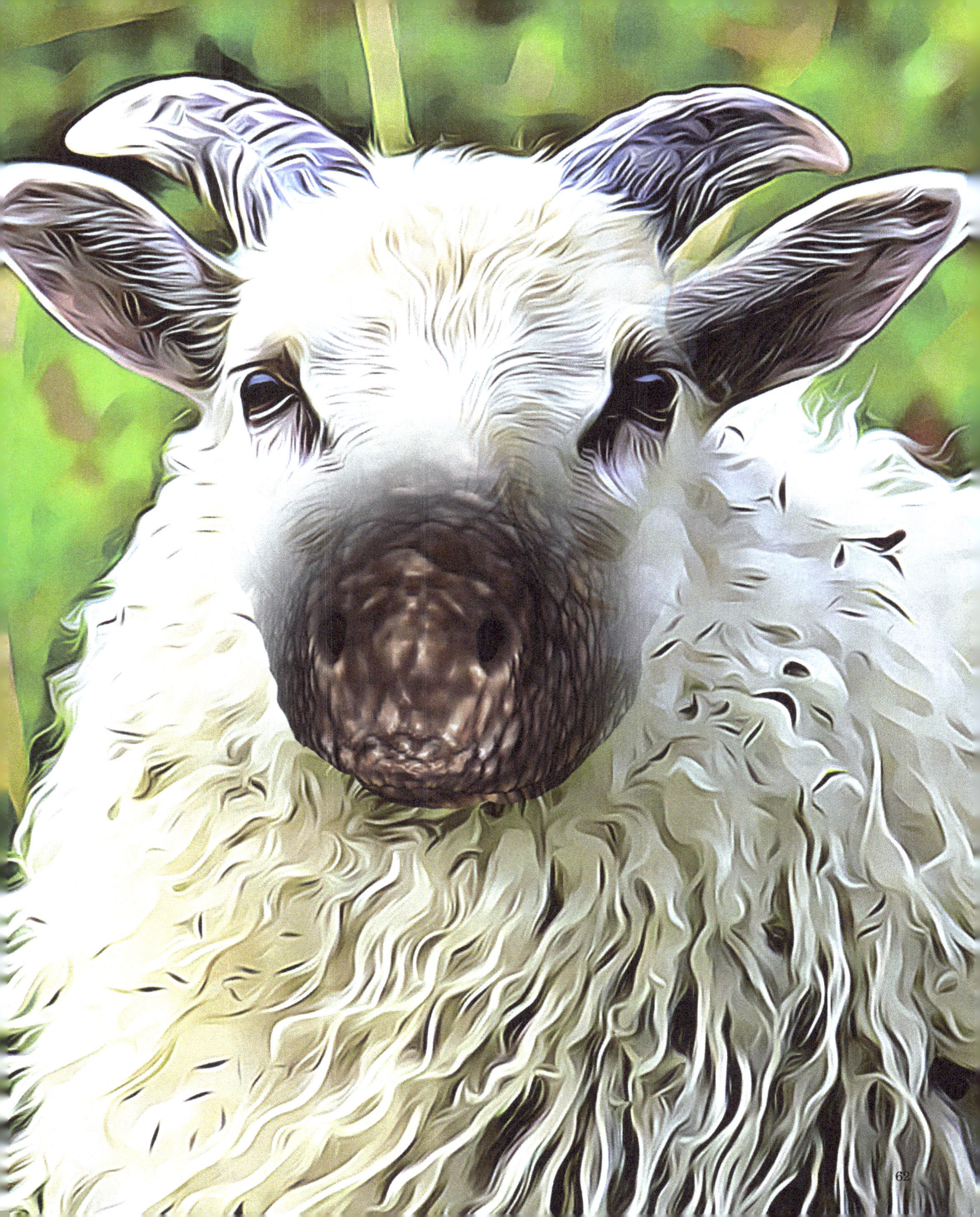

THE INTERPRETATION OF CHAPTER 14

The Rapture of the 144,000 Israelites

And I looked, and, lo, a Lamb stood on the mount Sion, and with him an hundred forty and four thousand, having his Father's name written in their foreheads. Revelations 14:1 (KJV)

Chapter 14 explains the rapture of the 144,000 Israelites from the earth. These Israelites are the same Israelites that were selected by God in Revelation Chapter 7 and they were given the opportunity to avoid participating in the future events that would bring about the end of the world. These Israelites were found to be without fault before God the father and Jesus the Lamb. The reason why God only allowed 144,000 Israelites to avoid the Tribulation Period is because the majority of the Israelites rejected Jesus as their Lord and Savior. The Israelites did not believe that Jesus was the Messiah and the fulfillment of the prophecy.

Because salvation during the church age can only come through Jesus, the unbelieving Israelites missed the opportunity to avoid the tribulation period.

Revelation 14:1-5   King James Version (KJV) Public Domain

14 And I looked, and, lo, a Lamb stood on the mount Sion, and with him an hundred forty and four thousand, having his Father's name written in their foreheads.

2 And I heard a voice from heaven, as the voice of many waters, and as the voice of a great thunder: and I heard the voice of harpers harping with their harps:

3 And they sung as it were a new song before the throne, and before the four beasts, and the elders: and no man could learn that song but the hundred and forty and four thousand, which were redeemed from the earth.

4 These are they which were not defiled with women; for they are virgins. These are they which follow the Lamb whithersoever he goeth. These were redeemed from among men, being the firstfruits unto God and to the Lamb.

5 And in their mouth was found no guile: for they are without fault before the throne of God.

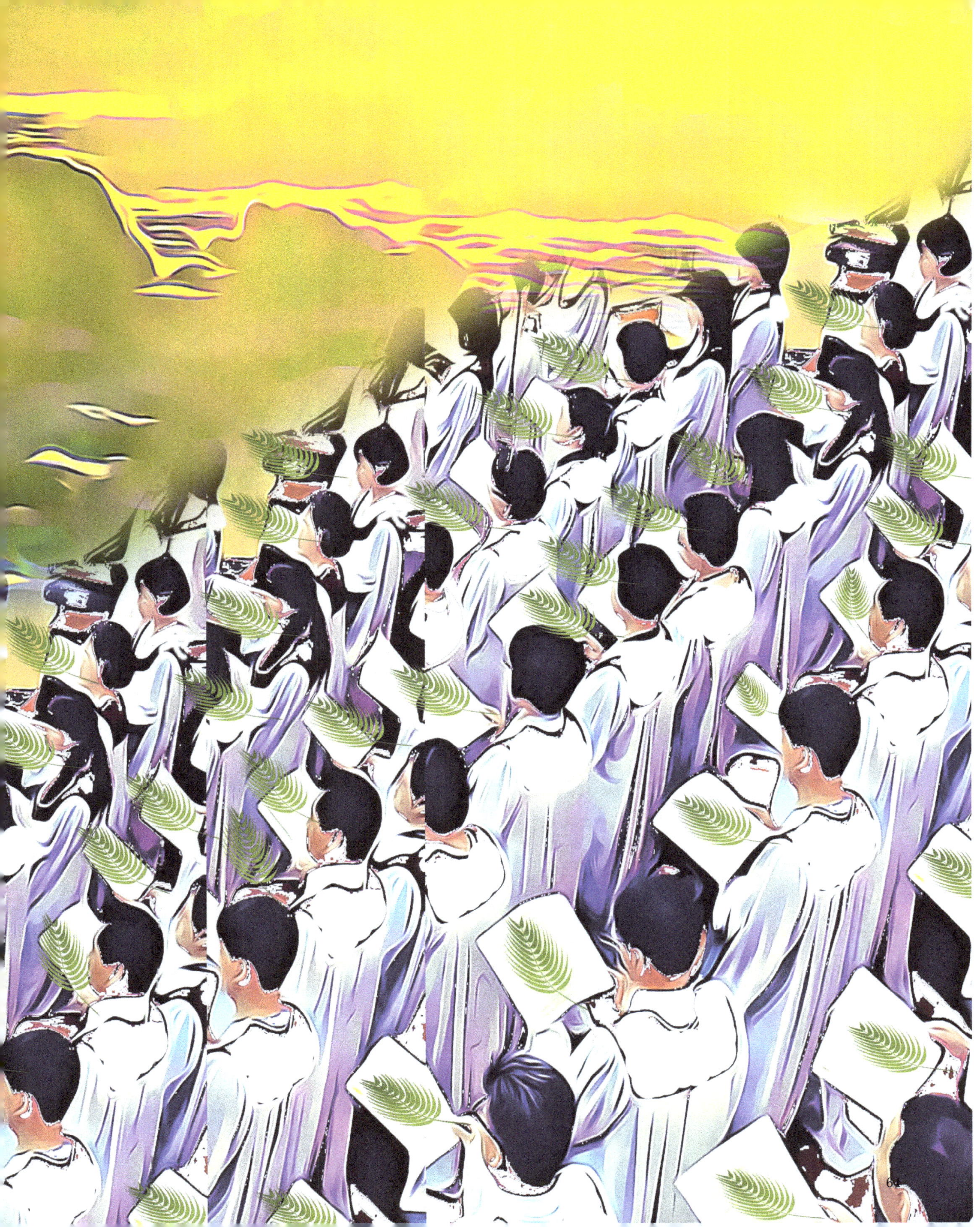

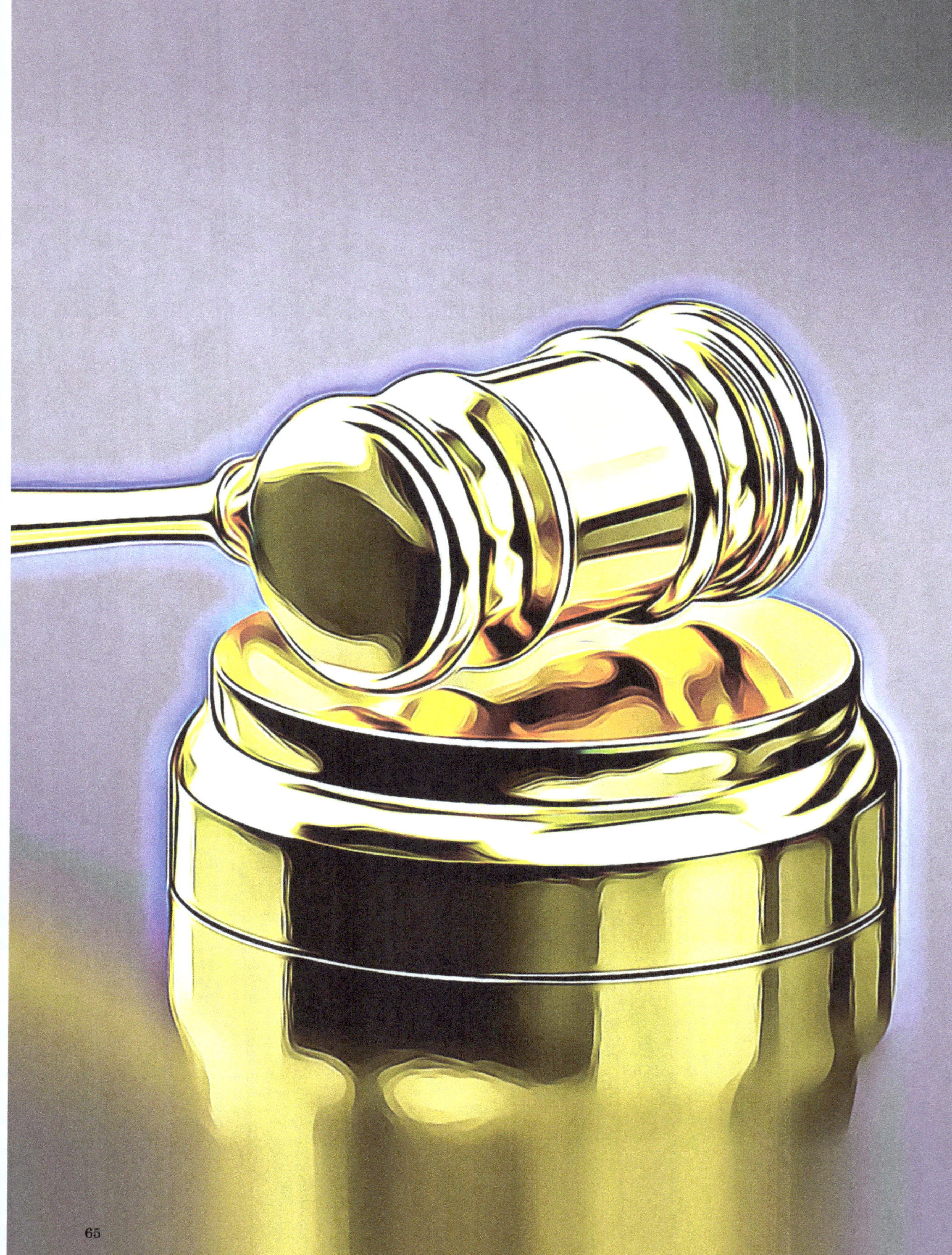

THE INTERPRETATION OF CHAPTER 14:6-11

Proclamation of the Final Judgment

Saying with a loud voice, Fear God, and give glory to him; for the hour of his judgment is come: and worship him that made heaven, and earth, and the sea, and the fountains of waters. Revelations 14:7 (KJV)

Revelation 14:6-11 explains the future events that would happen to the Anti-Christ kingdom and to the unrepentant men who accepted the mark of the beast.

Rev 14:8-10 (KJV) list the order of God's wrath as follows:
The Anti-Christ Kingdom will fall (The new city of Babylon would fall)
Those who receive the mark of the beast (Anti-Christ) will receive God's wrath

Revelation Chapter 14:6-11 King James Version (KJV) Public Domain

6 And I saw another angel fly in the midst of heaven, having the everlasting gospel to preach unto them that dwell on the earth, and to every nation, and kindred, and tongue, and people,
7 Saying with a loud voice, Fear God, and give glory to him; for the hour of his judgment is come: and worship him that made heaven, and earth, and the sea, and the fountains of waters.
8 And there followed another angel, saying, Babylon is fallen, is fallen, that great city, because she made all nations drink of the wine of the wrath of her fornication.
9 And the third angel followed them, saying with a loud voice, If any man worship the beast and his image, and receive his mark in his forehead, or in his hand,
10 The same shall drink of the wine of the wrath of God, which is poured out without mixture into the cup of his indignation; and he shall be tormented with fire and brimstone in the presence of the holy angels, and in the presence of the Lamb:
11 And the smoke of their torment ascendeth up for ever and ever: and they have no rest day nor night, who worship the beast and his image, and whosoever receiveth the mark of his name.

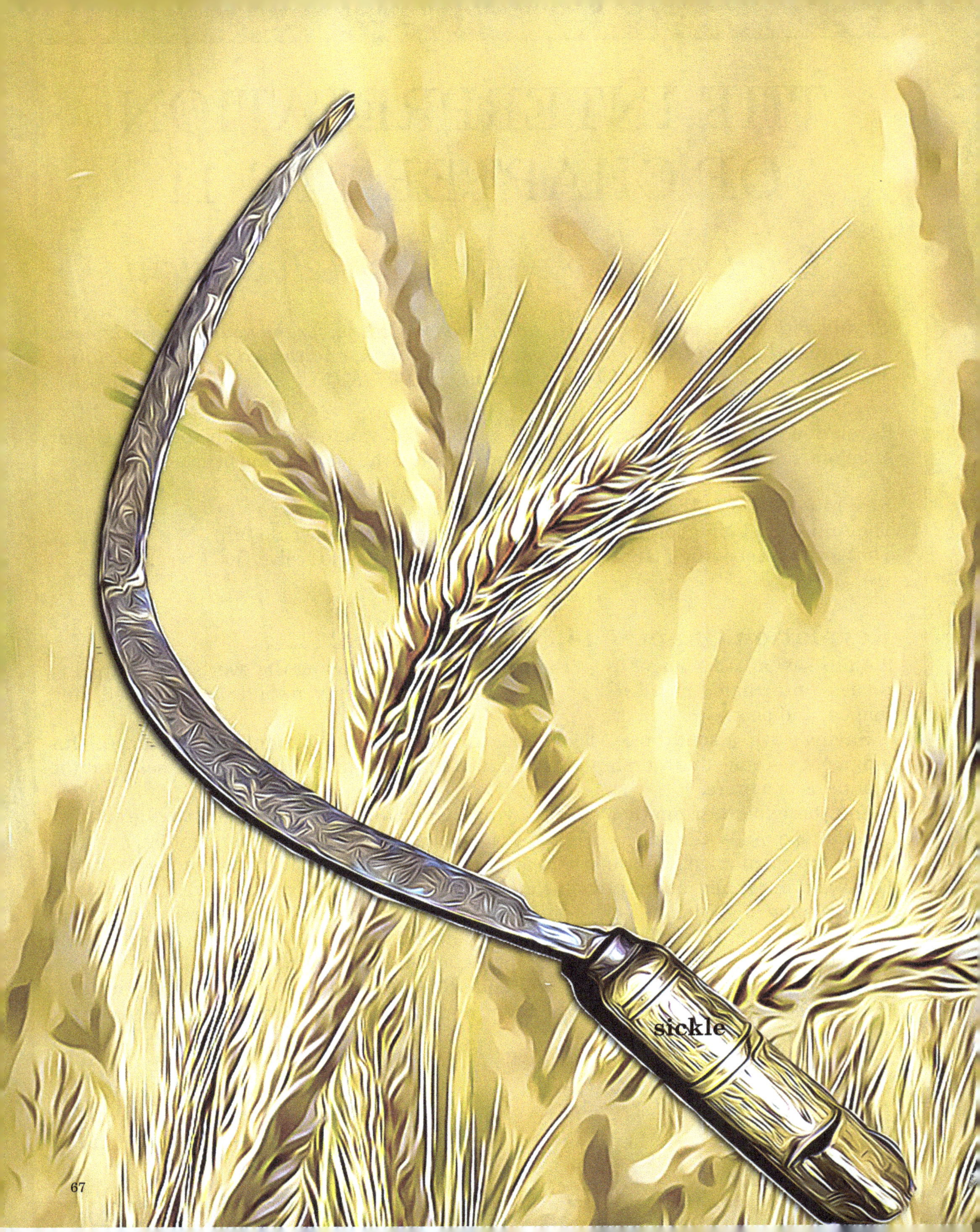
sickle

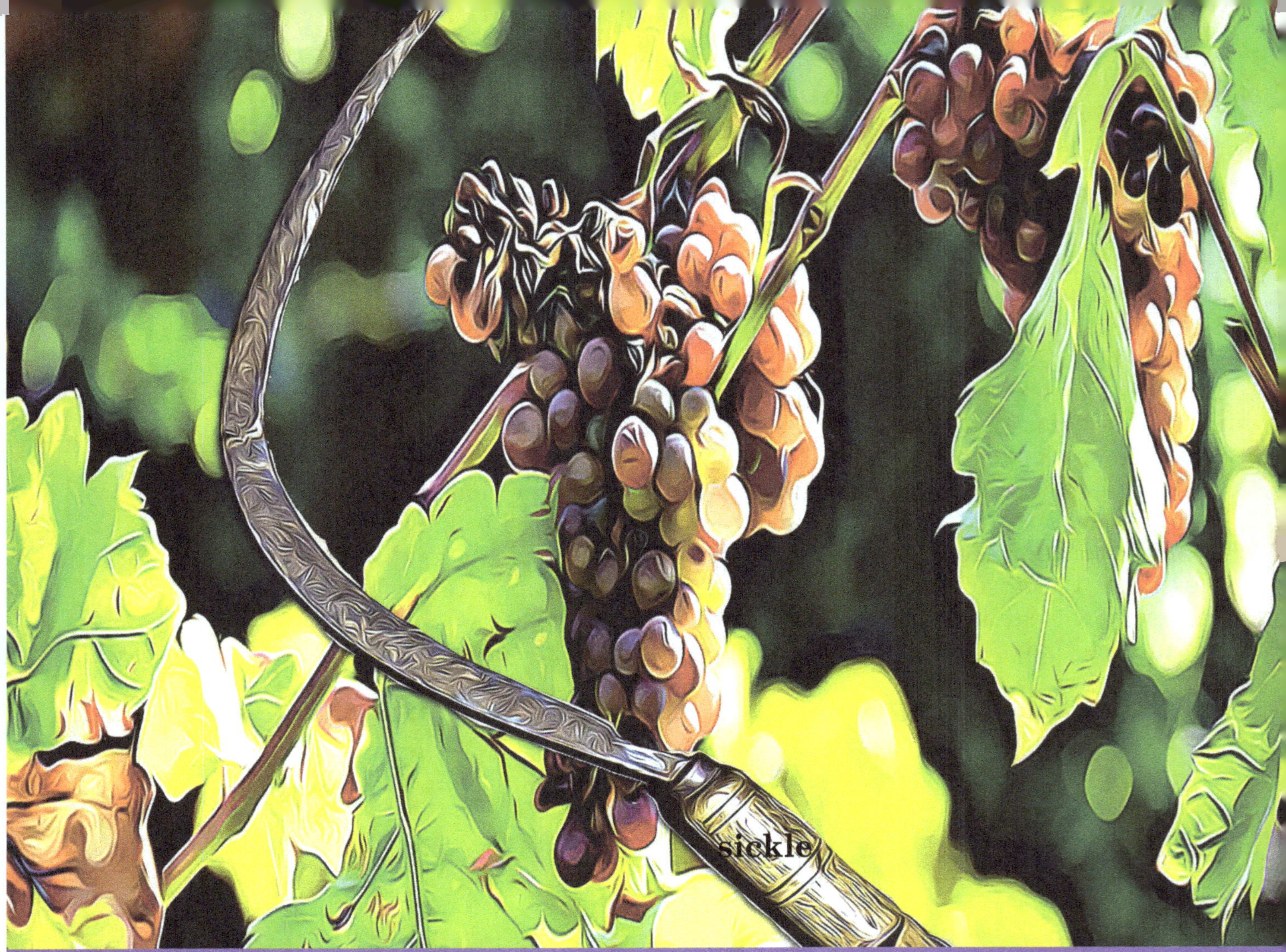

Interpretation - *The Death of the Martyrs during the Tribulation*

Chapter 14:17-20 explains the death of the martyrs. The martyrs are those who missed the opportunity for salvation through Jesus Christ but come to this realization only after the church is taken away from the earth. Although, the martyrs can no longer receive salvation through Jesus, God still gives them a chance to obtain salvation from eternal damnation through the refusal to accept the mark of the beast. However, the Anti-Christ will kill them over this same refusal and cause them to die as martyrs. The martyrs are symbolized as grapes that are thrown into the wine press of the wrath of God. The martyrs were thrown into God's wrath because unlike God's Servants who were raptured, the martyrs did not have Jesus to pay the price for their sins. The martyrs had to pay the price by sacrificing their own lives, which also meant they had to experience the wrath of God. However, although the martyrs experienced the wrath of God for failing to accept Jesus, God still gave them a chance to gain eternal life. The Anti-Christ murdered a multitude of martyrs in the outer parts of the city of Jerusalem. The martyrs' blood covered more than 183 miles (thousand and six hundred furlongs), which reached up to the height of a horse's reigns. The martyrs' blood symbolized wine in the same manner as Jesus blood symbolized wine **(Matthew 26:27-28 (KJV).** The murders of the martyrs caused God to unleash the wine of his wrath on all unbelievers, the Anti-Christ, and the False Prophet. Rev 14:10 (KJV).

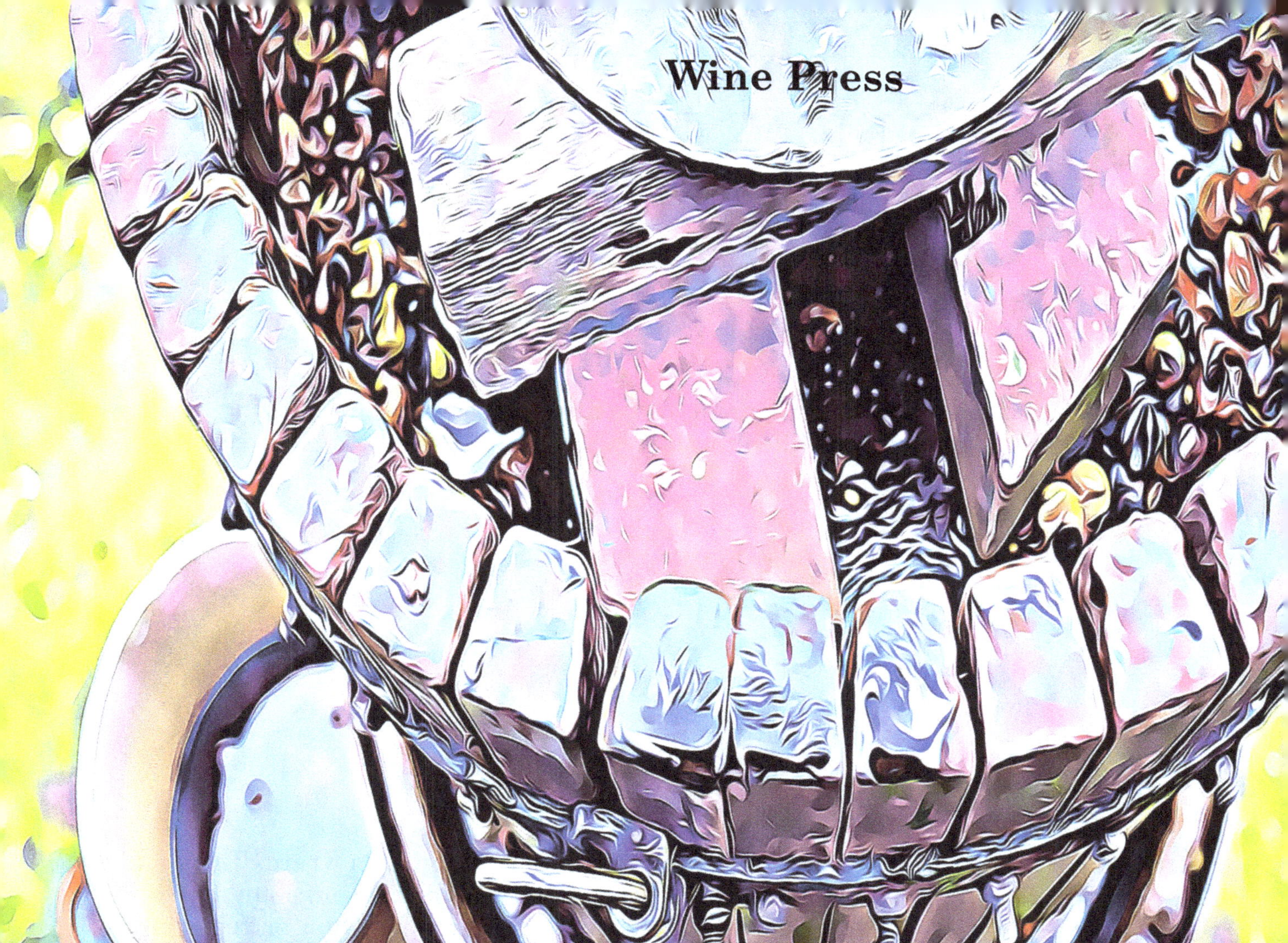

Revelation 14:17-20 King James Version (KJV) Public Domain

17 And another angel came out of the temple which is in heaven, he also having a sharp sickle.

18 And another angel came out from the altar, which had power over fire; and cried with a loud cry to him that had the sharp sickle, saying, Thrust in thy sharp sickle, and gather the clusters of the vine of the earth; for her grapes are fully ripe.

19 And the angel thrust in his sickle into the earth, and gathered the vine of the earth, and cast it into the great wine press of the wrath of God.

20 And the wine press was trodden without the city, and blood came out of the wine press, even unto the horse bridles, by the space of a thousand and six hundred furlongs.

Cross reference - Matthew 26:27-28 (KJV) - 27 And he took the cup, and gave thanks, and gave it to them, saying, Drink ye all of it; 28 For this is my blood of the new testament, which is shed for many for the remission of sins.

THE INTERPRETATION OF CHAPTER 15

Seven Angels with the Seven Bowls of Wrath

And I saw another sign in heaven, great and marvelous, seven angels having the seven last plagues; for in them is filled up the wrath of God. — *Revelation 15:1 (KJV)*

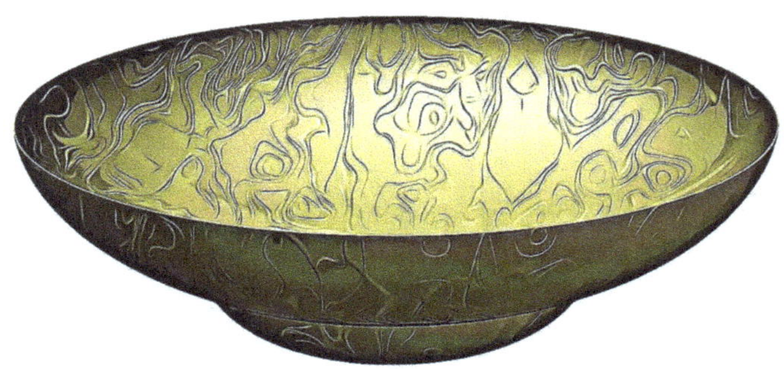

CHAPTER 15 opens with seven angels preparing to unleash God's wrath. The Prophet John saw all who were martyred from the earth celebrating in heaven. John stated that they had won the victory over the Anti-Christ for not worshiping him or receiving his mark on their foreheads and hands.

The martyrs sang as God prepared to judge the earth. God caused seven angels to have seven bowls filled with God's Wrath that was ready to be poured upon the earth and upon unrepentant men for their transgressions against the martyrs.

The seven bowls released seven plagues as follows:

1. Sores Upon the Men Who Accepted the Mark of The Beast
2. Seas Flooded, Blood Poisoned the Sea, Sea Life Dies
3. Rivers and Waterfalls are Turned into Blood
4. Unrepentant Men are Burned with Fire and Scorched with Heat
5. Darkness Fell on The Anti-Christ And His Kingdom
6. A Drought and The Release of The Unclean Spirits
7. The Great Earthquake and Hail Storm

Revelation Chapter 15 King James Version (KJV) Public Domain

1.   And I saw another sign in heaven, great and marvelous, seven angels having the seven last plagues; for in them is filled up the wrath of God.

2.   And I saw as it were a sea of glass mingled with fire: and them that had gotten the victory over the beast, and over his image, and over his mark, and over the number of his name, stand on the sea of glass, having the harps of God.

3.   And they sing the song of Moses the servant of God, and the song of the Lamb, saying, Great and marvelous are thy works, Lord God Almighty; just and true are thy ways, thou King of saints.

4.   Who shall not fear thee, O Lord, and glorify thy name? for thou only art holy: for all nations shall come and worship before thee; for thy judgments are made manifest.

5.   And after that I looked, and, behold, the temple of the tabernacle of the testimony in heaven was opened:

6.   And the seven angels came out of the temple, having the seven plagues, clothed in pure and white linen, and having their breasts girded with golden girdles.

7.   And one of the four beasts gave unto the seven angels seven golden vials full of the wrath of God, who liveth for ever and ever.

8.   And the temple was filled with smoke from the glory of God, and from his power; and no man was able to enter into the temple, till the seven plagues of the seven angels were fulfilled.

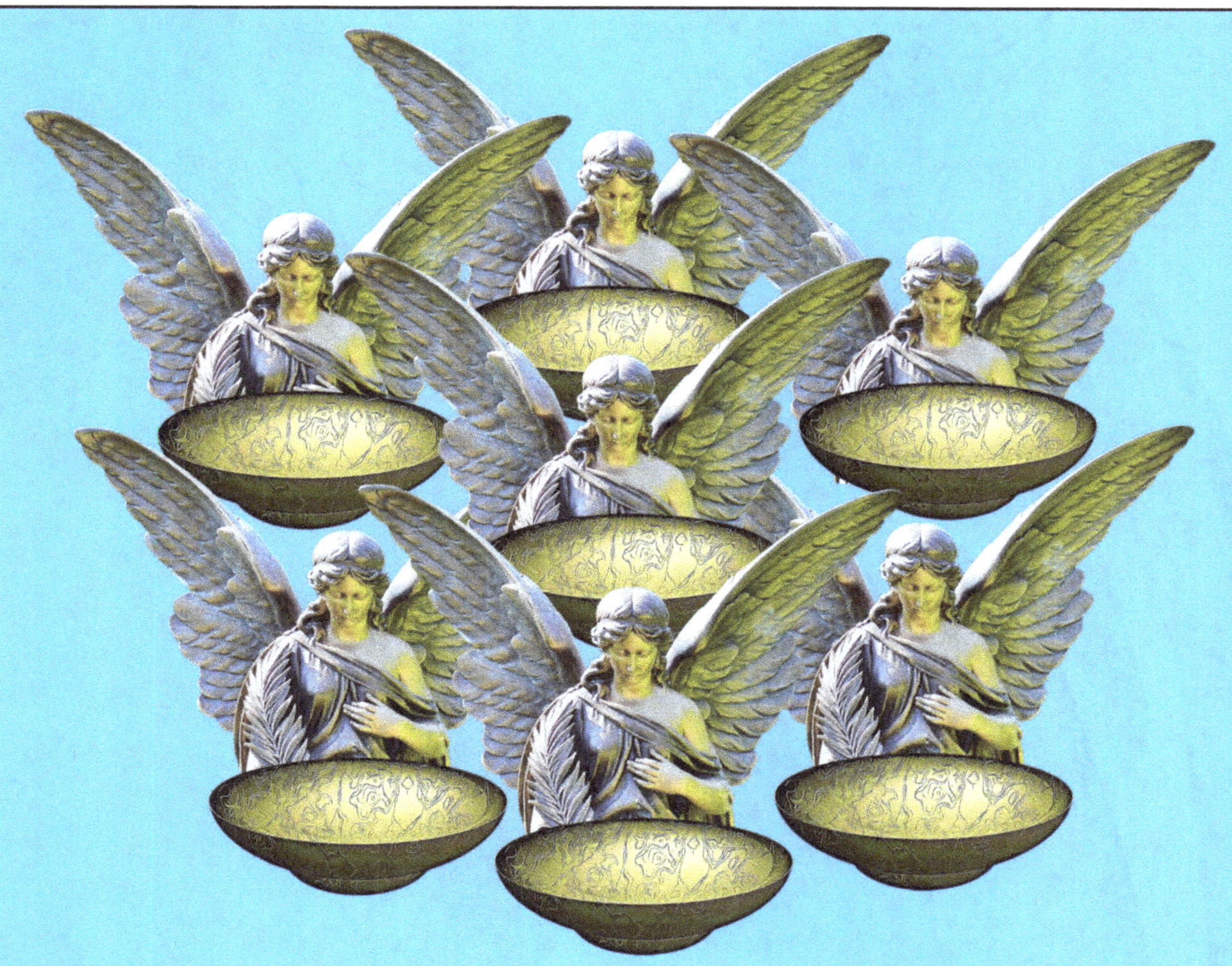

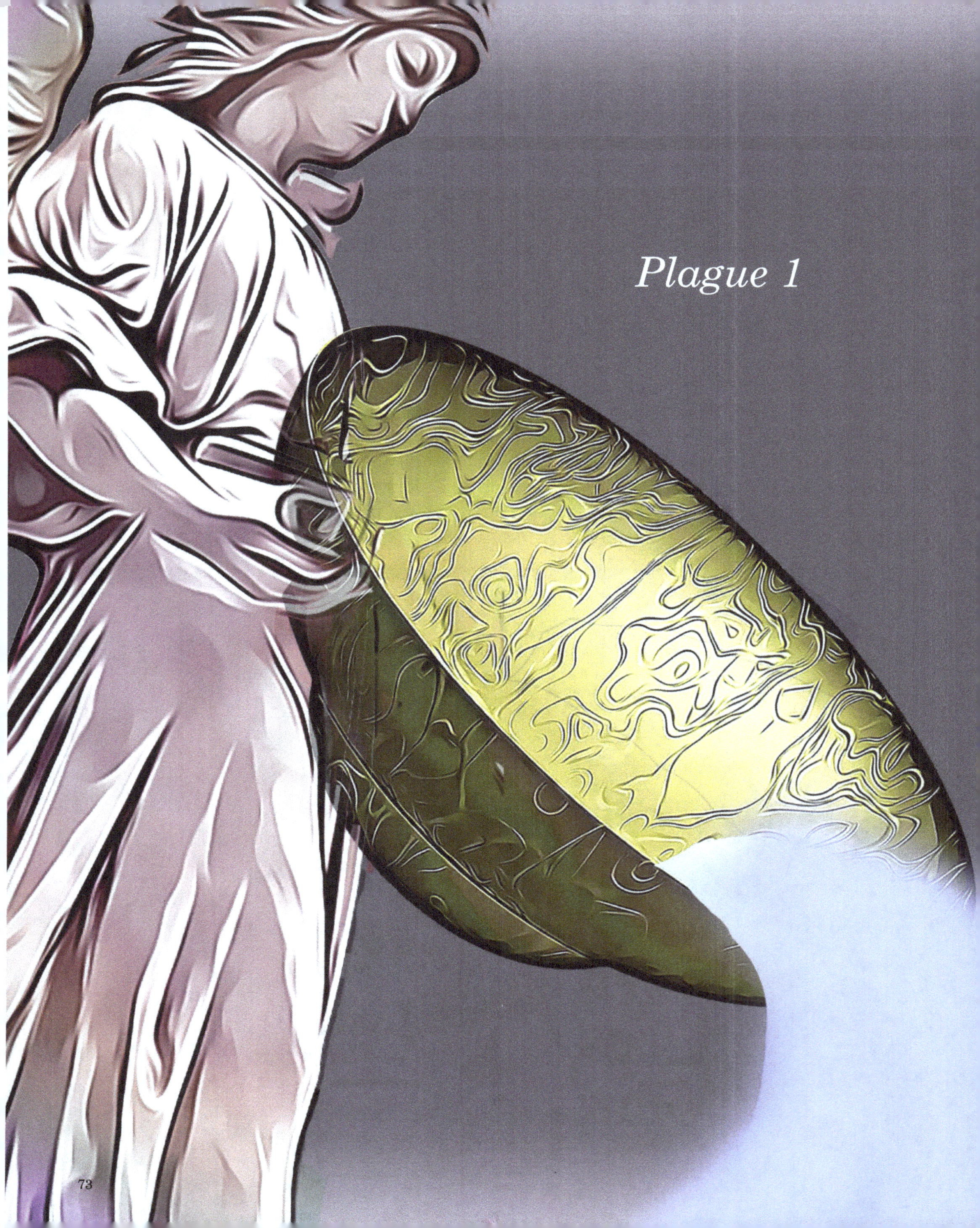

Plague 1

THE INTERPRETATION OF CHAPTER 16

Sores Upon Men and the Mark of the Beast

Revelation Chapter 16: 1-2 King James Version (KJV) Public Domain

1. And I heard a great voice out of the temple saying to the seven angels, Go your ways, and pour out the vials of the wrath of God upon the earth.

2. And the first went, and poured out his vial upon the earth; and there fell a noisome and grievous sore upon the men which had the mark of the beast, and upon them which worshiped his image.

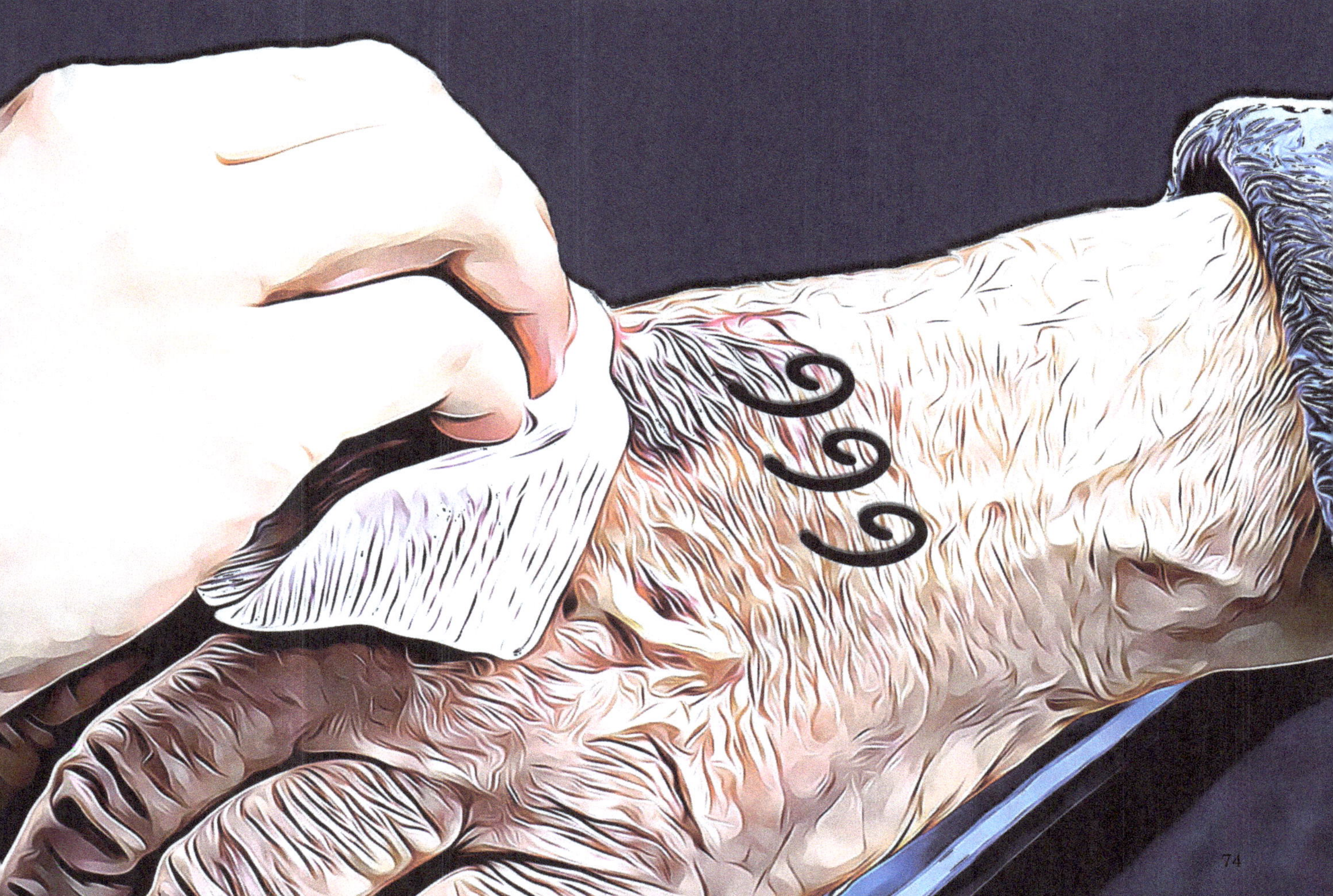

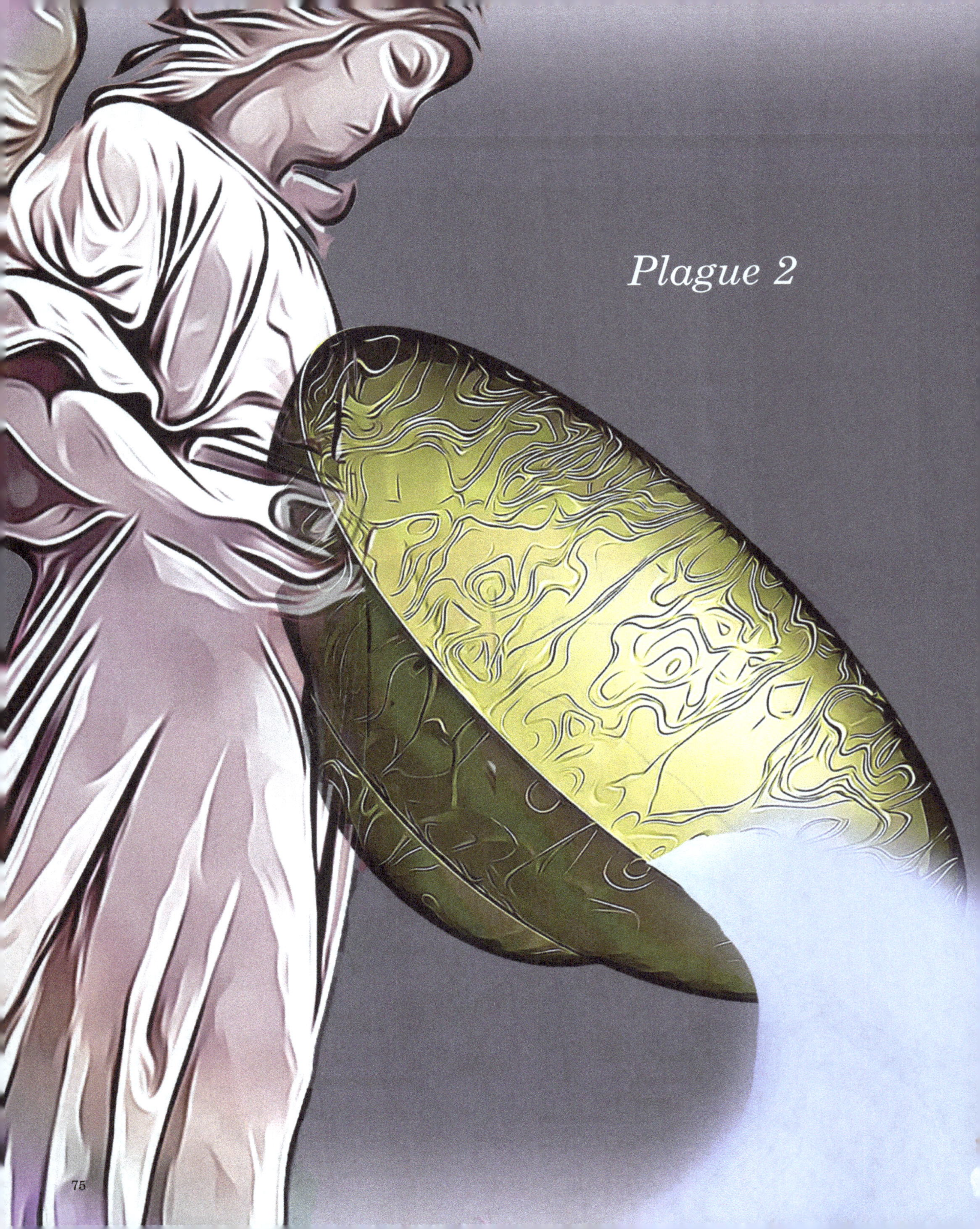
Plague 2

THE INTERPRETATION OF CHAPTER 16

Blood Poisoned the Sea

Revelation Chapter 16:3 King James Version (KJV) Public Domain

3. And the second angel poured out his vial upon the sea; and it became as the blood of a dead man: and every living soul died in the sea.

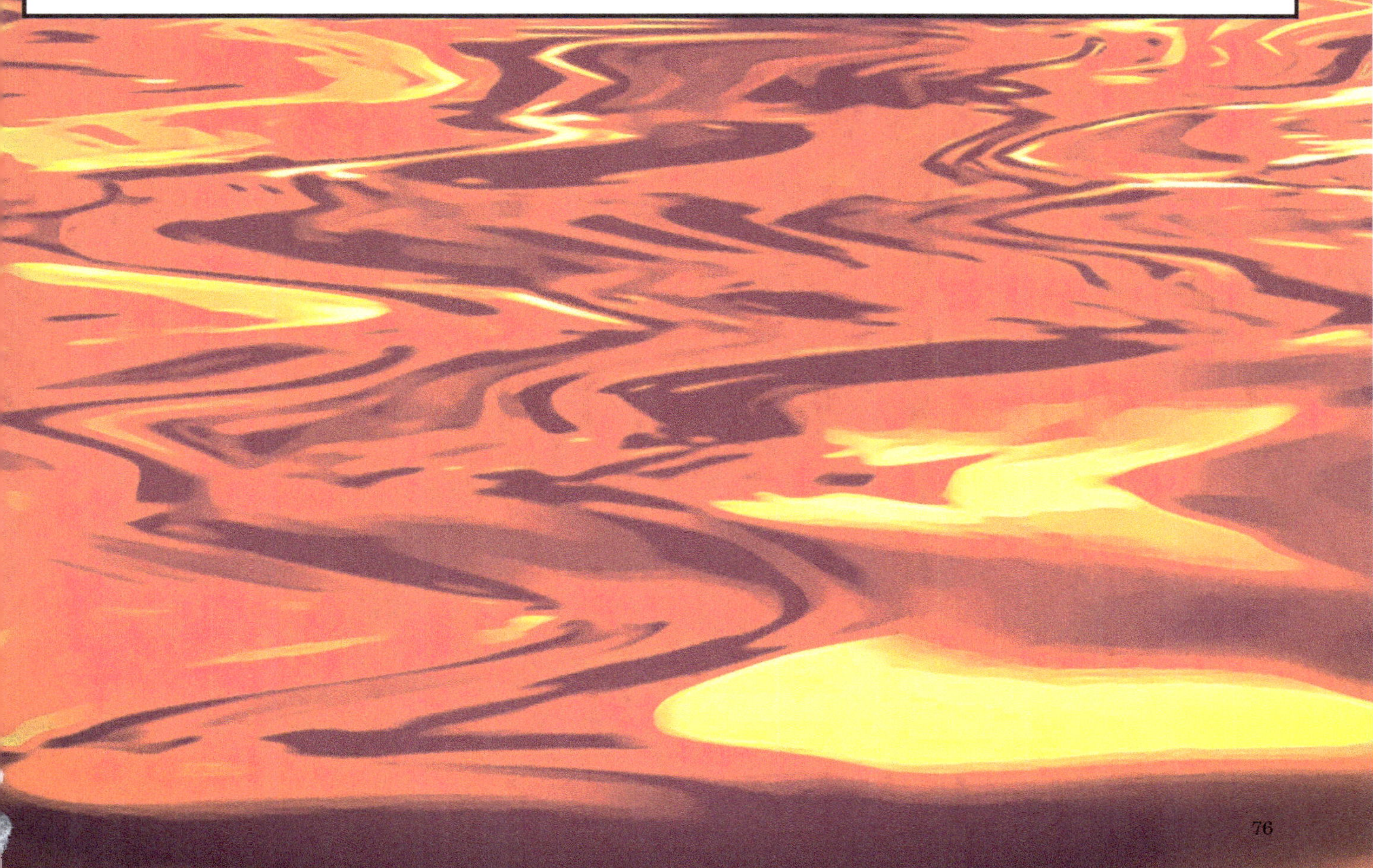

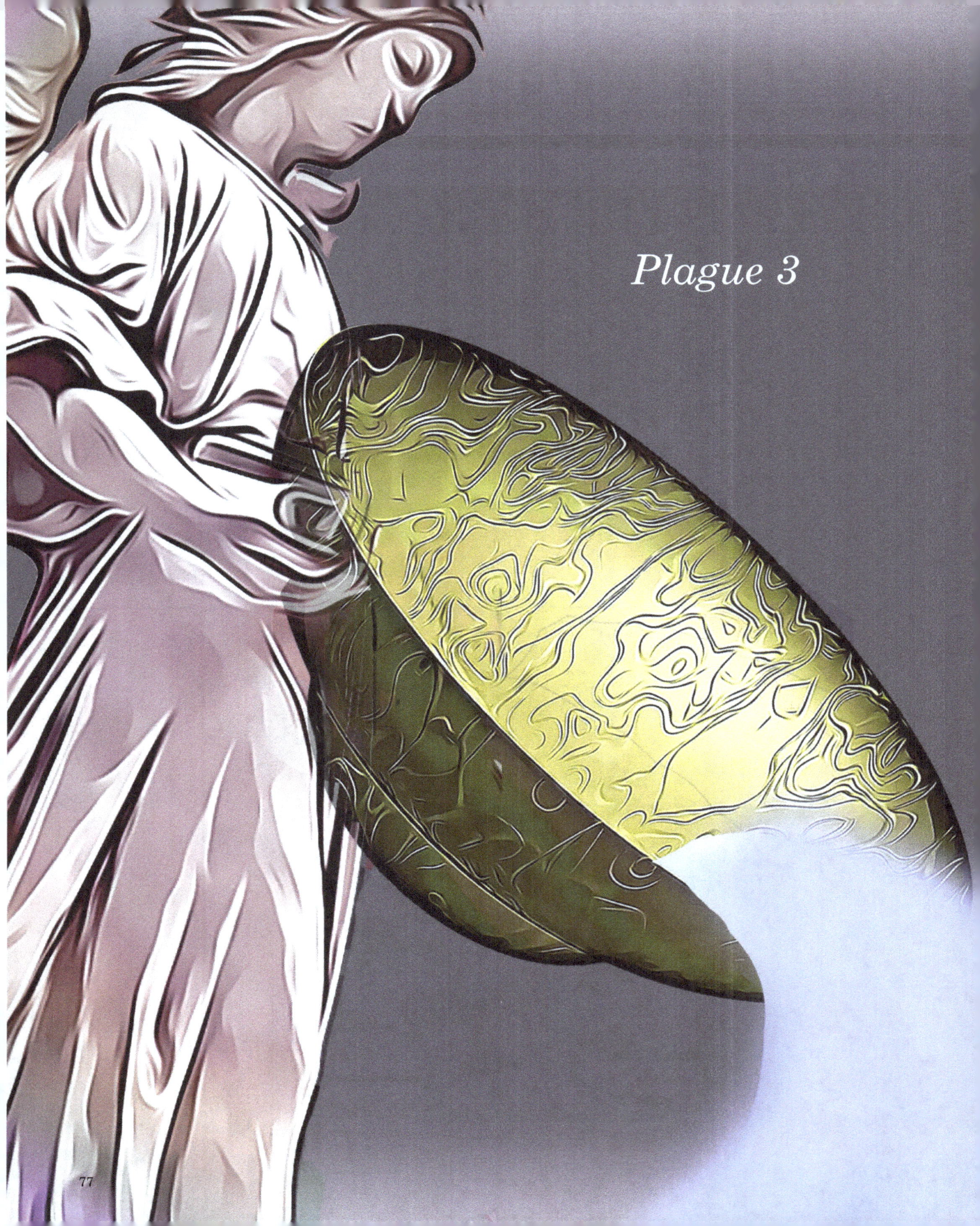

Plague 3

THE INTERPRETATION OF CHAPTER 16

Rivers and Waterfalls are turned to Blood

Revelation Chapter 16:4-7 King James Version (KJV) Public Domain

4. And the third angel poured out his vial upon the rivers and fountains of waters; and they became blood.

5. And I heard the angel of the waters say, Thou art righteous, O Lord, which art, and wast, and shalt be, because thou hast judged thus.

6. For they have shed the blood of saints and prophets, and thou hast given them blood to drink; for they are worthy.

7. And I heard another out of the altar say, Even so, Lord God Almighty, true and righteous are thy judgments.

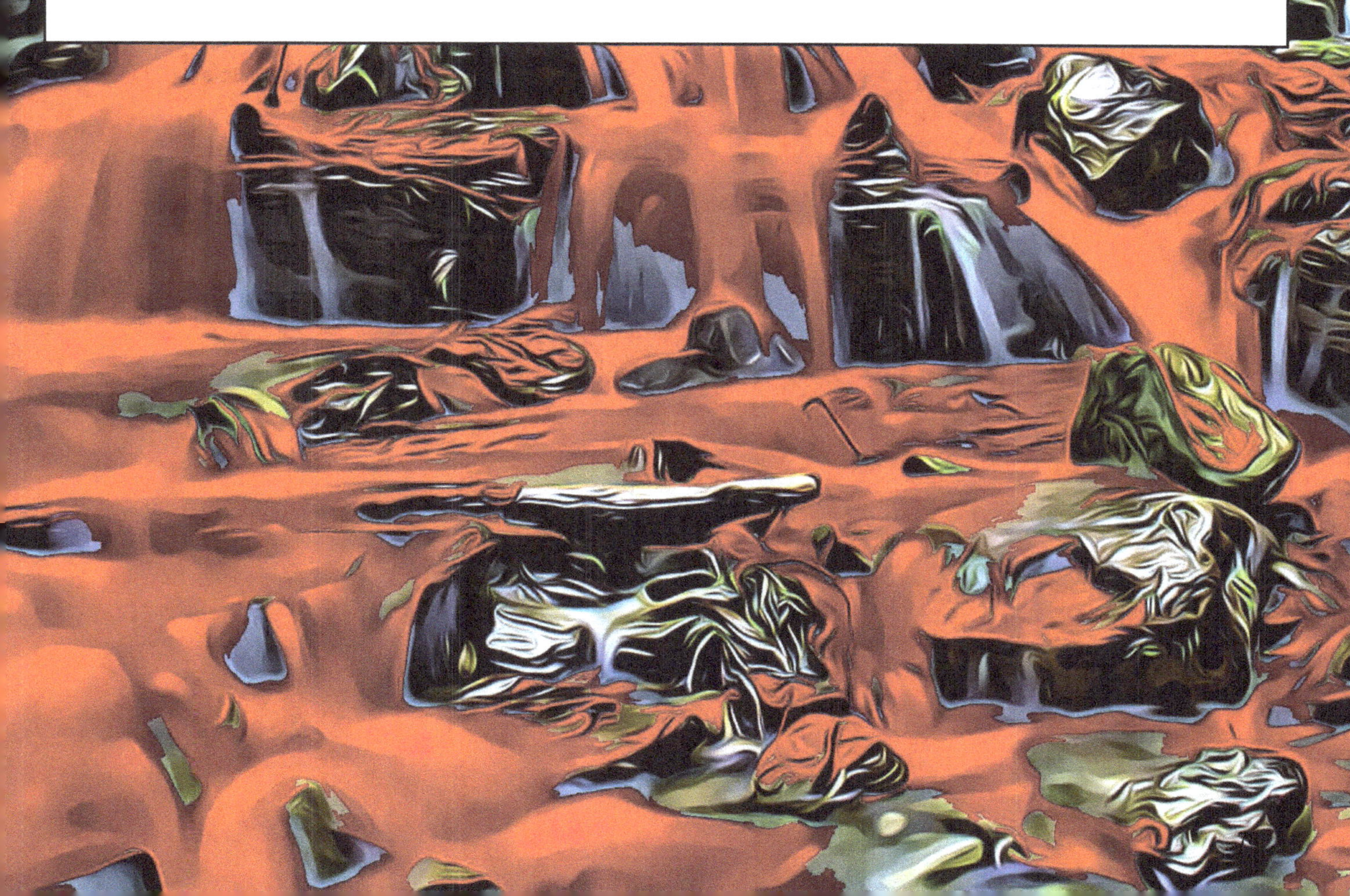

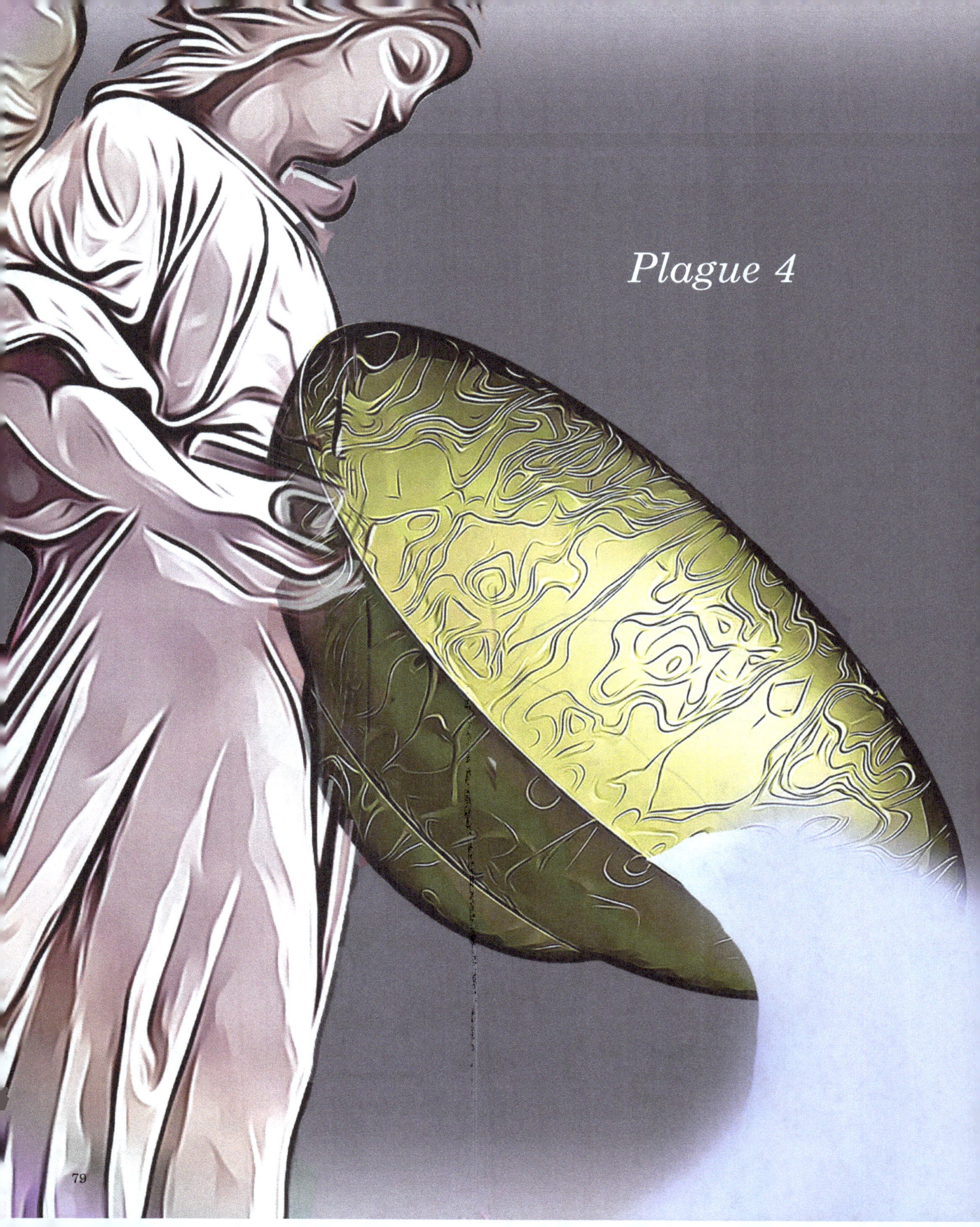

Plague 4

THE INTERPRETATION OF CHAPTER 16

Unrepentant Men Burned with Fire and Scorched with Heat

Revelation Chapter 16:8-9 King James Version (KJV) Public Domain
8. And the fourth angel poured out his vial upon the sun; and power was given unto him to scorch men with fire.
9. And men were scorched with great heat, and blasphemed the name of God, which hath power over these plagues: and they repented not to give him glory.

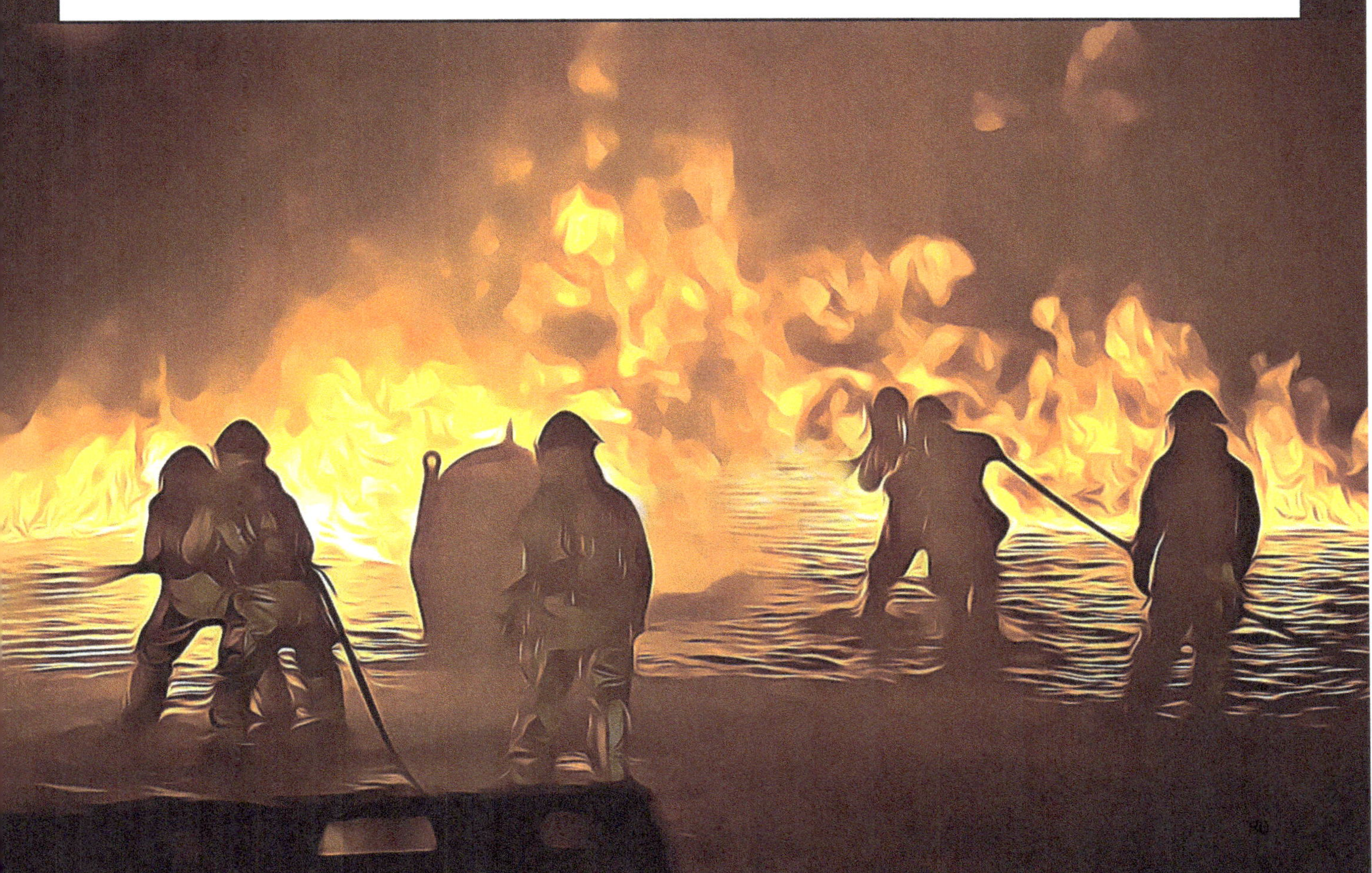

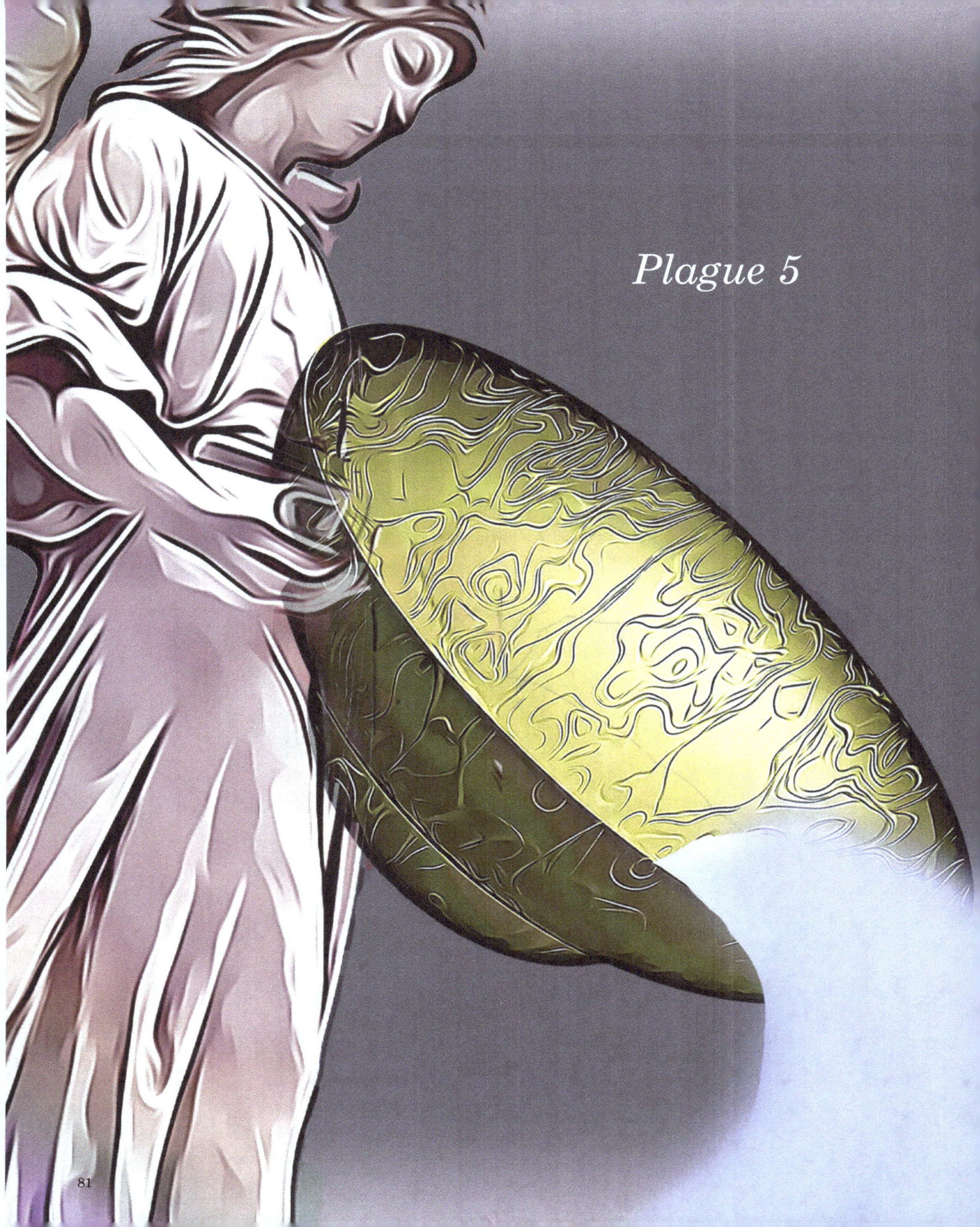

Plague 5

THE INTERPRETATION OF CHAPTER 16

The Darkness (God's Wrath) fell on the Anti-Christ and his Kingdom

Revelation Chapter 16:10-11 King James Version (KJV) Public Domain

10. And the fifth angel poured out his vial upon the seat of the beast; and his kingdom was full of darkness; and they gnawed their tongues for pain,

11. And blasphemed the God of heaven because of their pains and their sores, and repented not of their deeds.

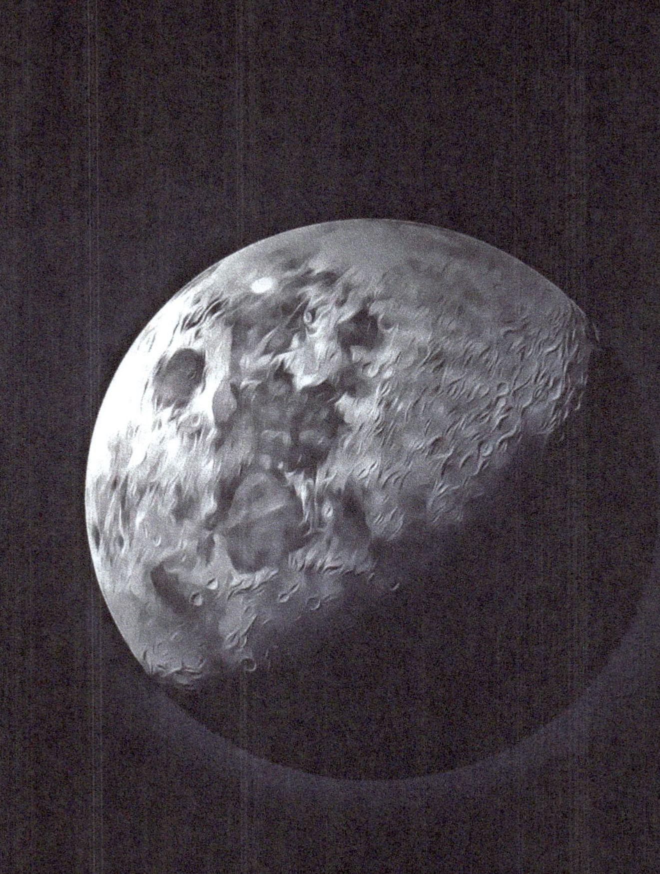

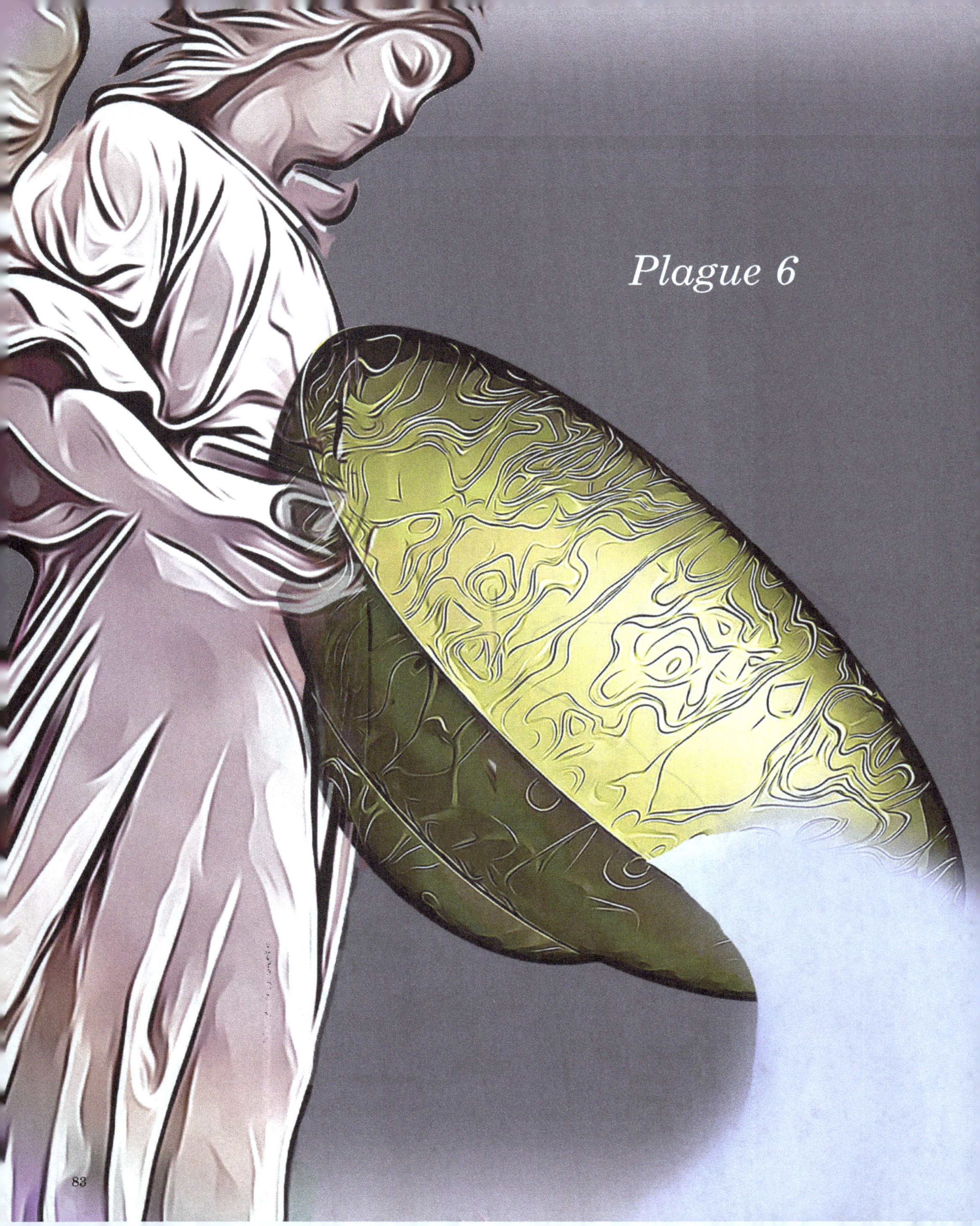
Plague 6

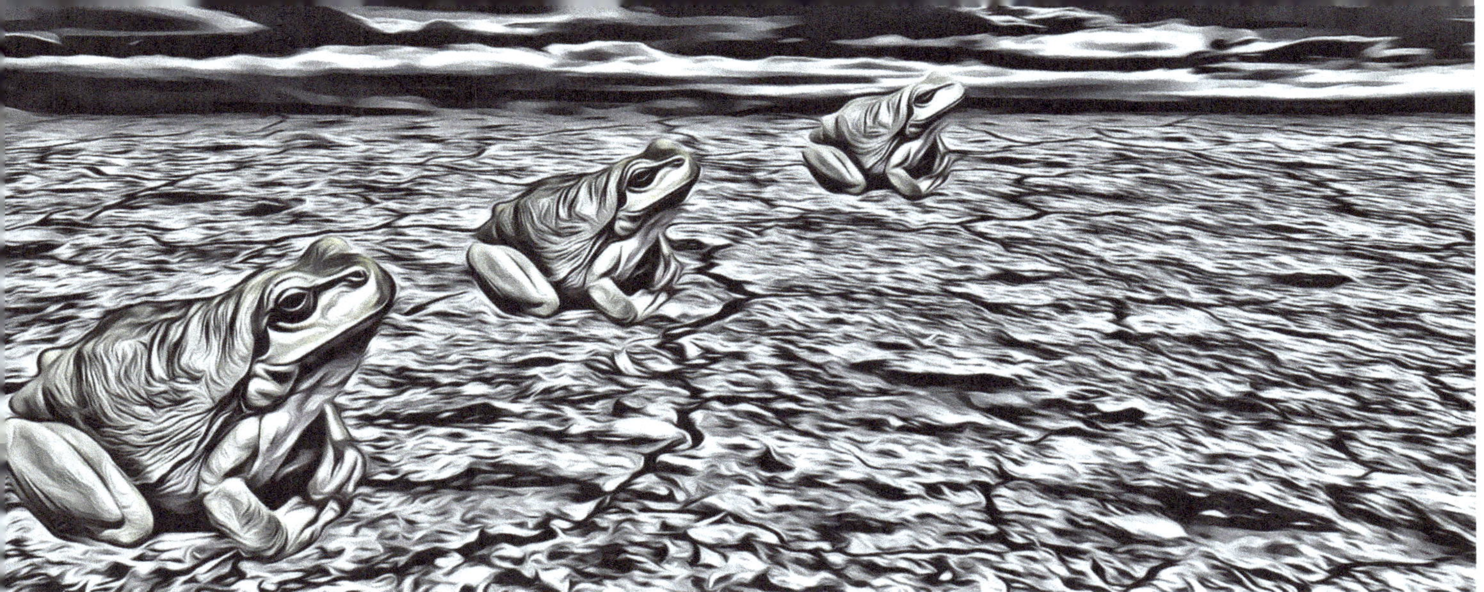

THE INTERPRETATION OF CHAPTER 16

Drought and Release of the Unclean Spirits

And I saw three unclean spirits like frogs come out of the mouth of the dragon, and out of the mouth of the beast, and out of the mouth of the false prophet. Revelation 16:13 (KJV)

The same devils that came from Satan, the Anti-Christ, and the False Prophet possessed kings from the entire earth to gather together against Jesus in the battle of Armageddon.

Revelation Chapter 16:12-16 King James Version (KJV) Public Domain

12. And the sixth angel poured out his vial upon the great river Euphrates; and the water thereof was dried up, that the way of the kings of the east might be prepared.

13. And I saw three unclean spirits like frogs come out of the mouth of the dragon, and out of the mouth of the beast, and out of the mouth of the false prophet.

14. For they are the spirits of devils, working miracles, which go forth unto the kings of the earth and of the whole world, to gather them to the battle of that great day of God Almighty.

15. Behold, I come as a thief. Blessed is he that watcheth, and keepeth his garments, lest he walk naked, and they see his shame.

16. And he gathered them together into a place called in the Hebrew tongue Armageddon.

In the Hebrew language it is called Armageddon - Revelation Chapter 16:16 (KJV)
In Hebrew it is displayed as הר מגידו, which translates in English as Mount Megiddo
Mount Megiddo or Tel Megiddo is in northern, Israel and is 66.31 miles from Jerusalem.

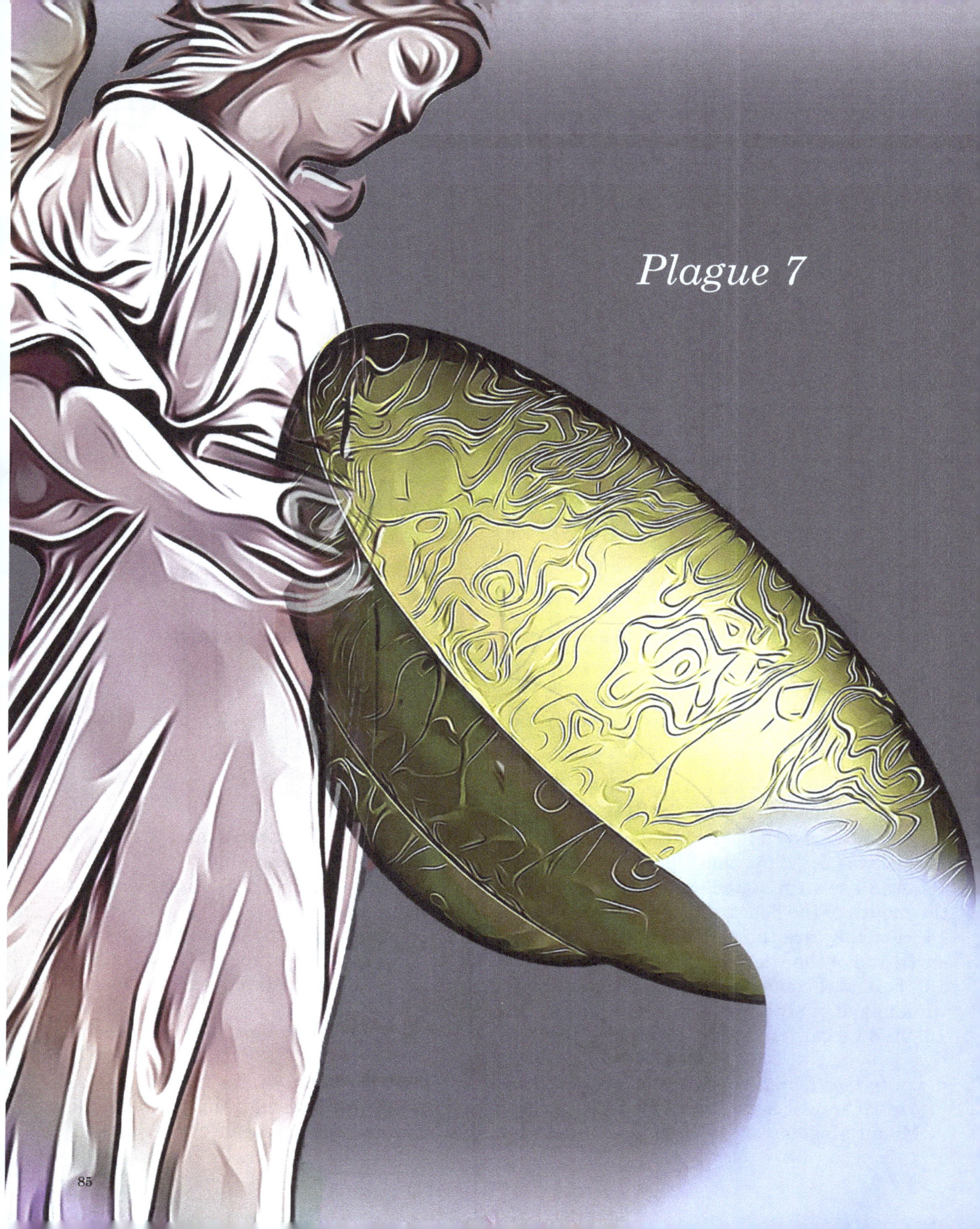

Plague 7

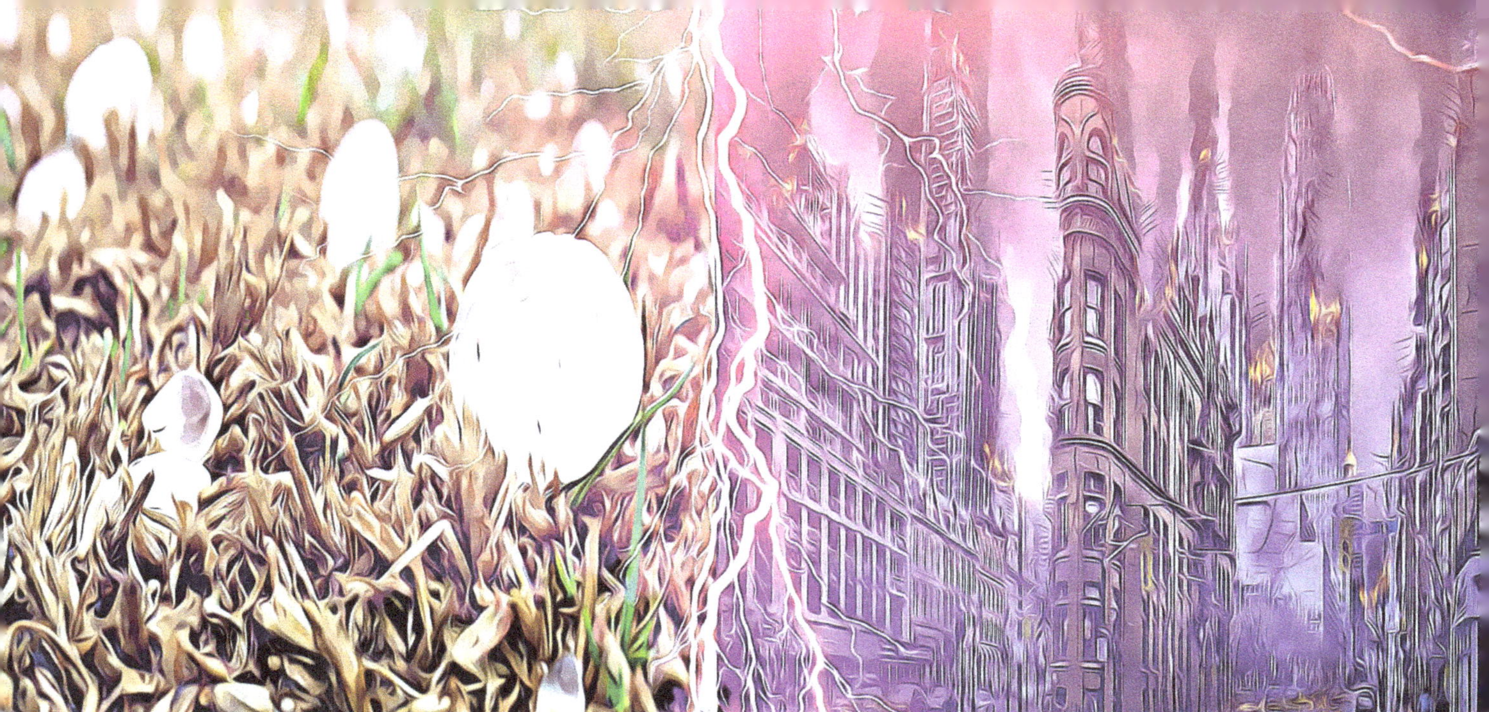

THE INTERPRETATION OF CHAPTER 16

The Great Earthquake and Hail Storm

Revelation Chapter 16:17-21 King James Version (KJV) Public Domain

17. And the seventh angel poured out his vial into the air; and there came a great voice out of the temple of heaven, from the throne, saying, It is done.

18. And there were voices, and thunders, and lightnings; and there was a great earthquake, such as was not since men were upon the earth, so mighty an earthquake, and so great.

19. And the great city was divided into three parts, and the cities of the nations fell: and great Babylon came in remembrance before God, to give unto her the cup of the wine of the fierceness of his wrath.

20. And every island fled away, and the mountains were not found.

21. And there fell upon men a great hail out of heaven, every stone about the weight of a talent: and men blasphemed God because of the plague of the hail; for the plague thereof was exceeding great.

THE INTERPRETATION OF CHAPTER 17
Judgment of the Great Whore

And upon her forehead was a name written, Mystery, Babylon The Great, The Mother of Harlots and Abominations of The Earth. — *Revelation 17:5 (KJV)*

CHAPTER 17 introduces the city that will fulfill the end time prophecy. This city will serve as the seat of the Anti-Christ during the tribulation period. The reason why this city is called "The Great Whore", "A Mystery", and "Babylon the Great" is because it committed the sin of idolatry. Many biblical scholars believe that the city in this chapter describes the city of Rome because Rome fits the description of a city physically sitting on seven mountains (Rev 17:9). However, this scripture is referring to the 7 earthly kingdoms backed by Satan that influenced the city into becoming "The Great Whore". The city described in this chapter is **Jerusalem** (Isaiah 1:21; Ezekiel 16:1–43; Ezekiel 23). Because of the evil influence of the 7 earthly kingdoms, Jerusalem went from being the beloved holy city to "The Great Whore". What a mystery! Jerusalem's new culture was accepting of the Anti-Christ. Rome could never fulfill the prophetic meaning of the seven mountains, only the geographical meaning. Jerusalem fulfills both the prophetic and geographical meaning. In addition, Jerusalem will fulfill the prophecy by becoming the city that reigns over the kings of the earth (Rev 17:18). This scripture is referring to the alliance of the 10 kings with the Anti-Christ. The bible states in Rev 11:2 that the Anti-Christ will be allowed to reign for 42 months in the holy city, Jerusalem. (Daniel 9:27; 2 Thessalonians 2:3-4)

SYMBOL	INTERPRETATION
The Woman	**The Woman represents the city of Jerusalem** Rev 17:18 (KJV) And the woman which thou sawest is that great city, which reigneth over the kings of the earth. *Cross-reference: Rev 11:8 (KJV)*
The Dragon	**The Dragon represents Satan and the 7 earthly kingdoms** Satan used these kingdoms to adversely influence Jerusalem.
The Seven Heads	**The Seven Heads represents the seven mountains (kingdoms)** that adversely influenced the city and not the geographical location. (*Ezekiel 23*) The seven mountains are as follows: 1) Egypt, 2) Assyrian Empire, 3) Babylon, 4) Persia Empire 5) Grecian Empire 6) Roman Empire 7) the Anti-Christ Kingdom.
The Seven Kings	**The Seven Kings:** Rev 17:10 (KJV) And there are seven kings: five are fallen, and one is, and the other is not yet come; and when he cometh, he must continue a short space. ------(**five are fallen** - Egypt, Assyrian Empire, Babylon, Persia, Grecian Empire) ------(**one is** - Roman Empire - At the time of John's writings, the Roman Empire was still in existence.) ------(**the other is yet to come** - This represents the Anti-Christ Kingdom)
The Ten Horns	**The Ten Horns represent the 10 kings** who made an alliance with the Anti-Christ Rev 17:12 (KJV) And the ten horns which thou sawest are ten kings, which have received no kingdom as yet; but receive power as kings one hour with the beast.

Revelation Chapter 17

1. And there came one of the seven angels which had the seven vials, and talked with me, saying unto me, Come hither; I will shew unto thee the judgment of the great whore that sitteth upon many waters:

2. With whom the kings of the earth have committed fornication, and the inhabitants of the earth have been made drunk with the wine of her fornication.

3. So he carried me away in the spirit into the wilderness: and I saw a woman sit upon a scarlet coloured beast, full of names of blasphemy, having seven heads and ten horns.

4. And the woman was arrayed in purple and scarlet colour, and decked with gold and precious stones and pearls, having a golden cup in her hand full of abominations and filthiness of her fornication:

5. And upon her forehead was a name written, Mystery, Babylon The Great, The Mother Of Harlots And Abominations Of The Earth.

6. And I saw the woman drunken with the blood of the saints, and with the blood of the martyrs of Jesus: and when I saw her, I wondered with great admiration.

7. And the angel said unto me, Wherefore didst thou marvel? I will tell thee the mystery of the woman, and of the beast that carrieth her, which hath the seven heads and ten horns.

8. The beast that thou sawest was, and is not; and shall ascend out of the bottomless pit, and go into perdition: and they that dwell on the earth shall wonder, whose names were not written in the book of life from the foundation of the world, when they behold the beast that was, and is not, and yet is.

9. And here is the mind which hath wisdom. The seven heads are seven mountains, on which the woman sitteth.

10. And there are seven kings: five are fallen, and one is, and the other is not yet come; and when he cometh, he must continue a short space.

11. And the beast that was, and is not, even he is the eighth, and is of the seven, and goeth into perdition.

12. And the ten horns which thou sawest are ten kings, which have received no kingdom as yet; but receive power as kings one hour with the beast.

13. These have one mind, and shall give their power and strength unto the beast.

14. These shall make war with the Lamb, and the Lamb shall overcome them: for he is Lord of lords, and King of kings: and they that are with him are called, and chosen, and faithful.

15. And he saith unto me, The waters which thou sawest, where the whore sitteth, are peoples, and multitudes, and nations, and tongues.

16. And the ten horns which thou sawest upon the beast, these shall hate the whore, and shall make her desolate and naked, and shall eat her flesh, and burn her with fire.

17. For God hath put in their hearts to fulfill his will, and to agree, and give their kingdom unto the beast, until the words of God shall be fulfilled.

18. And the woman which thou sawest is that great city, which reigneth over the kings of the earth.

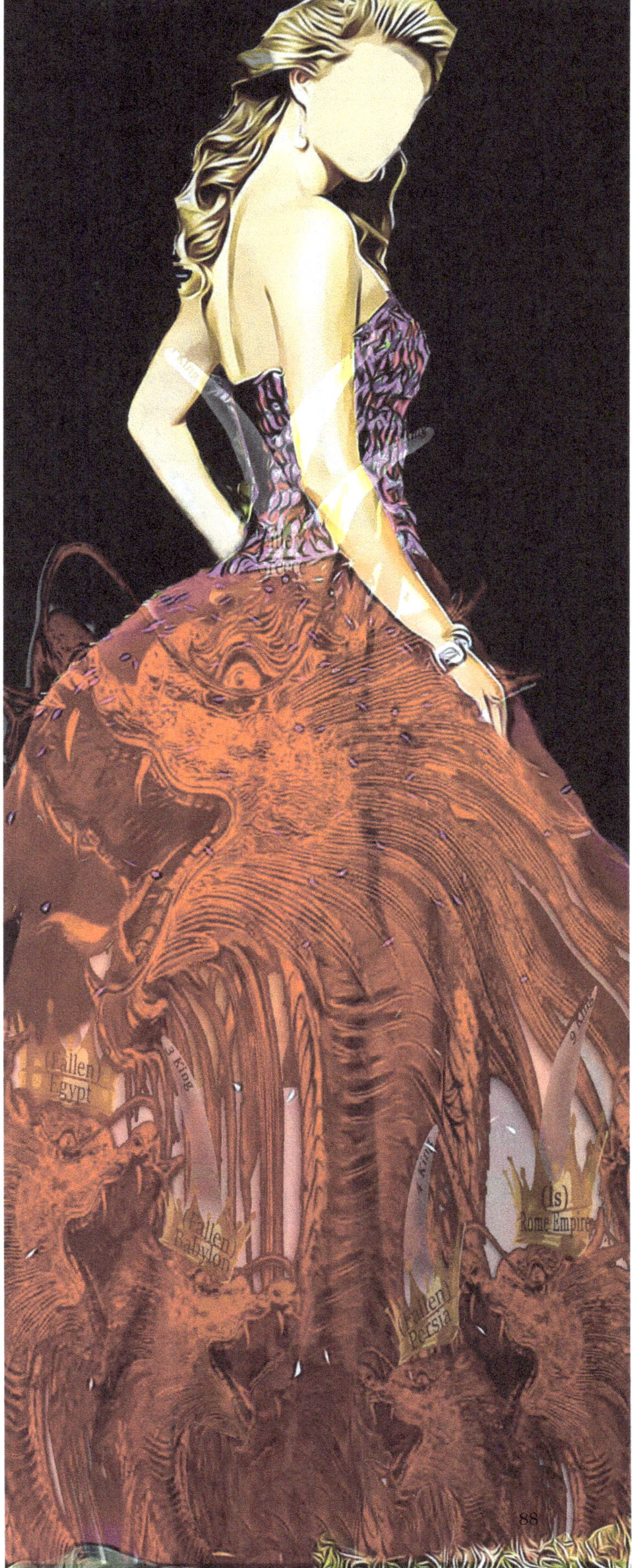

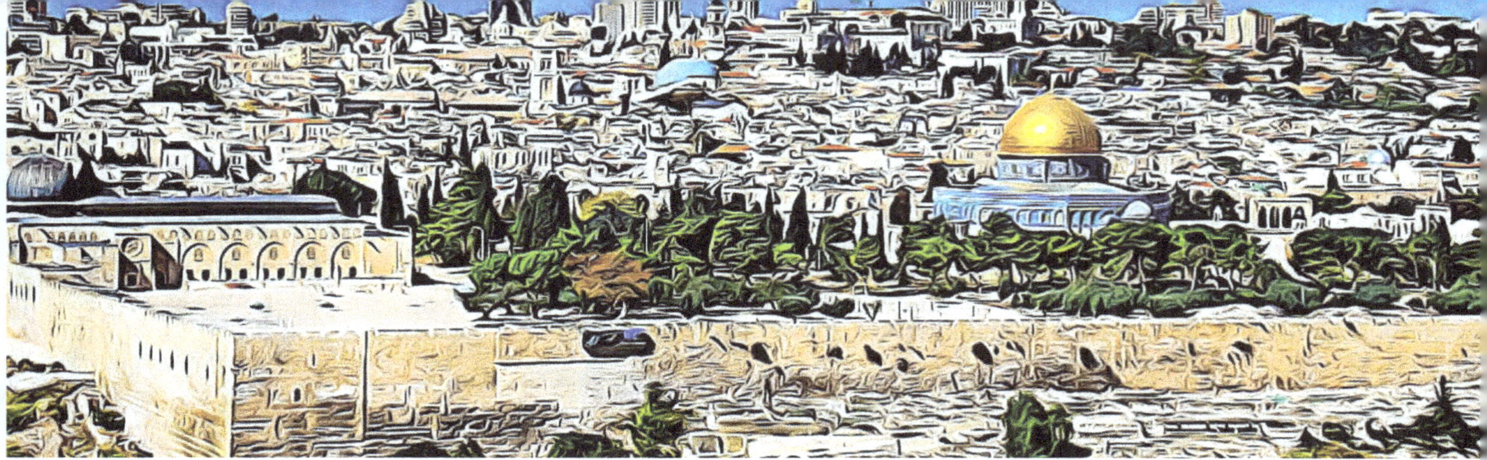

THE INTERPRETATION OF CHAPTER 18

"Babylon the Great" is Fallen

And he cried mightily with a strong voice, saying, Babylon the great is fallen, is fallen, and is become the habitation of devils, and the hold of every foul spirit, and a cage of every unclean and hateful bird. — *Revelation 18:2 (KJV)*

CHAPTER 18 describes the destruction of the great city of Jerusalem, nicknamed "Babylon the Great." After Jerusalem commits the sin of idolatry by worshiping the Anti-Christ in the third temple, God allows the angels to destroy the city of Jerusalem.

This Chapter explains how the city of Jerusalem will be burned down in one day. It describes how far Jerusalem had fallen away from God. This city was once considered the holy city based on Rev 18:23 (KJV). However, the light of a candle shall shine no more at all in Jerusalem and the voice of the bridegroom and of the bride shall be heard no more at all in Jerusalem for thy merchants were the great men of the earth; for by thy sorceries were all nations deceived.

As in Rev Chapter 1, the reference to the light of a candle refers to the temple in Jerusalem. This scripture is saying that the temple of God would be destroyed in this city, and no more praise and worship would come forth from this city.

Rev 18:24 further describes Jerusalem by revealing that both prophets and the saints were slain in Jerusalem. Rev 14:20 speaks of the martyrdom of the saints in Jerusalem. Also, the prophets Isaiah, Micah, and Zechariah ben Jehoiada (2 Chronicles 24:20-22) were martyred in Jerusalem. The two prophets were killed and resurrected in Jerusalem. Chapter 18 chronicles the end of the city of Jerusalem.

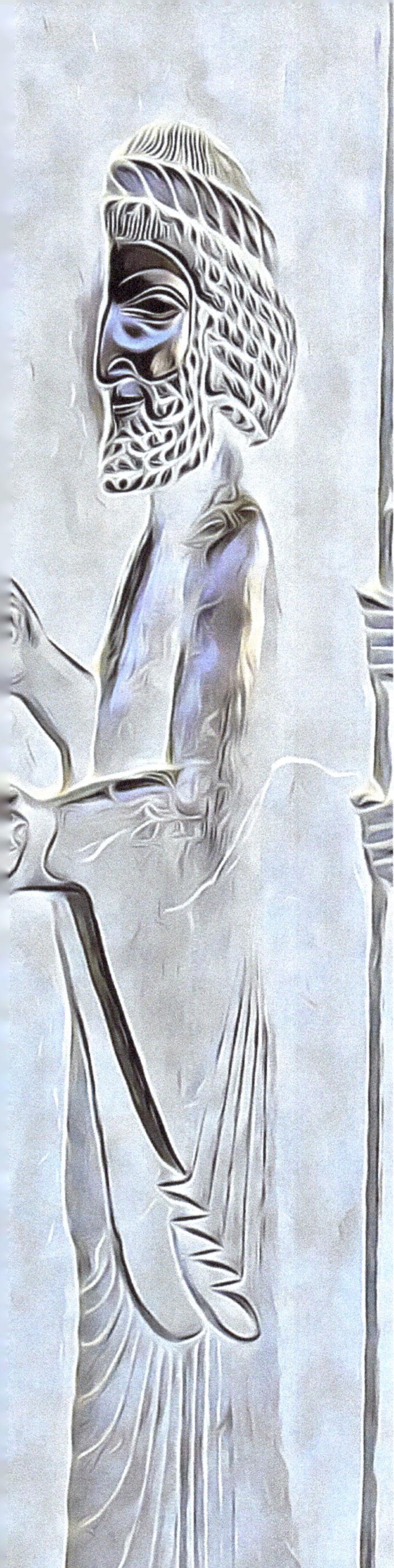

Revelation Chapter 18

1. And after these things I saw another angel come down from heaven, having great power; and the earth was lightened with his glory.

2. And he cried mightily with a strong voice, saying, Babylon the great is fallen, is fallen, and is become the habitation of devils, and the hold of every foul spirit, and a cage of every unclean and hateful bird.

3. For all nations have drunk of the wine of the wrath of her fornication, and the kings of the earth have committed fornication with her, and the merchants of the earth are waxed rich through the abundance of her delicacies.

4. And I heard another voice from heaven, saying, Come out of her, my people, that ye be not partakers of her sins, and that ye receive not of her plagues.

5. For her sins have reached unto heaven, and God hath remembered her iniquities.

6. Reward her even as she rewarded you, and double unto her double according to her works: in the cup which she hath filled fill to her double.

7. How much she hath glorified herself, and lived deliciously, so much torment and sorrow give her: for she saith in her heart, I sit a queen, and am no widow, and shall see no sorrow.

8. Therefore shall her plagues come in one day, death, and mourning, and famine; and she shall be utterly burned with fire: for strong is the Lord God who judgeth her.

9. And the kings of the earth, who have committed fornication and lived deliciously with her, shall bewail her, and lament for her, when they shall see the smoke of her burning,

10. Standing afar off for the fear of her torment, saying, Alas, alas that great city Babylon, that mighty city! for in one hour is thy judgment come.

11. And the merchants of the earth shall weep and mourn over her; for no man buyeth their merchandise any more:

12. The merchandise of gold, and silver, and precious stones, and of pearls, and fine linen, and purple, and silk, and scarlet, and all thyine wood, and all manner vessels of ivory, and all manner vessels of most precious wood, and of brass, and iron, and marble,

13. And cinnamon, and odours, and ointments, and frankincense, and wine, and oil, and fine flour, and wheat, and beasts, and sheep, and horses, and chariots, and slaves, and souls of men.

14. And the fruits that thy soul lusted after are departed from thee, and all things which were dainty and goodly are departed from thee, and thou shalt find them no more at all.

15. The merchants of these things, which were made rich by her, shall stand afar off for the fear of her torment, weeping and wailing,

16. And saying, Alas, alas that great city, that was clothed in fine linen, and purple, and scarlet, and decked with gold, and precious stones, and pearls!

17. For in one hour so great riches is come to nought. And every ship master, and all the company in ships, and sailors, and as many as trade by sea, stood afar off,

18. And cried when they saw the smoke of her burning, saying, What city is like unto this great city!

19. And they cast dust on their heads, and cried, weeping and wailing, saying, Alas, alas that great city, wherein were made rich all that had ships in the sea by reason of her costliness! for in one hour is she made desolate.

20. Rejoice over her, thou heaven, and ye holy apostles and prophets; for God hath avenged you on her.

21. And a mighty angel took up a stone like a great millstone, and cast it into the sea, saying, Thus with violence shall that great city Babylon be thrown down, and shall be found no more at all.

22. And the voice of harpers, and musicians, and of pipers, and trumpeters, shall be heard no more at all in thee; and no craftsman, of whatsoever craft he be, shall be found any more in thee; and the sound of a millstone shall be heard no more at all in thee;

23. And the light of a candle shall shine no more at all in thee; and the voice of the bridegroom and of the bride shall be heard no more at all in thee: for thy merchants were the great men of the earth; for by thy sorceries were all nations deceived.

24. And in her was found the blood of prophets, and of saints, and of all that were slain upon the earth.

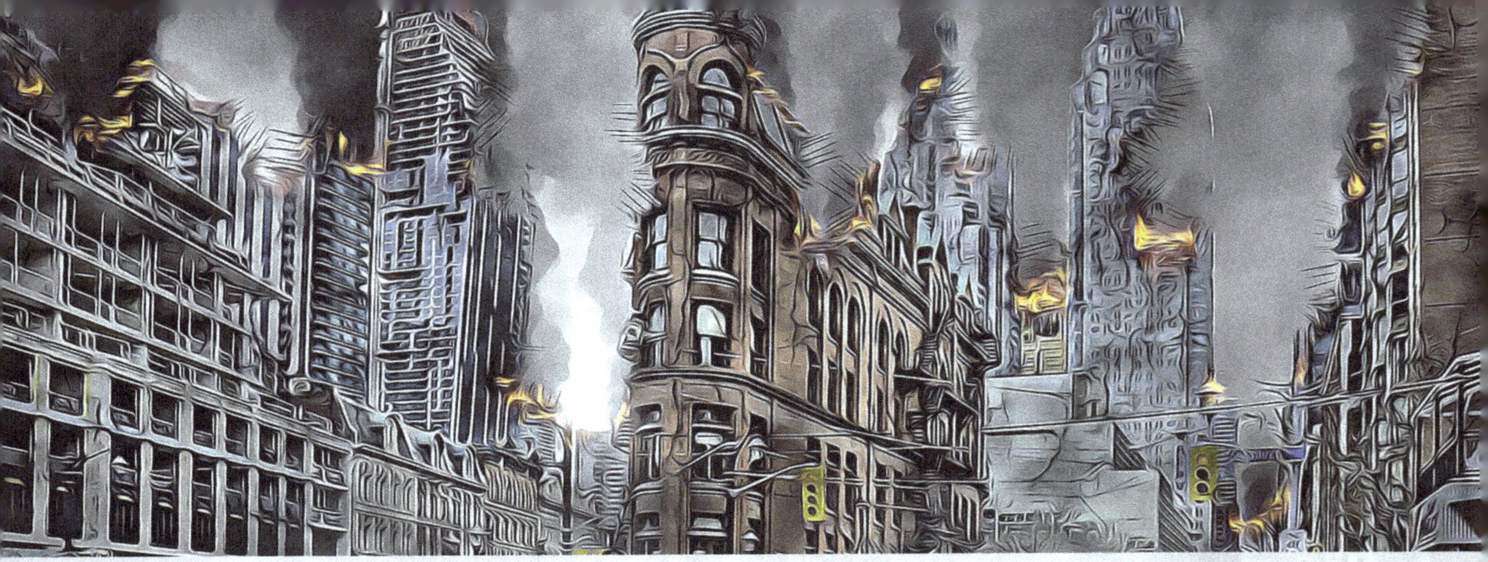

THE INTERPRETATION OF CHAPTER 19

The Marriage of the Lamb and Armageddon

Let us be glad and rejoice, and give honour to him:
for the marriage of the Lamb is come, and his wife hath made herself ready.
— *Revelation 19:7 (KJV)*

CHAPTER 19 describes the judgment of the 10 kings and end time war called Armageddon. This Chapter describes how Jesus will war against the Anti-Christ, the False Prophet, and Satan with the armies of God following His lead.

This battle is called the Battle of Armageddon, according to Rev 16:16. Armageddon translated in Hebrew means Megiddo. Many biblical scholars believe that the battle of Armageddon will occur physically at Megiddo. This could be accurately interpreted because Megiddo is only a little more than 66 miles from Jerusalem, the city that served as the seat of the Anti-Christ before it burned.

After Jerusalem burns and is destroyed, the Anti-Christ, the False Prophet, and Satan gather in Megiddo to battle Jesus and His army (The Lord's Army). Jesus, the King of Kings and Lord of Lords, defeats the Anti-Christ and the False Prophet and casts them alive into the lake of fire. The kings of the earth and those that worshiped the beast are also killed during this battle. However, Satan is not killed.

Revelation Chapter 19

1. And after these things I heard a great voice of much people in heaven, saying, Alleluia; Salvation, and glory, and honour, and power, unto the Lord our God:

2. For true and righteous are his judgments: for he hath judged the great whore, which did corrupt the earth with her fornication, and hath avenged the blood of his servants at her hand.

3. And again they said, Alleluia And her smoke rose up for ever and ever.

4. And the four and twenty elders and the four beasts fell down and worshiped God that sat on the throne, saying, Amen; Alleluia.

5. And a voice came out of the throne, saying, Praise our God, all ye his servants, and ye that fear him, both small and great.

6. And I heard as it were the voice of a great multitude, and as the voice of many waters, and as the voice of mighty thunderings, saying, Alleluia: for the Lord God omnipotent reigneth.

7. Let us be glad and rejoice, and give honour to him: for the marriage of the Lamb is come, and his wife hath made herself ready.

8. And to her was granted that she should be arrayed in fine linen, clean and white: for the fine linen is the righteousness of saints.

9. And he saith unto me, Write, Blessed are they which are called unto the marriage supper of the Lamb. And he saith unto me, These are the true sayings of God.

10. And I fell at his feet to worship him. And he said unto me, See thou do it not: I am thy fellow servant, and of thy brethren that have the testimony of Jesus: worship God: for the testimony of Jesus is the spirit of prophecy.

11. And I saw heaven opened, and behold a white horse; and he that sat upon him was called Faithful and True, and in righteousness he doth judge and make war.

12. His eyes were as a flame of fire, and on his head were many crowns; and he had a name written, that no man knew, but he himself.

13. And he was clothed with a vesture dipped in blood: and his name is called The Word of God.

14. And the armies which were in heaven followed him upon white horses, clothed in fine linen, white and clean.

15. And out of his mouth goeth a sharp sword, that with it he should smite the nations: and he shall rule them with a rod of iron: and he treadeth the wine press of the fierceness and wrath of Almighty God.

16. And he hath on his vesture and on his thigh a name written, King Of Kings, And Lord Of Lords.

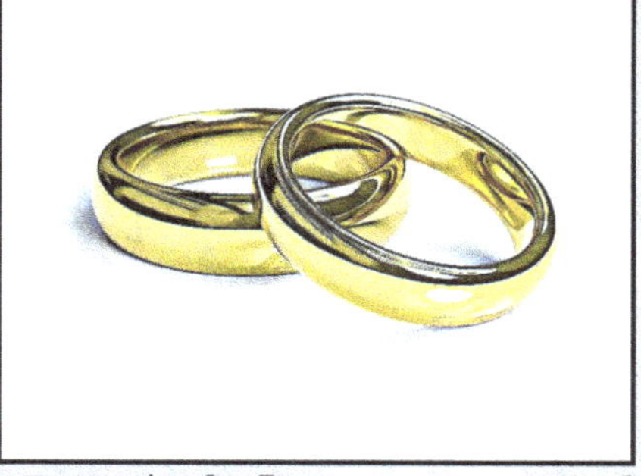

17. And I saw an angel standing in the sun; and he cried with a loud voice, saying to all the fowls that fly in the midst of heaven, Come and gather yourselves together unto the supper of the great God;

18. That ye may eat the flesh of kings, and the flesh of captains, and the flesh of mighty men, and the flesh of horses, and of them that sit on them, and the flesh of all men, both free and bond, both small and great.

19. And I saw the beast, and the kings of the earth, and their armies, gathered together to make war against him that sat on the horse, and against his army.

20. And the beast was taken, and with him the false prophet that wrought miracles before him, with which he deceived them that had received the mark of the beast, and them that worshiped his image. These both were cast alive into a lake of fire burning with brimstone.

21. And the remnant were slain with the sword of him that sat upon the horse, which sword proceeded out of his mouth: and all the fowls were filled with their flesh.

THE INTERPRETATION OF CHAPTER 20

Great Chain, Final Judgment, Final Battle

And he laid hold on the dragon, that old serpent, which is the Devil, and Satan, and bound him a thousand years. — Revelation 20:2 (KJV)

CHAPTER 20 describes Satan's judgment. An angel grabbed Satan and bound him to the bottomless pit for 1000 years. After 1000 years, Satan will be loosed for a season.

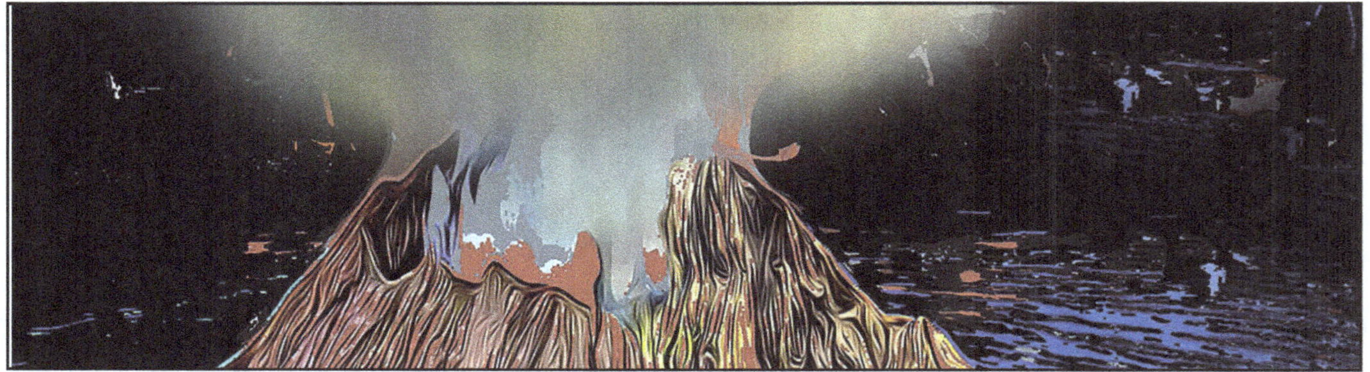

Those that were martyred during the tribulation were resurrected again in the first resurrection to reign with Jesus for 1000 years.

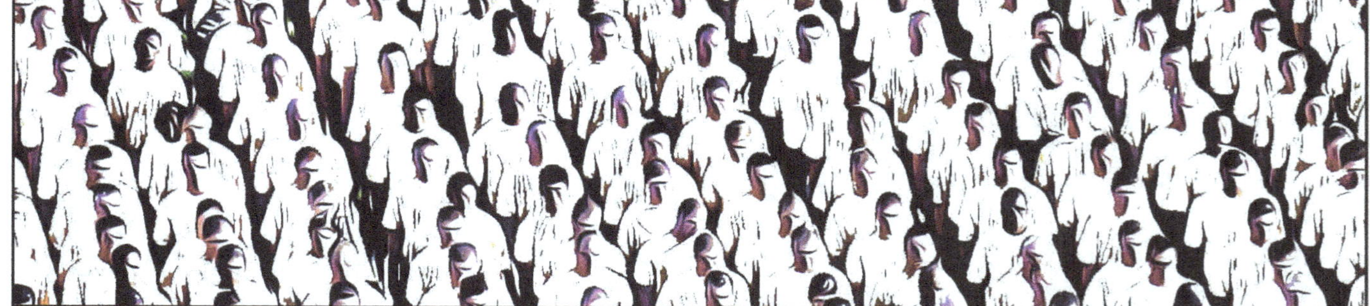

After Satan is loosed, he will gather from all nations evil men to battle Jesus once again at Gog and Magog. In this last battle, Satan surrounds the saints that were resurrected by Jesus in a rebuilt and revived city of Jerusalem, "the beloved city". Satan was not successful with his attack because fire came down from God out of heaven and devoured the evil followers of Satan. God also casts Satan into the lake of fire, where the Anti-Christ and False Prophet were also casts after the battle of Armageddon to be tormented forever. The heavens and the earth then will pass away and the judgment of the dead, according to deeds, begins. Those whose names were not written in the Book of Life are also cast into the lake of fire.

Revelation Chapter 20

1. And I saw an angel come down from heaven, having the key of the bottomless pit and a great chain in his hand.

2. And he laid hold on the dragon, that old serpent, which is the Devil, and Satan, and bound him a thousand years,

3. And cast him into the bottomless pit, and shut him up, and set a seal upon him, that he should deceive the nations no more, till the thousand years should be fulfilled: and after that he must be loosed a little season.

4. And I saw thrones, and they sat upon them, and judgment was given unto them: and I saw the souls of them that were beheaded for the witness of Jesus, and for the word of God, and which had not worshiped the beast, neither his image, neither had received his mark upon their foreheads, or in their hands; and they lived and reigned with Christ a thousand years.

5. But the rest of the dead lived not again until the thousand years were finished. This is the first resurrection.

6. Blessed and holy is he that hath part in the first resurrection: on such the second death hath no power, but they shall be priests of God and of Christ, and shall reign with him a thousand years.

7. And when the thousand years are expired, Satan shall be loosed out of his prison,

8. And shall go out to deceive the nations which are in the four quarters of the earth, Gog, and Magog, to gather them together to battle: the number of whom is as the sand of the sea.

9. And they went up on the breadth of the earth, and compassed the camp of the saints about, and the beloved city: and fire came down from God out of heaven, and devoured them.

10. And the devil that deceived them was cast into the lake of fire and brimstone, where the beast and the false prophet are, and shall be tormented day and night for ever and ever.

11. And I saw a great white throne, and him that sat on it, from whose face the earth and the heaven fled away; and there was found no place for them.

12. And I saw the dead, small and great, stand before God; and the books were opened: and another book was opened, which is the book of life: and the dead were judged out of those things which were written in the books, according to their works.

13. And the sea gave up the dead which were in it; and death and hell delivered up the dead which were in them: and they were judged every man according to their works.

14. And death and hell were cast into the lake of fire. This is the second death.

15. And whosoever was not found written in the book of life was cast into the lake of fire.

King James Version (KJV) Public Domain

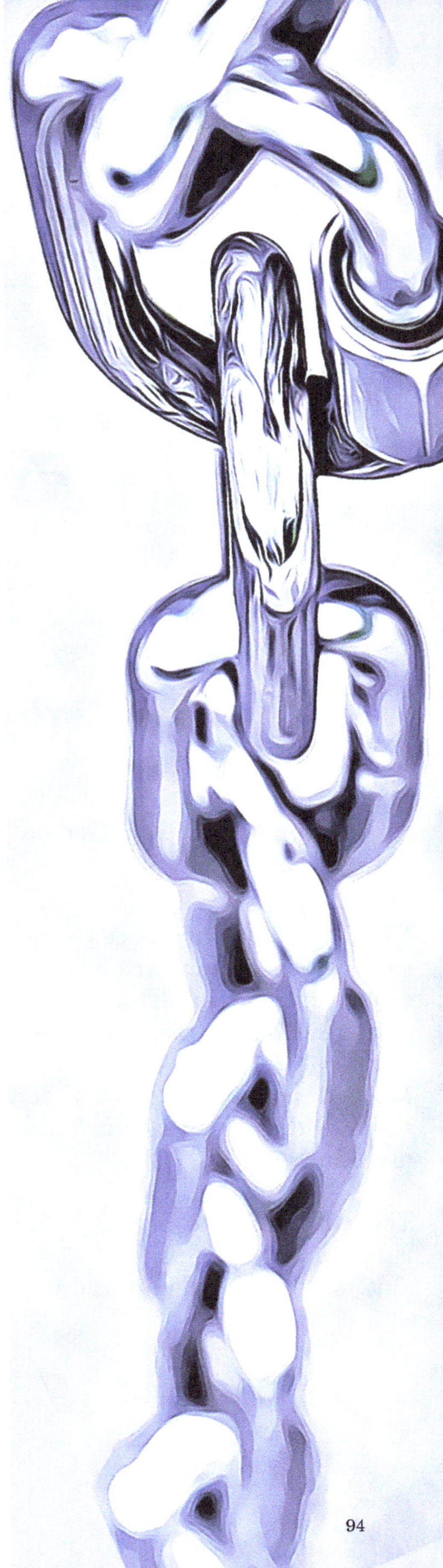

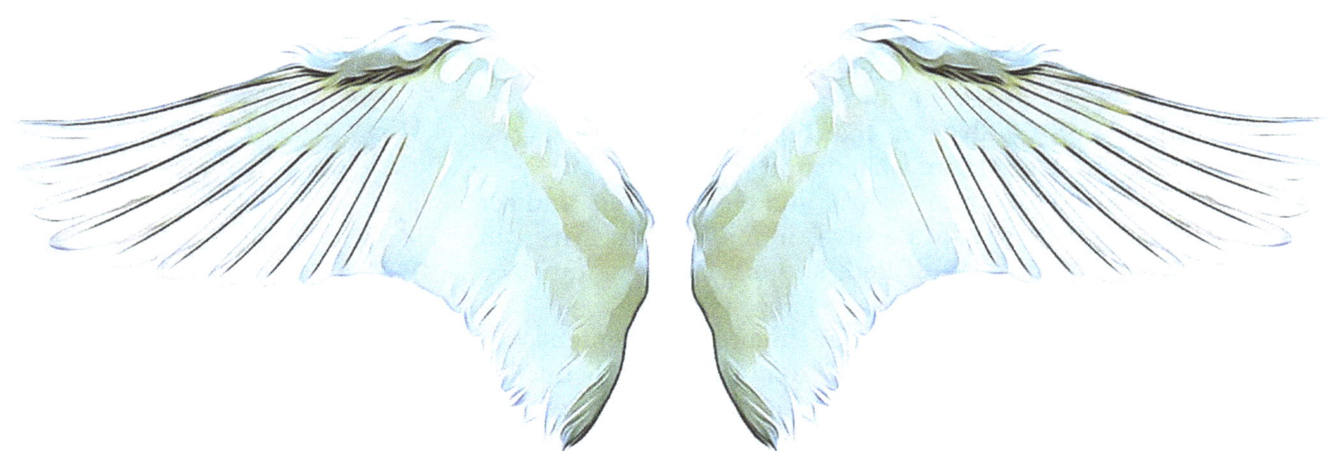

THE INTERPRETATION OF CHAPTER 21

The Coming of the New Jerusalem

And I John saw the holy city, new Jerusalem,
coming down from God out of heaven, prepared as a bride adorned for her husband.
— *Revelation 21:2 (KJV)*

CHAPTER 21 introduces a new heaven and new earth. Only those who are saved, hence, those whose names are written in the Lamb's Book of Life, are allowed to enter into the new city of Jerusalem. This new city came down from heaven, and was described as having the names of the 12 tribes of Israel and the 12 Apostles within its foundation.

More importantly, God's tabernacle dwells within the city. God's tabernacle is no longer separated from mankind. This was the initial relationship that God desired between He and mankind.

The whole theme of the Bible explains how far mankind had separated itself from God. However, in Revelation 21:3, God restored the relationship between Him and mankind and is able to dwell with mankind without separation.

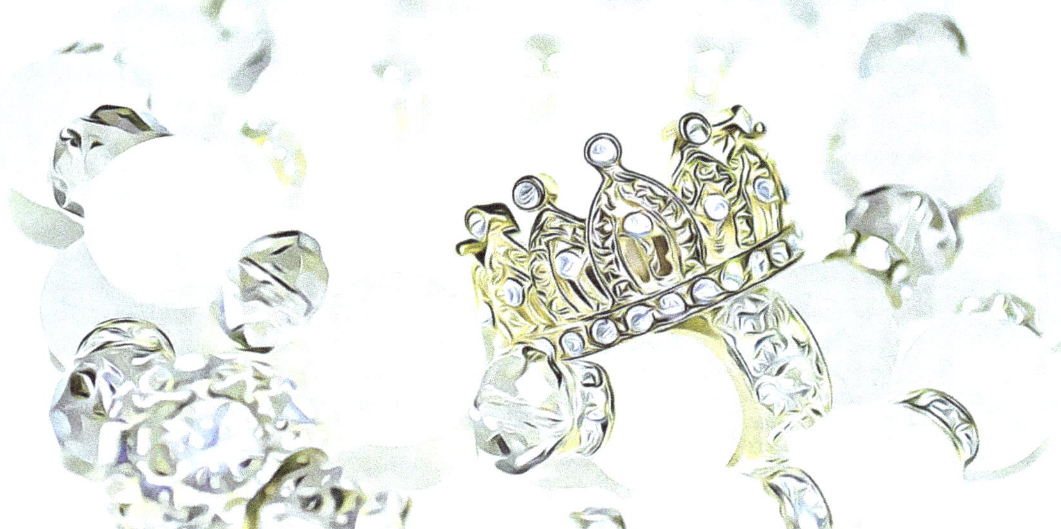

Revelation Chapter 21

1. And I saw a new heaven and a new earth: for the first heaven and the first earth were passed away; and there was no more sea.

2. And I John saw the holy city, new Jerusalem, coming down from God out of heaven, prepared as a bride adorned for her husband.

3. And I heard a great voice out of heaven saying, Behold, the tabernacle of God is with men, and he will dwell with them, and they shall be his people, and God himself shall be with them, and be their God.

4. And God shall wipe away all tears from their eyes; and there shall be no more death, neither sorrow, nor crying, neither shall there be any more pain: for the former things are passed away.

5. And he that sat upon the throne said, Behold, I make all things new. And he said unto me, Write: for these words are true and faithful.

6. And he said unto me, It is done. I am Alpha and Omega, the beginning and the end. I will give unto him that is athirst of the fountain of the water of life freely.

7. He that overcometh shall inherit all things; and I will be his God, and he shall be my son.

8. But the fearful, and unbelieving, and the abominable, and murderers, and whoremongers, and sorcerers, and idolaters, and all liars, shall have their part in the lake which burneth with fire and brimstone: which is the second death.

9. And there came unto me one of the seven angels which had the seven vials full of the seven last plagues, and talked with me, saying, Come hither, I will shew thee the bride, the Lamb's wife.

10. And he carried me away in the spirit to a great and high mountain, and shewed me that great city, the holy Jerusalem, descending out of heaven from God,

11. Having the glory of God: and her light was like unto a stone most precious, even like a jasper stone, clear as crystal;

12. And had a wall great and high, and had twelve gates, and at the gates twelve angels, and names written thereon, which are the names of the twelve tribes of the children of Israel:

13. On the east three gates; on the north three gates; on the south three gates; and on the west three gates.

14. And the wall of the city had twelve foundations, and in them the names of the twelve apostles of the Lamb.

15. And he that talked with me had a golden reed to measure the city, and the gates thereof, and the wall thereof.

16. And the city lieth foursquare, and the length is as large as the breadth: and he measured the city with the reed, twelve thousand furlongs. The length and the breadth and the height of it are equal.

17. And he measured the wall thereof, an hundred and forty and four cubits, according to the measure of a man, that is, of the angel.

18. And the building of the wall of it was of jasper: and the city was pure gold, like unto clear glass.

19. And the foundations of the wall of the city were garnished with all manner of precious stones. The first foundation was jasper; the second, sapphire; the third, a chalcedony; the fourth, an emerald;

20. The fifth, sardonyx; the sixth, sardius; the seventh, chrysolyte; the eighth, beryl; the ninth, a topaz; the tenth, a chrysoprasus; the eleventh, a jacinth; the twelfth, an amethyst.

21. And the twelve gates were twelve pearls: every several gate was of one pearl: and the street of the city was pure gold, as it were transparent glass.

22. And I saw no temple therein: for the Lord God Almighty and the Lamb are the temple of it.

23. And the city had no need of the sun, neither of the moon, to shine in it: for the glory of God did lighten it, and the Lamb is the light thereof.

24. And the nations of them which are saved shall walk in the light of it: and the kings of the earth do bring their glory and honour into it.

25. And the gates of it shall not be shut at all by day: for there shall be no night there.

26. And they shall bring the glory and honour of the nations into it.

27. And there shall in no wise enter into it any thing that defileth, neither whatsoever worketh abomination, or maketh a lie: but they which are written in the Lamb's book of life.

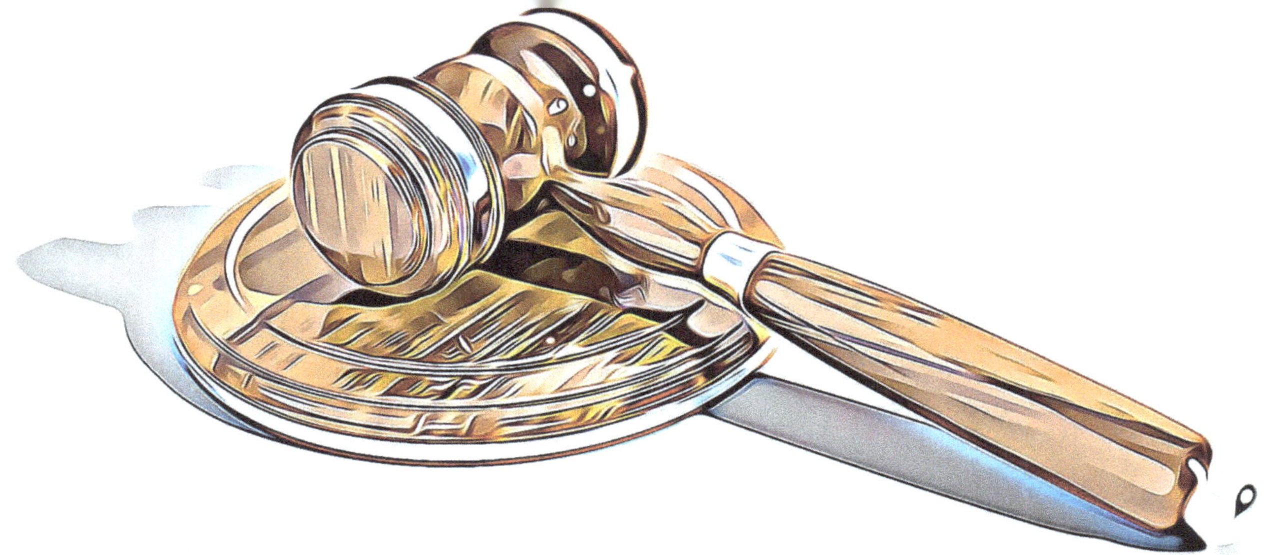

THE INTERPRETATION OF CHAPTER 22

The Conclusion of the Prophecy

Blessed are they that do his commandments, that they may have right to the tree of life, and may enter in through the gates into the city. — Revelation 22:14 (KJV)

CHAPTER 22 is the conclusion of the prophecy. Blessed are they that do his commandments, that they may have right to the tree of life. The angel continues to show John the splendor of the new heaven and new earth. Here, every saved person will live forever, eat from the tree of life, and drink from the crystal clear living waters. An angel concludes the prophecy by urging John to tell this prophecy to the churches. For the time is at hand to warn the hearers of this prophecy not to add or take away from its revelations, but to take heed because Jesus is soon to return.

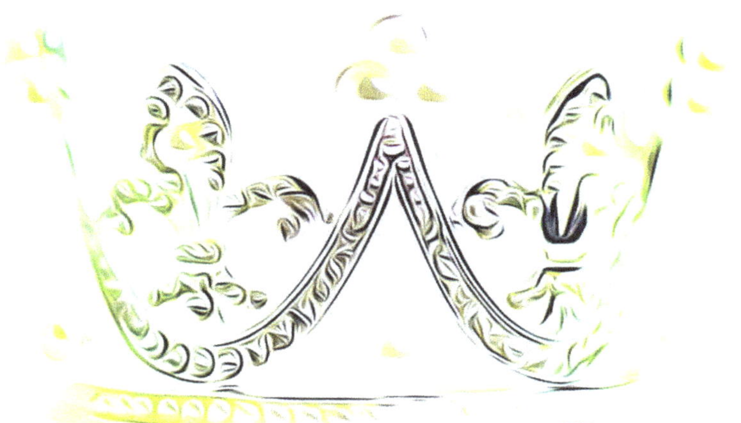

Revelation Chapter 22

1. And he shewed me a pure river of water of life, clear as crystal, proceeding out of the throne of God and of the Lamb.

2. In the midst of the street of it, and on either side of the river, was there the tree of life, which bare twelve manner of fruits, and yielded her fruit every month: and the leaves of the tree were for the healing of the nations.

3. And there shall be no more curse: but the throne of God and of the Lamb shall be in it; and his servants shall serve him:

4. And they shall see his face; and his name shall be in their foreheads.

5. And there shall be no night there; and they need no candle, neither light of the sun; for the Lord God giveth them light: and they shall reign for ever and ever.

6. And he said unto me, These sayings are faithful and true: and the Lord God of the holy prophets sent his angel to shew unto his servants the things which must shortly be done.

7. Behold, I come quickly: blessed is he that keepeth the sayings of the prophecy of this book.

8. And I John saw these things, and heard them. And when I had heard and seen, I fell down to worship before the feet of the angel which shewed me these things.

9. Then saith he unto me, See thou do it not: for I am thy fellowservant, and of thy brethren the prophets, and of them which keep the sayings of this book: worship God.

10. And he saith unto me, Seal not the sayings of the prophecy of this book: for the time is at hand.

11. He that is unjust, let him be unjust still: and he which is filthy, let him be filthy still: and he that is righteous, let him be righteous still: and he that is holy, let him be holy still.

12. And, behold, I come quickly; and my reward is with me, to give every man according as his work shall be.

13. I am Alpha and Omega, the beginning and the end, the first and the last.

14. Blessed are they that do his commandments, that they may have right to the tree of life, and may enter in through the gates into the city.

15. For without are dogs, and sorcerers, and whoremongers, and murderers, and idolaters, and whosoever loveth and maketh a lie.

16. I Jesus have sent mine angel to testify unto you these things in the churches. I am the root and the offspring of David, and the bright and morning star.

17. And the Spirit and the bride say, Come. And let him that heareth say, Come. And let him that is athirst come. And whosoever will, let him take the water of life freely.

18. For I testify unto every man that heareth the words of the prophecy of this book, If any man shall add unto these things, God shall add unto him the plagues that are written in this book:

19. And if any man shall take away from the words of the book of this prophecy, God shall take away his part out of the book of life, and out of the holy city, and from the things which are written in this book.

20. He which testifieth these things saith, Surely, I come quickly. Amen. Even so, come, Lord Jesus.

21. The grace of our Lord Jesus Christ be with you all....

Revelation Time Line
Chapters 12 -22

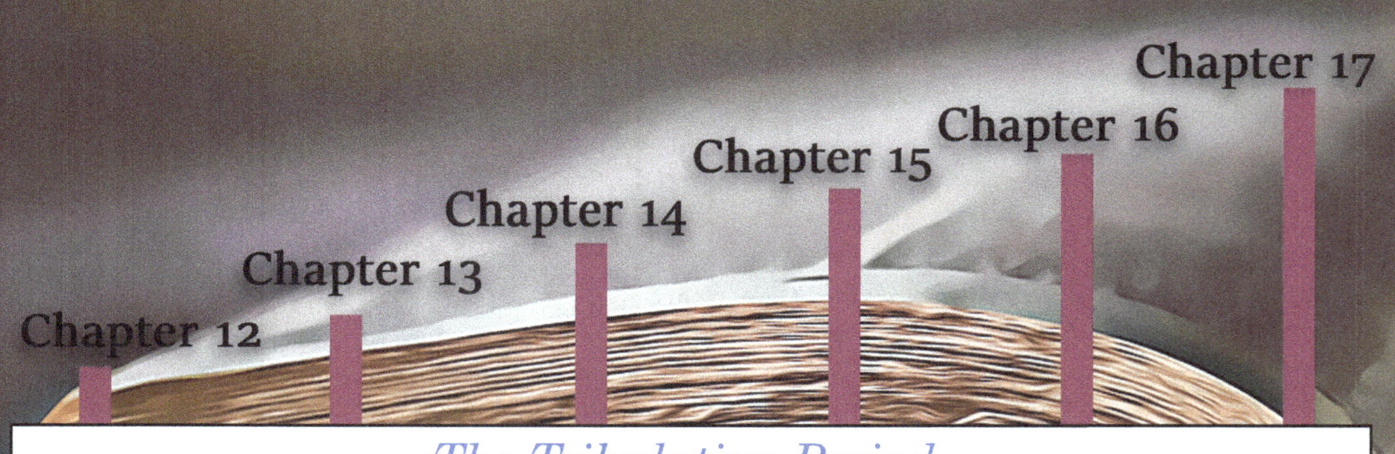

The Tribulation Period

Selection of the Nation to fulfill the prophesy	The 7 Earthly Kingdoms	Rapture of the 144,000 Israelites	Seven Angels with Seven Bowls of Wrath	Seven Bowls of Wrath Release Seven Plagues	Selection of the city to fulfill the prophesy
Israel	Anti-Christ Kingdom	Rapture of the Christian Church			The Anti-Christ introduces idolatry to Jerusalem
The Pregnant Woman	The Dragon	Death of the Martyrs			The Great Whore

The Book of Revelation covers the events that shall happen during the 70th week as mentioned in the Book of Daniel.

The 70th week is equivalent to one prophetic week or a period of seven years. **Chapters 12-22** focuses on the second 3 1/2 years of the 70th week, the Tribulation Period and Final Judgment. In these chapters we learn that the Anti-Christ will insult God in the rebuilt third temple in Jerusalem. The Anti-Christ will martyr those who refuse to take the mark of the beast "666." As a result, God will release his wrath and final judgment on all unbelievers, the Anti-Christ, the False Prophet, and Satan. End-time wars will bring about final judgment for the earth and all who occupied the earth. The final judgment of eternal life or eternal damnation will be issued according to deeds.

Final Judgment - Eternal Life or Eternal Damnation

Jerusalem, nicknamed, Babylon the Great is Fallen Jerusalem Burns Down	Anti-Christ and False Prophet casts into lake of fire. Martyrs resurrected, marry Jesus and reigns with him for 1000 years	The Great Chain bounds Satan for 1000 years during the martyrs and and Jesus 1000 year reign. Final judgment of the dead according to their deeds.	Heaven and Earth Pass Away Believers dwell with God in the new heaven, new earth, and in the new city of Jerusalem.	The Conclusion of the Prophecy

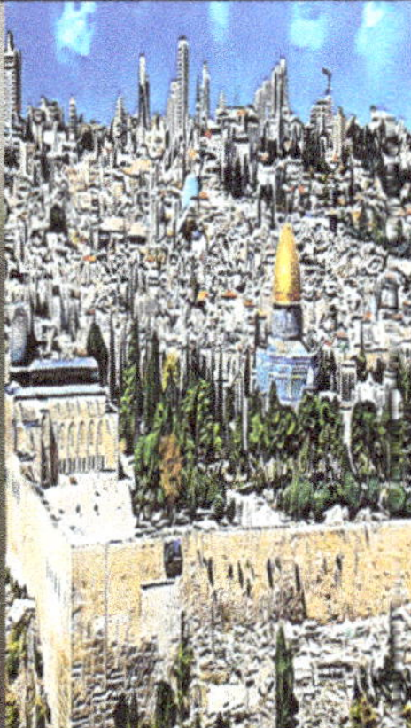
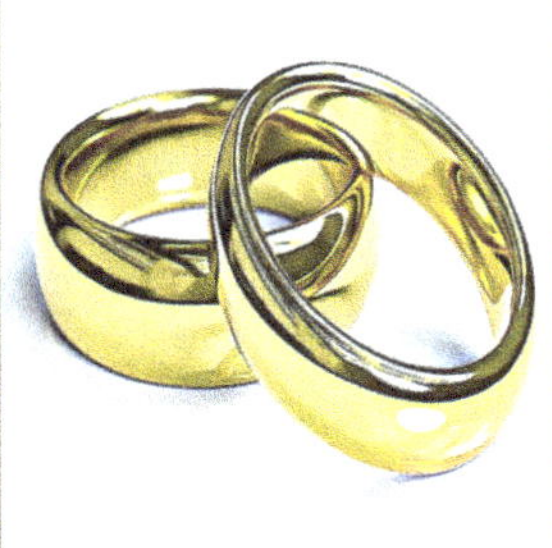
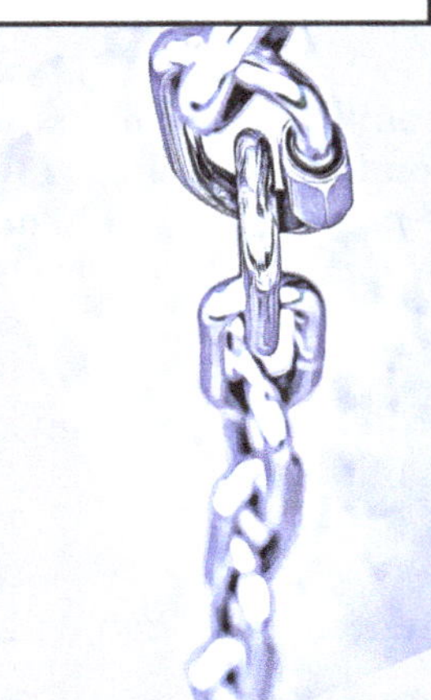
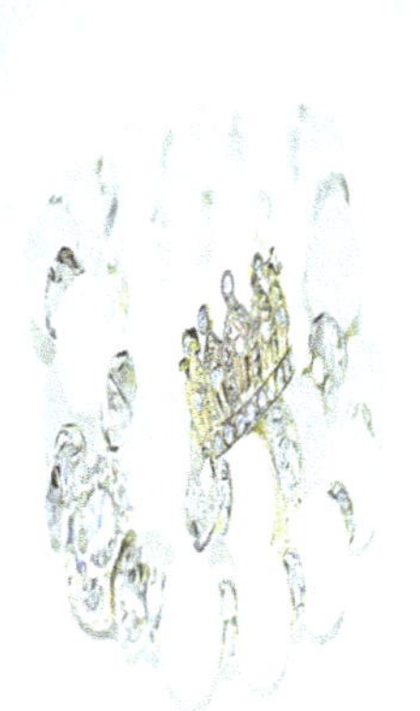
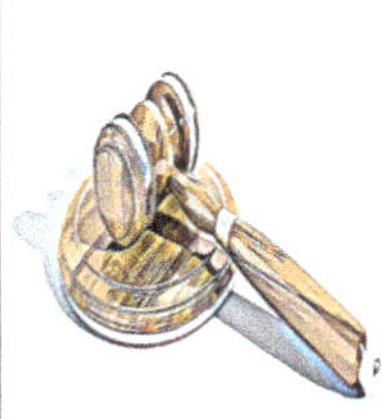

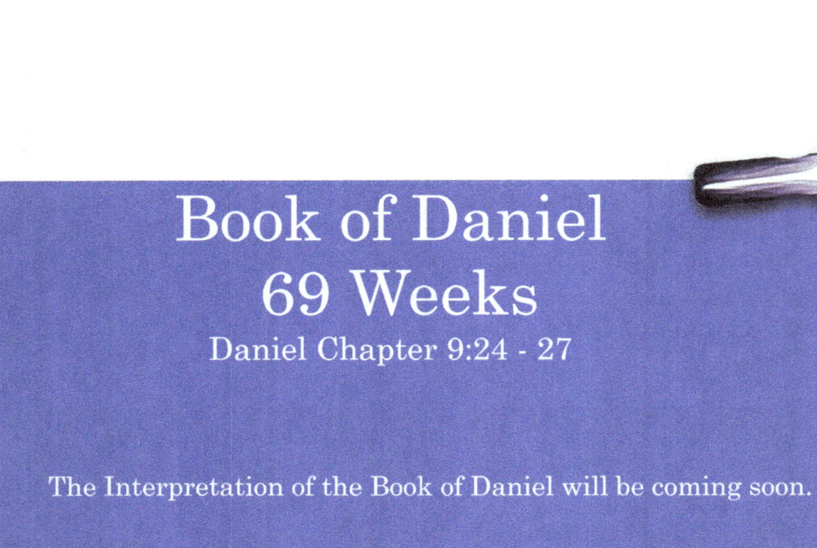

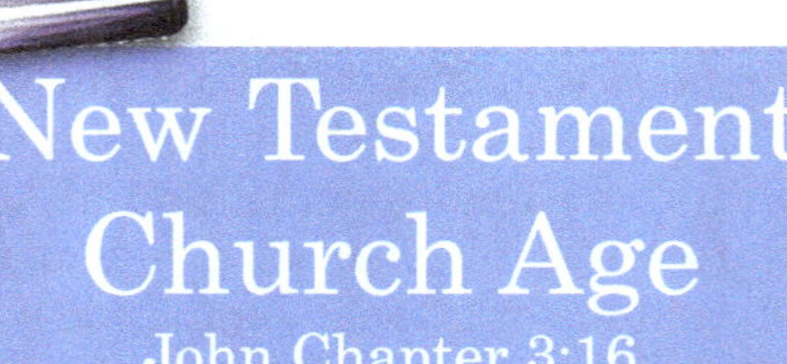

HOW SHOULD THIS INFORMATION BE APPLIED?

Church Age - During this period of time, Jesus is offering salvation. It is imperative that the readers of this book seize the opportunity to receive salvation from eternal damnation without having to pay the price and experience the wrath of God.

Be watchful for the following signs:
Watch for false prophets, wars, pestilence, famine, and increasing natural disasters;
Watch for the rebuilding of the third temple in Jerusalem;
Watch for the church as we know it and Christians to be taken away from the earth.
These are all signs that the end is near. I pray that the readers of this book accept Jesus as their savior so that they avoid the Tribulation period and eternal damnation.

Tribulation Period - During this period of time, accepting Jesus as your savior is no longer an option. By the time you realize that Christians were right, it is simply to late to get saved through the blood of Jesus. But hope is not lost, salvation is still an option, but it will costs you your own life. When the Anti-Christ offers you his provisions at the costs of receiving his mark on your forehead or hands, refuse and die as a martyr. Although this is not the best method, this will spare you from eternal damnation.

Be watchful for the following signs:
Watch for treaties between the nations within the Middle East (If you ever heard of the saying, "When you hear of peace in the Middle East, woe to the inhabitants of the earth.") *This is referring to the treaty of the 10 kings (10 horns) with the Anti-Christ.*
Watch for technology that will allow the capability to purchase items by merely scanning someone's forehead or hands, such as, RFID chips, barcodes, biometrics, Bitcoin, etc.) and the use of this technology to implement a worldwide economy.
Watch for the Anti-Christ to defile the rebuilt third temple in Jerusalem by declaring himself to be God;
Watch for governing bodies pressuring you to accept the symbol of a worldwide leader.
These are all signs that the end is near. I pray that if the readers of this book are living in the Tribulation Period, remember this prophecy. Refuse the mark of the beast and choose martyrdom, God will grant you salvation from eternal damnation.

Eternal Damnation - You did not accept Jesus as your savior and you die; or you are living during the tribulation period and you accept the mark of the beast.

Be watchful for the following signs:
Watch for a Final Judgment where your sentence is "You will be cast into the Lake of Fire."

THE FINAL MESSAGE

The Book of Revelation sums up why mankind should seek salvation through Jesus Christ, the reason Christianity exists, which is called the church age in this book, and the promise of Jesus' return. To the readers of this book, never allow this prophecy to fade away from your hearts. God will allow the final judgment to come to the earth and all will participate, whether you are a believer or not.

I urge you to err on the side of caution and strive to be on the winning side of judgment, which is by accepting Jesus Christ as your savior. To accept Jesus as your Lord and savior, read the book of Romans Chapter 10 verses 9-10 and follow the instructions provided.

May God add a blessing to the readers of this book and may the grace of our Lord Jesus Christ be with you always. Amen.